LAUGHING TORSO

LAUGHING TORSO

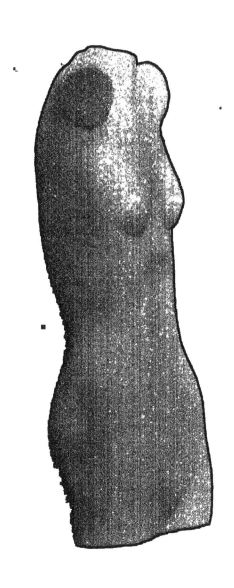

LAUGHING TORSO

REMINISCENCES OF

NINA HAMNETT

With 23 Illustrations

Ray Long & Richard R. Smith, Inc.
NEW YORK · · · 1932

PRINTED IN THE UNITED STATES OF AMERICA, BY THE
NATIONAL PROCESS COMPANY, Inc., NEW YORK, N. Y.

TO HAROLD NICOLSON

AND

TO DOUGLAS GOLDRING

WITHOUT WHOSE KINDNESS AND ENCOURAGEMENT

I SHOULD NEVER HAVE WRITTEN

THIS BOOK

September 1931.

CONTENTS

ILLUSTRATIONS

LAUGHING TORSO

ONE morning towards the end of the year 1889, a
lady who lived in a terrace of houses on the top of a
high rock surrounded by battlements descended into
the kitchen to order the food for the day. She was
in a few months' time to have a child. She was
suddenly seized with a strong feeling that she must
come upstairs, cross the garden and look down on
the seashore. The impulse became so strong that
she went upstairs, crossed the garden and looked
over the battlements. Standing on the shore far
below was a man with dark hypnotic eyes. This
man, whenever he saw her, stared at her in a way
that frightened her; he had lived a long time in the
East.

The child she was about to bear was myself. I
have often wondered if that man hypnotized her in
any way that may afterwards have affected me or
induced me to start on a career that was so different
from that of my family or my upbringing. On
February the fourteenth, 1890, I was born.

Everybody was furious, especially my Father, who
still is. As soon as I became conscious of anything
I was furious too, at having been born a girl; I have
since discovered that it has certain advantages. My
first recollection of anything is walking downstairs,
step by step, to join a little boy who was standing at

the bottom of the stairs holding out a china vase with pink and blue flowers on it. That was my second birthday. We then went to Saltash, where, seated on the front doorstep one day, I went for a walk with a strange lady and was later discovered by my nurse all dressed in white chasing a flock of sheep down a hillside followed by an angry shepherd. At this time my brother was born, and as everyone was very much occupied I had a good time rooting up all the carnations in the front garden that my Father, whom I disliked, had recently planted. Next door lived a boy of about six. I spent much time trying to pull him through the wire-netting which separated our gardens, but without success; he is now, I believe, a Brigadier-General in the Royal Engineers. We then went to York. I was taken out one evening in my nurse's arms to see the Duke and Duchess of York driving through the streets and was thrilled by the lights and the crowd; this was their honeymoon visit to York. They are now King George and Queen Mary.

There was a lunatic asylum next door and sometimes a fair; the noise of the fair and the lunatics kept us awake at night. On Christmas Day I was given a glass of champagne, which gave me a pleasant and gay feeling. I was then sent back to Tenby and to my Grandmother, who was the most stupid and sentimental of women and loathed my Father. I was free and allowed to do as I liked. I rode every day on a donkey, accompanied by a donkey-boy and my nurse. I liked the donkey-boy, but the nurse and he talked all the time. I felt the

2

MYSELF AT SALTASH
1891

terrible misery of being so young and ignorant and having no conversational powers: I decided that something must be done to improve things. I fell in love with a little boy of seven and ran all over the town after him saying, " Tony, I *will* kiss you," but I never caught him. Many years later, when I was eleven I was asked to a party and everyone said, " Aren't you going to kiss Tony? " and we both nearly died of shame. He is to-day a successful rancher in South America. I was now four, and had the first feeling of shame. I spent most of my time writing stories and drawing. I wore socks, and one day my Grandmother said, " You are too big to wear socks and people will think it shameful and will stare at you." I hung my head and blushed and had to wear black woollen stockings. A birthday party was given for me and I was given an oyster to taste; I spat it on the floor and was carried out screaming. I objected to girls, and was asked to a refined Christmas tree party where I was given a beautiful pink doll. I made so much disturbance that I was taken home at once in the Bath chair that always took us to parties.

There was a woman with a horrible face who passed the house every morning; I always waited for her to poke my tongue out and make grimaces; I found out later that she was a Sunday School teacher. She complained to my Grandmother, who had me locked into a back room during the time she passed the window. Life with my Grandmother was, on the whole, too easy, and, finding my behaviour impossible to cope with, she sent me to

Chatham to my Father. There I had a donkey to ride on which was kept in the barracks and all was well until the soldier servant gave her oatmeal that had not been soaked and she swelled up and burst and I was very sad.

Life at Chatham was not pleasant. My Grandmother arrived and then there was one perpetual argument as to how I was to be brought up, violent arguments that nearly came to blows; one particularly awful moment when I locked myself into the W.C. and the battle raged in the passage outside. There was a picture of Lord Nelson when young, a coloured plate from the *Illustrated London News*, on the wall that I had to gaze at trembling. I think I could draw that picture now. The only friendly person in the house was the soldier servant whom I would grab whenever he came into the nursery and tie him to a chair with a skipping rope. My Father was selfish and bad-tempered and beat me. I must admit that I was a dreadful child but I think he rather overdid it. He had a bag of bamboo canes which were sent to him from India. If I had behaved badly during the morning I was locked into his dressing-room to wait for him to come home. How I hate still the smell of shaving soap and pomade. When he arrived, he made a noise like a hungry lion, took the bag of canes, and tried each one out on his hand to see which was the most effective, then as I skipped about and screamed he would cut me on the legs or anywhere he could. I had to go to bed on one occasion as my legs were cut and bleeding; such was the Spartan upbringing

4

of the 'nineties. A large doll was brought for me with a view to instilling some feminine feeling into me, but being of an imitative disposition I placed its head in the fire-place with its legs sticking over the nursery fender, stole one of my father's bamboo canes, turned up its skirts, and beat it so that its head was battered on the grate; it was mended but as this occurred again and again the family gave it up. One nursemaid left after another. A very tall one came and I found that her white apron made a very nice slide, so she went too.

We went to the grand review on the Lines; I sat beside the coachman. In the carriage was my Mother, my Grandmother, an old lady and an old gentleman. The ladies wore hats like birds'-nests. When the guns went off I gave a loud howl and fell backwards into the carriage on to the birds'-nests. I was left at home next time.

In 1898 my Father was sent to Belfast where we had a house near the Ormeau Road. I was sent out one Saturday evening to fetch a medicine glass as my sister was ill and the servants had gone out. It was a terrifying experience, every house seemed to be a pub and outside lying against the barrels of whisky were drunken men and women: I had to dodge them and wind my way through them.

I and my brother went to an Irish mixed school, we were regarded as foreigners, and as I did not feel able to deal with the pupils I did my best to have my revenge on the music mistress who, poor woman, had a miserable time and probably still hates the English. In Belfast I first felt real affection. An

5

Irish lady my family knew had three little girls; I stayed with them as often as I could escape from home and was really happy.

When we left Ireland I had to be carried on to the boat wailing loudly with misery. We went back to Tenby and my parents went to Malta, leaving me with my Grandmother. I spent most of my time and money on fishing; I sat daily on the end of the old pier alone with a line and caught pollack and sometimes sprats which were generally too small to cook. One day I met a butcher boy whose face I had never liked, so I kicked his tray of meat over and hit him in the stomach; I was rescued by two nuns and taken home to my infuriated Grandmother. I made friends with bathing-machine boys whom I found sympathetic and a pleasant change from home life. I learnt the pleasing expression of " Bloody b——r " from them, which I found acted very effectively on a nasty park keeper. I also had a dispute with my Grandmother who locked me into a bedroom and spoke about the devil, so I threw a basin, a jerry, a jug and two bananas out of the window and knocked her down. Every day I rode on a fat pony kept by the sweep but I only rode it because I liked the sweep, who was a nice kindly old man and not because of his pony, which was old and fat.

CHAPTER II   THE CALMING INFLUENCE OF THE
PRIVATE ACADEMY FOR YOUNG LADIES

ONE day a grim aunt appeared; she said that
boarding school was the only place for me, so I
was sent to a high-class Academy for young Ladies
at Westgate-on-Sea. I was plunged in gloom. My
Father wrote quoting from Thackeray, I can't remember the exact quotation, but it was about the
boy who was sad at school, not because he was sorry
to leave his parents, but because the school was a
very uncomfortable place. He was right, but it
pained me at the time and I did miss the bathing-
machine boys. My Grandmother had fitted me out
in a splendid manner. I had a bag with my initials
on it, a writing-case from the Army and Navy Stores
with initials too, and a fine Bible with large print
handsomely bound in leather with my name in gold.
I was thrilled to see my name in print. I shared a
room with another girl. Apart from her beautiful
red hair which was curly and hung down to her
waist, I decided that she was the same kind of gutless
half-wit as the rest of the sex. I cried all that night
and she cried too. I cried, mostly from rage and a
feeling of being caged in: she cried because she
loved her parents. I cried daily for a week.

On Sunday we went to church. The altar walls
and ceiling were painted blue with silver stars; after
gazing at the stars during the sermon I had an idea.
" Why not run away? " At seven-thirty the next
morning I saw that my room-mate was still asleep;

7

I looked round the room and saw the Bible with my initials in gold; I put it under one arm and a pair of indoor slippers under the other. I took seven and sixpence which was my pocket money for some time, climbed over the garden wall, and started in the direction of the station. I must have been rather a noticeable figure at that hour as I had the school colours on my hat. I got to the station and asked about the trains to London, where my Grandmother was staying. By this time I had worked up a considerable amount of affection for her. Alas! no trains for an hour and a half; what should I do? I took a road behind the station. I passed by a farmyard and looked through the iron gates. I saw chickens and pigs feeding. I felt awfully hungry and envied them. I passed a road of villas and could see the detested *bourgeois* eating eggs and bacon through the lace curtains. I came to a field of turnips and sat down on the roadside. I had heard that turnips were good to eat so I chipped a bit off one and found it extremely disagreeable. I thought that it must be nearly time for the train to go and got up to walk on, suddenly a hand was laid on my shoulder: the HEAD MISTRESS!

The mistresses—three sisters—were charming and very intelligent women, and although I won a prize for writing an essay on a play of Shakespeare's, my performances in the schoolroom were far from satisfactory. I was by this time quite resigned to my fate and began rather to enjoy it. In the winter term I overheard a discussion on theatricals and to my joy was told that the theatre was to be hired for

8

two nights and that I was to play the leading part in *Jack and the Beanstalk.* "Fame at last." I danced extremely well. The most brilliant pupil was a child of ten, my own age, with blue eyes and short golden hair, a relation of the mistresses, who was very conceited and was furious that she was not given the leading part. I met her in Paris a few years ago. It still rankled. Like most blondes later in life, she resembled instead of a ripe fruit or flower, those pale faded waxen fruits and flowers in Victorian glass cases. Blondes should dye their hair and paint their faces or get married and have children. Rehearsing was fun and the costumes were made by the mistresses and the great night came. I wore red tights and high-heeled red shoes and a little cap with a feather and felt that I was about to conquer the world. I went through my part and climbed the beanstalk—a rope covered in leaves which hung over a beam and was held by two old gentlemen in the wings. I was very well received, I danced a hornpipe and brought the house down. I was called for over and over again. The only time I shall know what real Fame is, to stand in front of an enthusiastic and cheering audience. Some rich people wanted to get me an engagement in London and others to dance at concerts but alas! my family again. "Ladies do not go on the stage." I was furious, besides a lady was the last thing that I wanted to be.

CHAPTER III   AT A PUBLIC SCHOOL

My family had decided that the school at West-
gate was very expensive and decided to get votes for
me to go to the Royal School, Bath; this was for
officers' daughters; it meant passing a rather stiff
exam., so I returned to Tenby. My Father was in
South Africa at the War, so things looked good.
Some nice little boys and I organized an army with
a view to beating up some members of the lower
classes who had taken exception to us. They despised girls but said that I and a girl friend of mine,
the only one who was not a fool that I could find,
could join, provided that we put red crosses on our
arms and attended to the wounded, which we had
to do after the first encounter. Our army went out
on the prowl every Sunday. One day we marched
out on to the sand dunes. We approached a high
rock and to our horror when we got near we were
bombarded with huge stones and large lumps of
turf; we were forced to retreat. One day the
enemy appeared unexpectedly. My noble army all
ran away and left me. They tied my hands behind
my back with rope and marched me back triumphantly through the streets where I met my Grandmother!

We had a charming milkman who had a milk cart
with big cans which I could hide behind when I did
the rounds with him and saw any undesirables
about.

My Brother's school had just started a girls' class,

MYSELF AND MY BROTHER IN FANCY DRESS
TENBY, 1899

so I was sent there. The Headmaster's wife was terrifying but kind and intelligent. I could not do arithmetic, so cried with rage whilst she roared at me.

The Headmaster appeared from time to time and when my sums were shown to him he would exclaim "Moly Hoses!" which we thought very dashing and clever. My friend who wore the red cross in our ill-fated army was brilliant at arithmetic and what was my astonishment when one day in the middle of an impossible sum the Mistress glared at my friend and pointing to me said, "She has more brains in her little finger than you have in your whole body." That gave me confidence in myself and I took to writing stories. I could never arrive at any satisfactory result as I never could think of anything to write about and had to console myself with doing drawings, which I considered to be an inferior art. I passed the examination with honours, I think principally on my *viva voce* examination in scripture. I was examined by a charming and sympathetic Welsh clergyman who found my views on the Bible quite unusual.

Every Saturday since I can remember, my Grandmother insisted on my accompanying her to the cemetery to visit the tomb of my Grandfather. She was of a sentimental disposition and lived only for the dead. It was a dismal proceeding. I had to fill the iron anchor and cross with water and arrange the flowers. After a speech about death and the uselessness of living, we went home. The flowers chosen were often "Stars of Bethlehem," which smelt strongly of onions: it seemed an odd way of demonstrating one's affection and I was glad that the dead had lost their sense of smell.

My Grandfather was a remarkable man and if he had only lived—he died in 1893—we would all not have got into so much trouble. Any artistic talent that I have I inherited from him. He was a naval officer and did all the surveying in the 'seventies of Heligoland, Western Wales, and Western Australia. He drew all the maps himself with beautiful drawings of islands and little landscapes. I believe that they are still in use at the Admiralty. In those days naval officers took their wives and families with them when they went abroad. They sailed to Australia in a sailing ship with two masts; this took three months. Perth was then a convict settlement and all the servants were convicts. My Grandfather bought for a few hundred pounds land that is now the main street of Perth; he sold it for a few thousand pounds. When they sailed back there was a terrible storm and one mast was washed overboard and they knelt down and said their prayers; a shark followed the ship and the second mate went mad and jumped overboard. They got home safely, however. My Grandmother was a Canadian and was one of three very beautiful sisters; she met my Grandfather when he was in Canada with his ship and married him. One of her ancestors was Joseph Howe, who federated the Canadian States and had a dispute with Mr. Gladstone, who was forced to apologize (*Dictionary of National Biography*). She had many ancestors: in

12

fact there was no end to the ancestors who came over on that very overcrowded ship, the " Mayflower." She was what the Americans would describe as " dumb."

From here I went to Bath. This was very different from my private school; there were a hundred and fifty girls and I was delighted with it: the girls complained bitterly that it was a charity institution; the only advantage being that we were not made to wear uniforms and be completely like workhouse inmates.

My first term I won the foreign languages prize because I had had the verb " To be " and the verb " To have " dinned into my head for two years. I had no particular talent for languages. I drew maps for a friend of mine and she did my arithmetic. At Christmas I played the " Mad Hatter " in *Alice in Wonderland,* and had a great success; the Archdeacon of Bath always sent his old top hats to the school for theatricals, so I wore one. One day during preparation someone handed me a copy of Edward Lear's *Nonsense Rhymes.* I thought them so funny and made such a disturbance that I was sent out. A friend and I started to write a magazine together, I doing the illustrations, having abandoned writing. This was stopped as it was considered unconventional. Bath made me horribly ill and depressed; I developed glands and had to stay at home for a term.

My family were at Portsmouth waiting for the return of my Father from South Africa and I was sent to the Portsmouth School of Art. This was in

1903. I was given coloured pictures of Venice to copy in water-colours; it bored me after a time and so I used to wander about the Art School. I found a passage, on the walls of which were nude studies done by the students which fired me with enthusiasm. I found myself in the Antique Room with white plaster casts of Venus, Hercules, and the Dancing Faun. I had an irresistible desire to get a hammer and chip off the plaster fig leaves that seemed to me to be ugly and silly.

I met at this time a family who were very kind to me. The sister had hair nearly down to the ground, reddish gold and most beautiful. She had a wonderful voice and used to act in amateur theatricals; she was always getting engaged to naval officers but none of them came up to her ideal. I believe she is still a maiden. Her family would not allow her to become a singer notwithstanding the fact that they were almost penniless; because " Ladies did not go on the stage." She would probably have become a famous singer. I fell in love with her brother Morris who was nineteen, six foot three, and a dream of beauty. He was in the Rifle Brigade and looked magnificent in his uniform. I stayed with them sometimes when my family went to London, and as his sister sat each evening with me when I was in bed and talked about life he would rush into the room and fire a revolver out of the window. This seemed to me the height of daring and manliness. One day he invited me to go for a drive in a horse trap of the American pattern that one sees in old cowboy films. It had big spidery wheels and held two people. We drove to Portsdown Hill. He put his arm along the back of the seat, I was terrified. My Father had warned me that one should " Never let a man touch you "; I did not know what he meant but I sat straight up on the end of the seat until the arm was removed. I was sadly disillusioned the following Christmas, when we had moved to Plymouth. A photograph album was sent to me and inside was written, " Nina with love from Morris," but it was in his sister's handwriting. He is now the father of a large family.

CHAPTER IV   I BEGIN TO BE AN ARTIST

In 1905 my throat was so bad that I had to leave school, which I did, shedding a tear on the Head-mistress's shoulder. My Father was stationed in Dublin opposite Guinness's Brewery, and I was sent to the Dublin School of Art. I liked the Irish, they were free, easy, and amiable. I was known as " the foreigner." I drew extremely well and the other students came round to admire my drawing. I did a charcoal drawing of the head of Michael Angelo's " David," half life size, the curls nearly killed me but I was very proud of it and took it home triumphantly. My Father then went to the Curragh Camp where I had a splendid time and hunted with the Kildare. I had to ride the army horses, which had very hard mouths, but I rode well and did not mind.

Then the crash came and my Father ruined the family. We crept away one night in a jaunting car along the wet and lonely roads. We were not feeling very cheerful and the only vehicle we met was another car with a coffin on it. My Grandmother had a big flat at Chiswick and she and my Father fought daily as they tried to plan out our future. This was in 1905. My Father said to me, " Now you must earn your own living. I believe that it is quite respectable for ladies to study to become clerks in the Post Office." I was sent to the Regent Street Polytechnic, the commercial side. The Headmaster was a Yorkshireman and an old beast.

16

The students were mostly board-school children whose talent for adding up and doing sums staggered me. I gave one look of despair at the figures and took to drawing on the blotting paper. At the end of the term the Headmaster told my Father that I was a hopeless case and quite incapable of getting on in any walk of life. As I persisted in drawing, my Grandmother decided to send me to an Art School. About this time I was confirmed. I never knew quite why or what it was all about, but I was sent alone to a very sympathetic clergyman. We prayed together and I had to write an essay on one's Duty to one's Parents. This I did so well and filled it with such noble and pious sentiments that he told my Grandmother that I had something of a real Saint in my disposition. It occurred to me that if leg-pulling was as easy as all that the future might not be so bad. I was dressed in white and taken to a church at Chiswick where the Bishop of London confirmed me.

Some friends of my Grandmother's knew A. B. Cull, now a famous marine artist; he said that five years' free education was to be had at the Royal Academy Schools. He had just finished the course there himself. The examination was difficult and he said that once having passed the examination one's artistic future was easy! I was sent to prepare for this exam. at the Pelham School of Art in South Kensington. The students were very refined and snobbish, the girls were mostly of well-to-do families who, I think, sent their daughters there to await the happy moment when they would find husbands. I was deadly serious and determined to get on. The old man who kept the school was a sweet old Scotsman who painted curious pictures of Highlanders and romantic scenes at dawn. They did not seem to me to mean very much. I drew from the antique with energy. Mr. Cope, now Sir Arthur, conducted the life class. He used to roar, " Line! Line! " at the young ladies and they would burst into tears.

I lived at the flat at Chiswick with my Grandmother. I wore a stiff linen collar and tie and corsets with bones in them. A few years later I cast them aside. My Grandmother and an elderly cousin said that it was indecent and disgraceful and women's backs were not strong enough to support themselves; I am now forty-one and my backbone has not yet crumpled up.

In the flat underneath lived a very charming family. They knew H. M. Bateman, which thrilled me, and I would go down in the evenings and hear about the great man, of whom I am still a very great admirer. One of the sons, Charlie, was a medical student. I fell violently in love with him. I was ugly and shy, and he used to take beautiful and well-dressed girls to dances. This made me sad. I was studying Anatomy at the time and going to lectures at the Royal Academy. The grand passion gave me such interest in Anatomy that I learnt and knew by heart every muscle and its attachment. I borrowed his bones, a skull, a backbone, and a chain of vertebrae on a string which hung over the end of my bed at night. I placed the skull affection-

MYSELF AT SEVENTEEN
1907

ately on the table at my bedside. My Grandmother thought that I was mad. Poor Charlie! he is now dead.

I was now sixteen. I drew from the nude at the Art School, but I had never dared to look at myself in the mirror, for my Grandmother had always insisted that one dressed and undressed under one's nightdress using it as a kind of tent. One day, feeling very bold, I took off all my clothes and gazed in the looking-glass. I was delighted. I was much superior to anything I had seen in the life class and I got a book and began to draw.

I went away for the summer to Margate and painted four water-colour landscapes, for which I got a silver medal at Christmas.

A girl student one day gave me a small book by Camille Mauclair on the French Impressionists; I thought they were most interesting and so different from Highlanders in action.

I travelled home one day in the same carriage as a girl who had won the gold medal at the Royal Academy Schools for portrait painting. I was much impressed at first but bitterly disillusioned when I showed her the book and found that she had never heard of Edouard Manet.

One of our students had found a Sketch Class where clothed models, workpeople, and interesting character models posed from five till seven. It was at the London School of Art, where John Swan, the animal painter, and Frank Brangwyn were the professors, and Joseph Simpson took the sketch class. Simpson was a brilliant caricaturist and draughtsman. I went along with her and when I got there I knew for certain that the Royal Academy was no place for me and decided at all costs to leave Pelham Street. This was not so easy, as my Grandmother was thinking of the five years' free education at the Royal Academy Schools rather than my artistic development.

I wrote to Mr. George Clausen, the Academician, who occasionally gave criticisms at Pelham Street. I went with some of my drawings to his studio in St. John's Wood. He was very encouraging and sympathetic and when I asked his opinion on the advisability of going to the London School of Art he seemed to think that it was a good idea. The result was that my Grandmother was induced to pay my fees for a short time.

The next term I went to " Brangwyns," as we called it.

Here at last was paradise. It was run as a French Academy. The class had a Massier who posed the models and the professor came once a week.

Swan was a remarkable personality and was very hard to please. One day a negro model was posing and I was doing a large drawing in charcoal. Swan appeared and said, " Go and wash your hands and face and if you can draw like that you are all right."

Most of the students imitated Brangwyn and their work was atrocious. They imitated his mannerisms instead of learning from his real qualities. He was not a good professor, he had too much personality to teach well.

Later George Lambert and William Nicholson

were the professors. Nicholson always wore a white duck suit, with a spotted tie and socks to match, and came on a push bike.

As we decorated the walls with palette scrapings I am afraid he never left as spotless as he arrived. He taught still life. We began with a white plate and a stout bottle with some white drapery against a grey wall. Nicholson always said when he saw a somewhat shaky plate, "Draw the plate round, it looks more professional," so he got a pair of compasses. He was an excellent teacher.

George Lambert was the best professor I have ever had. He drew beautifully and took endless pains over anyone whom he thought had talent. Lambert took a whole morning painting a leg for me.

Everyone was terrified of Swan and we all ran like rabbits when we saw him coming. One bold student wrote on the door of his Life Class, "Abandon hope all ye who enter here," but as it was high up I don't think he ever saw it.

A girl who was with me at Brangwyns had a room in Chelsea and we shared models. She and her brother Henry Savage knew Richard Middleton, the poet, very well. I found her extremely interesting. She was very well read and talked a great deal about people like Frank Harris and Edward Thomas and we wallowed in the "Shropshire Lad" and the poems of John Davidson.

Wilenski, the critic, was a student there too. He wore a large sombrero and a black cloak and carried a silver-headed stick. He had studied abroad and painted purple and green studies and was the admiration of the whole school, but we were rather frightened of him and regarded him as a superior being who understood the mysteries of life. Jan Gordon was there also.

One day there came to the school a strange young man with a funny hat made of cloth in the pattern of an American sailor's hat. He had a long nose and stuttered. He was at once named " The Genius.'' He certainly had talent. I fell in love with him. I used to visit him in Chelsea; we were very pure.

I used to come home late at night. My Father screamed about virtue. We were only too virtuous. He kissed me one day. We read d'Annunzio. I wished I were older. I bought a large black hat like a coal-scuttle and a dress with a slight train and tried to feel fatal.

We went to the Coliseum to see Sarah Bernhardt. We imagined that we were greater than all the lovers in history. We remained pure because I don't think he quite knew what to do about it, anyway he lacked initiative and so nothing happened. We drank *crème-de-menthe* and felt really devilish.

He painted a picture of me lying on a sofa with an out-stretched hand like a fork. I forget what it represented; I think one of the phases of the soul. I was convinced that I had a fatal and hopeless passion.

About this time I met Arthur Ransome who had written a book called *Bohemia in London*. I walked into a friend's room and a man in knickerbockers,

MYSELF TO-DAY
1932

with a very large moustache, was there. He produced a flute from his pocket and I danced. We
were later introduced. This was Ransome. I
went to his flat one day; as he opened the door
there was an awful smell of shag and beer. Ransome
said, " I am awfully sorry but a friend of mine, a
gipsy, arrived here with his donkey-cart filled with
ferns which he hawks round. I have not seen him
for years." Ransome invited him in and they
talked Romany, drank beer, and smoked shag.
Later, when they came out, the donkey-cart had
been taken to the police station.

Ransome was editing a series of translations of
short stories by foreign authors. One day he asked
me to dine with him at the " Good Intent," on
Chelsea Embankment, he was meeting a young man
who was in Fleet Street. I was much impressed as
I had just read *The Street of Adventure*, by Philip
Gibbs. The young man was Hugh Walpole. They
talked and I listened and felt that life had really
begun.

*   *   *   *   *

Nineteen hundred and nine. A very talented girl
at the Art School, who had been born and brought
up in Russia, asked me to spend the summer vacation
with her family. I was delighted and took the last ten
pounds out of the savings bank and we took a ship
from the Millwall Dock to St. Petersburg.

We were given in charge of the Captain, but he
could never find us in the evenings. We discovered
some students in the Second Class with guitars and

we spent our evenings singing and drinking port. The farther the ship got away from England the better I felt, and my Father and my Grandmother seemed like some nightmare of a forgotten age.

At Kronstadt a steamboat approached filled with the wildest-looking men dressed in green uniforms, with high boots, large flowing beards, carrying swords. These were the Customs officers. They climbed over the side of the ship and looked through our things.

When we got to St. Petersburg we drove in a droshky to my friend's family's flat, a magnificent apartment with salons and many rooms. The next day we went to a place on the Gulf of Finland. This part of Finland is not very beautiful. Nothing but pine trees and forests. I stayed there for two months.

For one week they came to Petersburg to show me the sights.

I went to the first night of the ballet *The Sleeping Beauty*. Pavlova was the *Première Danseuse*, Karsavina the second, and the *Corps de Ballet* was wonderful. Any one of them would have been a star now.

My friend had two unmarried sisters and they had two very beautiful Russian friends who were both unmarried. Every day roses and poems were brought to the Russian girls by students and young officers. I was very envious, but they were bored and sent them away. The students came in their blue uniforms and talked and talked; they never seemed to repeat themselves. They all talked French and most of them English. After their visits we were quite exhausted and they never seemed to have really said anything at all. We had violent arguments in the evenings over the respective values of Dostoievsky and Shakespeare.

A Russian uncle appeared one day, his name was Alexander. There was a piano in the house called the Castrule, which is the Russian name for sauce-pan, because it made such an odd noise. Uncle Alexander sat down to it after luncheon one day and played without stopping for eight hours; he played rather like a barrel organ. He was very sweet and had an enormous grey beard and steel-rimmed spectacles.

I went to my first cinema in Finland. There were no street lamps so we started in a procession with sticks and Chinese lanterns attached by strings. We saw the old Italian funny films where cart wheels dropped off and old ladies were left sitting on them being whirled round and round.

There was a Kursaal where we were taken and given one glass of Swedish punch each—quite enough, as it was very intoxicating and would certainly have gone to our heads. Sometimes they had fêtes and we would dance the Mazurka with Finns and Russians. That was fun and much better than Charlestons and jazz dances. The Finns are mostly very ugly and quick-tempered. One of our friend's cooks disappeared suddenly and we heard that she had been displeased with the butcher and had thrown a large mutton bone at him, doing considerable damage, and had been locked up for a month. There were Northern Lights at night, not

25

very strong but most irritating, as one woke up at one a.m. and thought it was five, and the nights were interminable.

I learnt a little Russian and was sent out to buy stamps and cigarettes. In September I sailed from St. Petersburg. On the boat I met a woman who, like my friends, had been born and brought up in Russia, although of English parents. We became great friends. Her family had cotton mills in Russia. As I shall explain later she was the means of my going to Paris.

I would very much have liked to have stayed in Russia, but there was no chance of an English person getting anything to do. The only thing was to go into a home for decayed gentlewomen and wait for an opportunity to teach English.

I went back to my Grandmother's and felt extremely discontented. I returned to Brangwyns, and as my Grandmother refused to pay any more fees, the manager of the Academy was kind enough to allow me to work there for nothing on the condition that I acted as Massier for the still life class. We painted onions and potatoes and strawberries. The braver and better off students painted melons and pumpkins out of respect for Brangwyn.

I still continued to visit my friend the " Genius " and worked in his studio. He was still painting souls in torture. I did not belong to the imaginative school of painting, so drew charwomen and small children.

One day I was in the King's Road, Chelsea, and someone said, " There goes Augustus John! " In

1906, when I first went to Pelham Street, I had heard
of him and went to his first Exhibition at the Carfax
Galleries. There were drawings and water-colours
and I was thrilled by them and visited the Exhibition many times. I saw a tall man with a reddish
beard, in a velvet coat and brown trousers, striding
along; he was a splendid-looking fellow and I
followed him down the King's Road keeping a
respectable distance behind. I did not discover
until I met him in 1914 that he came from Tenby
and had had the same German and dancing mistress
as I had had twelve years before.

Epstein lived in Cheyne Walk and I would stand
outside hoping to get a glimpse of him. I saw him
through the window one day.

Life was dull and I knew nobody of any real
interest. I went to the local Public Library and
read everything. I had to find out something about
life at all costs, and in order to meet interesting
people decided that I must not be an ignorant bore.

I went and lived with my family. In the evenings,
when I was reading, my Father would come in and,
seeing reproductions of Whistler etchings on the
wall, would scream, "Whistler! Ha! Ha! If you
continue this rot I will have you put into a lunatic
asylum." What with this and my hopeless passion
I became paralyzed. I lost the use of my hands
completely. I was taken to a doctor friend of my
Father's, an unpleasant man who might have been
my Father's twin brother. What I really was suffering from was virginal hysteria and boredom, but this
monster invented a disease called Spinal Adhesion

27

and made me lie down for hours. This made me worse.

I went to Margate with my Mother who I had really never known before. I found her charming and we got on very well. I read philosophy and poetry; my Mother thought that I was overstraining my brain and suggested a little light literature, Ethel M. Dell, etc. I was horrified and continued to read Kant, Schopenhauer, and Baudelaire. I got slightly better and on my return got worse. My Father had a friend who worked with Dr. Forbes Winslow and went in for hypnotic suggestion. I was taken there; he had a medium who went into a trance, she held my hands and he said to her, " She has nothing the matter with her whatever." The medium then came out of her trance, let go of my hands, and the doctor said, " What you want to do is some work, any kind, but occupy your mind." From that moment I recovered.

A second cousin of mine was an opera singer; he had sung at Covent Garden. He had a fine baritone voice but he was not strong and had to spend most of his time touring the Colonies with Madame Albani and singing " Land of Hope and Glory," which urged large crowds to a feeling of patriotism bordering on frenzy. I never liked him; when I was fifteen he would stare at me in a way that made me embarrassed. He was at this time Thomas Beecham's manager and a play called *Proud Maisie*, by Hemmerde, was running at the Aldwych Theatre. I wrote to him asking him if he could get me a job to walk on. I had finished with the Art

School and was at home with no money to buy paints or canvas and very miserable. My cousin wrote and asked me to go to his office. To my joy he said that I could start that night and walk on in the chorus at £1 a week. I was delighted to earn £1 a week at anything, it was a fortune. The play was an eighteenth-century Scottish play, with powdered and bewigged ladies, of whom I was one, and Highlanders in kilts. I thought with a smile of the old Professor at Pelham Street and his pictures of Highlanders in action. There was plenty of action in this play. We had Henry Ainley, Leon Quartermaine, and Alexander Carlisle in the caste, a splendid caste, but the play was not a success. The hero and adored of all the chorus was Leon Quartermaine; Henry Ainley was quite out of the picture. My first night I was standing in the wings and Ainley, seeing a new face, came up to me and, putting his hand under my chin, tilted up my face, looked at it, and walked away. I was in a dressing-room with eleven other girls; they showed me how to make up and were very kind. The management provided eleven wicker-work frames to wear under the dresses and make the panels at the side stick out, and eleven pairs of white drawers with white lace on the legs. These hung on a rail. We had to hold empty golden glasses and sing a drinking song. All the girls had young men who waited for them. They brought them flowers and accompanied them home. I was very much distressed. I had quarrelled with the " Genius " and had no one at all. At the end of the week I got my £1. At the end of the

29

second week the play came to an end. All the chorus were upset and recommended me to visit Mr. Blackmore in Garrick Street. It was strange after my youthful cravings to find myself acting on the stage of a London theatre, but the glamour had already worn off, and even two weeks showed me that I had done well to paint and not to act.

I put on my coal-scuttle hat and the dress with the train, and sat down in Mr. Blackmore's waiting-room. There were dowdy-looking painted ladies of all ages, and a good many rather horsey and beery-looking men, nothing at all like the present-day chorus boy. We all waited, in fact we waited and waited. After waiting about three weeks, one day a page boy, who used to come round daily and peer into our faces, tapped on the window of Mr. Blackmore's office, and as the window was lifted up, shouted, " A little bit of fluff, sir." I then realized that if I sat there for forty years I should never be a " Little Bit of Fluff." I returned to painting. I worked at home and joined the Polytechnic evening life classes at Turnham Green. A neighbour sat for me and I did a pastel of her head which was accepted by the Liverpool Art Gallery.

CHAPTER V   I COME OF AGE

I WAS now twenty-one. I was introduced one day
to a poet. He had long hair. He lived with an
extremely beautiful girl who was an actress. She
had golden eyes and the most perfect eyebrows; she
had long black hair down to her waist. He wrote
hundreds and hundreds of poems to her. She had
plenty of money always. The poet talked of Aleister
Crowley, of whom I had heard a good deal. He
was supposed to be very clever and very wicked. I
was taken to his studio and introduced to him. I
found him extremely intelligent and he did not
strike me as being very bad. He asked me to paint
four panels with signs representing the elements,
earth, air, fire, and water; while I was painting
Fire, apparently the Fire Element escaped, and three
fires started in mysterious ways in the studio on the
same day. It was said that Crowley was so wicked
that no young thing could remain alone in the same
room with him in safety. One day I was painting
by the fire and his secretary went out, leaving me
alone with him. He was lying on the hearthrug in
front of the fire asleep. He woke up, stared at me,
and said, " ARE YOU ALONE? " I said, " YES,"
and he lay down and went to sleep again. Crowley
had some drug from South America; it was quite
harmless and one saw colours. He never offered to
give me any. One day a rich marmalade manufacturer, who had come to study magic, was given
some. He was stone deaf and was sitting by the

fireplace with a dreamy look on his face; he had just taken some. Every now and then Crowley would write on a piece of paper, " What are your impressions? " and the marmalade manufacturer wrote, much to Crowley's disgust, " I see coloured patterns like the tiles in the Victoria and Albert Museum."

I visited the poet and the beautiful girl quite often. She had a big studio in Chelsea. She seemed often depressed and one day said to me, " I am going away to-morrow for a long time, perhaps for ever, come in the morning and I will give you some clothes." I was delighted as I had very few clothes. I felt rather worried about her but did not know what I could do. The next day I went to the studio. Outside pinned on the door was an envelope and inside was the key. I was rather frightened. I opened the door and inside was a large red curtain. I hesitated for a moment, terrified; I pulled it aside and on the sofa she lay dead, with a mother-o'-pearl revolver and her slippers beside her on the floor. Her face was quite white and her golden eyes were half closed. She had placed the revolver to her chest, inside her dress, and shot herself through her heart and lungs. I called the caretaker and he fetched the police. I, of course, had to be a witness. This depressed me for some time.

The following summer my family went to Margate for two weeks. I did not want to go, so my Father gave me two pounds and I took a furnished studio in Chelsea for ten shillings a week and worked. I was quite alone, everyone was away, and I had no one to talk to at all for two weeks, but I could work and was quite happy. About this time my Grandmother died. Nobody was at all sorry. She had to be taken back to Tenby to be buried with my Grandfather. The family went to Paddington to see her off. I found my friend the " Genius " and we ate ham and drank coffee in the Fulham Road. He took a room in Charlotte Street and we became friendly again; the great passion had vanished and he rather bored me. He talked very much about a woman older than himself whom he had met in Cornwall. He had a little picture of hers that I thought very good. He said that she had a wonderful voice and was also very musical. I felt quite jealous. One day I met her and we became great friends. The " Genius " has long since vanished, but often I see his friend. I am afraid we are unkind enough to make fun of him.

One day I visited the Chelsea Palace and saw Fred Karno's *Mumming Birds*. Then there was a man who just walked up and down the stage. He did not speak but he was so funny that the whole house roared. This man, I found out afterwards, was Charlie Chaplin, who must have already done a good many films. At this time two aunts of mine took pity on me to the extent of providing me with 2s. 6d. a week each to help my artistic career. Also a girl whom I had met at Brangwyns had a maiden aunt who suffered from suicidal mania and was certified insane. I taught her painting and cheered her up considerably; she paid me 5s. a lesson, so I was quite well off. This poor woman's life had been

33

completely ruined by her parents' stupid way of bringing her up. When she was a girl she was never even allowed to go to dances, her Father was a clergyman. She had no friends and at the age of twenty fell in love with the coachman. There was a scandal in the village and she never recovered. She drew rather like a child and some of her pictures of ships and the sea were quite good. She eventually died and so my finances were again in a bad way.

My paternal Grandfather was an Indian Civil Servant. He had had at one time a considerable sum of money in a bank that went smash. There still remained a few hundred pounds which the grandchildren would eventually get. A sympathetic uncle by marriage arranged that I could get fifty pounds in advance. This was a fortune and I was overjoyed. I took a room in Grafton Street, Fitzroy Square, for seven and sixpence a week. There were bugs in it. I chased them with a can of petrol. I slept there sometimes but generally went home as I could not afford much to eat during the day-time and there was always food at home. My Father by this time had quite given up any hopes of my becoming a decent human being or marrying a nice man and settling down in the suburbs. He secretly hoped that I would get into some awful mess and then he would be able to say, " I told you so, this is what Art leads to." He and his horrible doctor friend would discuss me with leers and winks and talk about what they thought went on in Art Schools.

In Gower Street was the Slade School. The

London School of Art and the Slade were rivals and we despised the students there. There were dances at the Botanical Gardens. Marquees were put in the gardens and everyone went in fancy dress. We wore very few clothes but the Slade wore Aubrey Beardsley costumes and were covered up to their necks. Our school had the reputation for being immoral whereas we were very innocent and respectable. So much so that one day a girl was discovered kissing a young man behind a door and she was practically cut by the whole school. I now began to feel that having finished with Art Schools I must leave the student stage and become an artist. This I realized was a difficult thing to do as many students at the Art School—and they were of all ages—seemed to have remained students all their lives. I painted a life-size portrait of myself in the looking-glass. The colour was very dull but it was very well drawn. I painted a pale-faced and half-starved looking woman in black, holding a yellow tulip. She was one of Crowley's poetesses and he called her the " Dead Soul "; it was a very good description.

One day when I was going home in the tube I sat opposite a girl. She had a most wonderful face, like the portrait of the girl in the National Gallery by Ghirlandaio; she was rather fatter and I decided that at all costs I must paint her portrait. I followed her out at Hammersmith and touched her on the arm. I said, " Do let me do a painting of you." She looked rather frightened, but I pressed my name and address into her hand. She had a sister who knew some artists in Chelsea and wondered what strange kind of individual I could be. She wrote asking me to tea. The family were charming people. My future model's name was Dilys and her father was Welsh. She came and sat for me and I painted a life-size portrait which delighted us both. I gave it to a second-rate woman novelist who, I believe, put it in the dustbin.

At this time Mark Gertler was very much talked about. He was painting pictures of Jewish characters in Whitechapel which were very interesting, and I saw an exhibition of his things at Chenil's in Chelsea. There was a self-portrait there of a young man with a fringe and very blue eyes. One day I met him and a girl called Carrington, who had won a Scholarship at the Slade. She had fair hair which was cut like an Italian page. She was one of the first women in England to cut off her hair and was very much stared at as she never wore a hat. I invited them both to tea and felt rather as if I had invited a god and goddess. Carrington appeared in one red shoe and one blue. We talked about Art and the future, and I preserved Gertler's tea-cup intact and unwashed on the mantelpiece. It remained there for about a month; I felt that it ought to be given to a museum. He asked me to come to tea. He lived in Bishopsgate with his sister and brother-in-law. I found myself in a Jewish market where hardly anyone spoke English. I finally got to his house. He went downstairs and fetched up a tray with the tea on it; he put it down on the floor and said, " Help yourself! " I met at this time a girl

36

RICHARD SICKERT, R.A.

with long red hair. She was a friend of Gertler's and was an actress. She was acting at the St. James's Theatre, where a Shakespeare season was being given by Granville Barker. I met Cathleen Nesbitt with her, too, and one day Dennis Neilson Terry came to her flat. He had to give a recitation and chose one from the Bible. He recited it to us. In the middle was an awful shriek and he shrieked so loudly that the people upstairs came down thinking someone was being murdered.

I met a woman who took me to one of Walter Sickert's Saturday afternoons. I thought him a wonderful person and he seemed to like me. He came to my room in Grafton Street and liked my work. I used to go to see him nearly every Saturday. I met Lucien Pissarro, who also came to my room and liked my work. I met Wyndham Lewis, T. E. Hulme, and Epstein. At this time a society was started called the " Independants," which was founded on the principle of the Salon des Indépendants in Paris. Anyone could send five pictures on the payment of a small fee. The Albert Hall was hired for the occasion and I sent five pictures, including the " Dead Soul," my portrait of " Dilys," and two others, and it was a most interesting exhibition. The sculpture was downstairs and many famous foreign artists showed there. My pictures were hung upstairs in a group and I thought they looked very nice. All my friends from Brangwyns showed there. I had two press cuttings, one in the *Times*, of which I was very proud. Clutton Brock was then the art critic. I met him some years afterwards and he was always very kind to me in his criticisms.

Some months before in a paper called *Rhythm*, which I took in, I saw some drawings that interested me very much. They were by a young man called Henri Gaudier Brzeska. Downstairs there were statues by him, one was of a wrestler, and four others. I used to visit the show several times a week and when I was tired of walking round I sat down on a chair in the midst of his statues. One day a young man, looking like a foreigner with a little beard, looked at me in an amused kind of way. I thought that this was probably the sculptor, but was too shy to tell him how much I liked his works. He walked away and afterwards I went upstairs and to my delight found him standing in front of my pictures. One day an elderly woman whom I knew asked me if I knew a sculptor who could give her lessons at five shillings a time. I knew the bookseller, Dan Rider, who lived near Charing Cross Road. He was a fat little man who roared with laughter the whole time. He knew Frank Harris very well. He also knew Gaudier Brzeska. I went to see him and I said, " Is Brzeska rich? " and he said, " He is very poor "; so I said, " There is a lady who would like lessons in sculpture." This was in 1913, when five shillings meant more than it does now. It was not very good payment but I wanted to meet him. Dan Rider arranged a meeting at his book shop. I turned up and was introduced to him. I said, " Come back to my place and we will talk about the lessons in sculpture." We walked up

Charing Cross Road. He said, " What do you do? "
I said that I painted and had exhibited at the
Independants at the Albert Hall. He said, " There
were so many pictures." I said nervously I had a
picture of a " Dead Soul," holding a yellow tulip.
He said, " Yes, of course, I remember it, you are the
young girl who sat with my statues; my sister and
I called you ' La Fillette.' " We walked on. He
gave my friend lessons, and one day came to my
room and said, " I am very poor and I want to do a
torso, will you sit for me? " I said, " I don't know,
perhaps I look awful with nothing on," and he said,
" Don't worry." I went one day to his studio in the
Fulham Road and took off all my clothes. I turned
round slowly and he did drawings of me. When he
had finished he said, " Now it is your turn to work."
He took off all his clothes, took a large piece of
marble and made me draw, and I had to. I did
three drawings and he said, " Now we will have
some tea." From the drawings he did two torsos.
The other day Harold Nicolson published one of
the drawings in the *Evening Standard* and said that
the torso was of myself. Henri was very poor and
lived with an elderly woman who, he told me, was
his sister. We used to wander round Putney and
look at stonemasons' yards, where tombstones were
exhibited, in the hopes of finding odd bits of stone in
reach of the railings. One day we found a nice
piece of marble and that night we arranged to
meet. At 10.30 we went to the yard. I watched
for a policeman and he took the piece of marble and
put it in his pocket.

39

Out of this piece of marble he made the first torso of me, which is now in the Victoria and Albert Museum. I thought he was the most wonderful person that I had ever met. The sister was rather terrifying and Polish. At that time young men had the idea that Polish women were the only women in the world. They certainly had brains, but also temperaments and many "complexes." She and Henri lived in rooms in Putney and Henri had a workshop under one of the arches of Putney Bridge. I spent every Sunday afternoon with him. We bought chestnuts and roasted them and he drew me in my clothes. Henri had a bright red shirt. A friend of mine had invented a shirt, the neck was cut square, it was what is now called a jumper. Henri had a red one and wore it inside his trousers. I wore mine outside my skirt and people stared at us in the street. Henri talked about the "*sales bourgeois*." In the next arch of Putney Bridge there lived an academic sculptor who did monuments. He did not carve stone, so Henri despised him. He had a band of Italian workmen who came and did the dirty work for him, that is to say, they hacked out the stone. When the sculptor was out Henri would buy the workmen some Chianti and learn from them how to carve stone. He bought a forge cheaply and put it in his backyard. There he used to forge the tools that he sculpted with. It was a wonderful machine with large bellows and made a great noise. Henri said to me, " Don't mind what people say to you, find out what you have in yourself and do your best, that is the only hope in life."

One day I sold six of Henri's drawings to a friend of mine for £1 each. He said, " Don't tell my sister you sold six, say it was only five and we will go to the ' Swiss ' in Soho and have some drinks." I dined with him and his sister in their rooms in Putney. There was a row during dinner and they threw some beefsteaks at each other. After dinner she said to Henri, " You bore me, take Nina away and give her something to drink," so we went to the " Swiss." After we had had some beer Henri said, " She is not my sister, she is my mistress," and I choked down some sobs. She did not seem to mind my going out with Henri and in fact rather encouraged it, so I thought that it didn't matter. Henri bought a large knife with a curved blade. He had met W. B. Yeats who told him about the ghosts of his ancestors. Henri said, " I have never met a ghost and if I did I should take this bloody great knife and kill him." Henri never met a ghost, but I did later on, and I didn't have a knife.

Henri knew Ezra Pound very well and liked him. Ezra said, " You must sculpt me," and bought him a block of marble. He said, " You must make me look like a sexual organ." So Henri got to work with a piece of charcoal and drew on the stone. He chipped and chipped and it was magnificent and it has been offered to and refused by many museums. It is now in a front garden in Kensington, surrounded by geraniums. Henri slept generally under the arch on an iron bed, one of the kind that servants used to sleep on and could be folded up. It looked very uncomfortable. He disapproved of comfort. " Artists should be poor and not indulge in comforts of any kind." One night we went to an anarchist meeting in Soho. They had weekly meetings and each week in a different language. This night it was in German. Henri knew five languages and translated for me. I did not know much about anarchy but I thought that any kind of revolt against anything was good. I decided that it was dreadful not to have been born in Whitechapel and that the proletariat were the only people who were capable of anything. Henri came to my room sometimes. He arrived one day and took out of his pocket a large statue. I could see it sticking out as it was about a foot long. It was " The Singing Woman " and is now in the Tate Gallery. We put it on the table and admired it. Henri talked about art and said, " Painting is an art for women, Literature is an art for old people, but Sculpture is the art for strong men."

I still had my room in Grafton Street. One day somebody said, " You might get a job to paint furniture and do decorative work at the Omega workshops in Fitzroy Square." The man who owned it was Roger Fry. I knew his name very well as he organized the first Post-Impressionist show in London in 1911.

Feeling brave one morning I went to Fitzroy Square and asked to see Mr. Fry. He was a charm-ing man with grey hair, and said that I could come round the next day and start work. I went round and was shown how to do Batiks. I was paid by the

42

hour. I made two or three pounds a week and felt like a millionaire. I brought Henri round one day and he did a design for a tray which was eventually carried out in inlaid woods.

CHAPTER VI   LIFE

I was now twenty-two, and having read many
books, thought that it was time to consider the
problem of sex. I was almost completely ignorant.
I decided that the next man I met and whom I liked
I would hand myself over to. I went to see an
elderly woman in Chelsea and asked her what
happened. She gave me such a terrifying description that when the moment arrived for the presenta-
tion of my virginity I required more courage than
a soldier has when " Going over the top."

One day I went to see Crowley in the Fulham
Road, where I met a most beautiful creature. He
had long green eyes and hands like the Angel in the
National Gallery by Filippino Lippi. He seemed
to like me too. He took two rooms near Fitzroy
Square; one night I arranged to see him at 10.30.
I arrived and he said, " Will you take your clothes
off? " So I did and the deed was done. I did not
think very much of it, but the next morning I had
a sense of spiritual freedom and that something important had been accomplished.

I read frequently the poems of Paul Verlaine, and
translations (of which there were not many) of
Arthur Rimbaud. One day I read Berrichon's
book on Rimbaud and discovered to my amusement
that the rooms where I had left my virginity behind
were those that Rimbaud and Verlaine had stayed
in in London. One day I said to Walter Sickert,
" Do you think that they will put up a blue plaque

on the house for me or will they put up one for
Verlaine and Rimbaud? " and Walter said, " My
dear, they will put up one on the front for you and
one on the back for them." My beautiful admirer
tired of me very soon. I discovered afterwards that
he liked only pure young girls who very quickly
bored him. We went to Paris and I stayed at the
same hotel with a Russian woman who was a friend
of his, and who came over with us. I did not see
much of him. We stayed there for five days.
Epstein and his wife were there and I met Brancusi
the sculptor. At this time Epstein's Memorial to
Oscar Wilde was put up in Père Lachaise. For some
reason it was considered indecent and covered up
with a tarpaulin, so every afternoon Epstein, his
wife, Brancusi, a Spanish painter, his wife and I,
would go to Père Lachaise and snatch the tarpaulin
off. Eventually the French police were told about
it, and, when we next arrived, hiding behind the
tombstones were policemen who rushed at us and
covered the statue up again.

I liked Paris and determined to return there as
soon as I could collect sufficient money. Montparnasse was cheap and everyone worked all day
and came to the Rotonde in the evening. I was still
rather in love. After five days my money gave out
and I came back to London with the Russian woman.
I have always regretted not having stayed another
night as I could have seen Isadora Duncan dance,
and at that time she was in her prime. When I got
back to Grafton Street I burst into tears. I cried
every day for four days.

I had always wanted to cut off my hair—I never had very much—but my friend had said, " You must never cut your hair off." The first thing that I did was to get it cut. To my delight it curled and I wore a fringe. I felt a sense of freedom. A large fair man, who was a poet, was brought to see me the day after I had come back. He came to see me every day at five o'clock, and after the fourth day my sobs ceased at that hour. He took me to dinner one evening at a restaurant called the Eiffel Tower. Some artists and poets went there. We had a very good dinner and the proprietor seemed very pleased to see him. I soon recovered from my passion and started to work again. He wrote me a poem which I still have, but as his handwriting is rather difficult I can only make out some of it.

I sent a picture to the New English Art Club which was accepted and which was hung on the line. Epstein saw it and liked it very much and spoke about me to people. I knew a man called Redmond Howard; he was the nephew of John Redmond. He was a journalist and, like the rest of us, generally in financial difficulties. Once he pawned all his possessions and was left only with a top-hat and a frock coat.

John Flanagan, the painter, lived in Fitzroy Street and he had supper parties consisting of sausages and mashed. One day a man came to my room and bought a drawing. Howard turned up and I said, " Let's go for a drink." He replied, " If you don't mind do buy me a pair of socks instead." We went to Berwick market and got a pair of socks.

46

The old Jew who had the stall said to me, " Vill you 'ave some silk stockings—very cheap? " I said, " Oh no, that would be extravagant." And he said, " Oh no, it vill be an investment," and I was so flattered that he mistook me for a lady of loose morals that I took Redmond out and we spent all the money.

One of the first night clubs was started in London at this time, 1913. It was started by Madame Strindberg, the second wife of the Swedish playwright. She had been a famous actress and beauty in Vienna when she was young. I had been taken to the Café Royal some weeks before by Henri where we would drink *crème-de-menthe frappée*.

I had met Lilian Shelley, a beautiful girl who was on the stage. She sang at the " Cave of the Golden Calf," the name of the night club. It was decorated by Wyndham Lewis and several other artists, and Epstein had done sculptures for two of the columns. It was a really gay and cheerful place. Madame Strindberg brought a flock of Galician gipsies over and they played accordions and sang and danced. There were beautiful ladies and young Guardsmen and artists, and everyone had a good time. Madame Strindberg had a monkey and every evening at 10.30 Lilian Shelley, who sang " Popsy Wopsy " and " You made me love you " every night at the cabaret, was sent to the Savoy Hotel to feed it. Madame Strindberg gave dinner parties there. She was very fond of inviting people who disliked each other. These parties frequently ended in a free fight.

I wore in the daytime a clergyman's hat, a check

coat, and a skirt with red facings, including the button-hole, which was faced with red too. Walter Sickert always asked me, " When had I won the Legion of Honour? " I wore white stockings and men's dancing pumps and was stared at in the Tottenham Court Road. One had to do something to celebrate one's freedom and escape from home.

One day the woman whom I had met in the ship when I returned from Russia, came to my room. She said, "What are you going to do now?" I said that I would like to go to Paris. She said, " I have twenty pounds in the bank doing nothing. Would you like to take it and go to Paris? " I said that I would. She sent me a cheque for thirty pounds and one day I packed my bags and went to Paris alone. In Paris I knew one of the beautiful Russian girls with whom I had been in Finland, and a gipsy. I arrived knowing only the French that I had learnt at the Royal School. I went to a hotel in the Boulevard Raspail and took a room. The bed was very short and had a feather mattress, the room looked on to a courtyard and smelt horrible. The next day I visited my Russian and the gipsy who lived in the same hotel. I told them that I did not want to know any English-speaking people. The first evening I arrived in Paris, I went to a little restaurant in the Rue Campagne Première which was kept by an old Italian woman called " Rosalie." She looked very distinguished and had a wonderful Roman nose. She had been a great beauty and a model of Whistler's. Epstein had recommended it to me. I sat down alone and began my dinner. Suddenly the door

opened and in came a man with a roll of newspaper
under his arm. He wore a black hat and a corduroy
suit. He had curly black hair and brown eyes and
was very good looking. He came straight up to me
and said, pointing to his chest, "*Je suis Modigliani,
Juif, Jew*," unrolled his newspaper, and produced
some drawings. He said, "*Cinq Francs.*" They
were very curious and interesting, long heads with
pupil-less eyes. I thought them very beautiful.
Some were in red and blue chalk. I gave him five
francs and chose one of a head in pencil. He sat
down and we tried to understand each other and I
said that I knew Epstein and we got on very well,
although I could not understand much of what he
said.

He used to drink a great deal of wine, and absinthe
when he could afford it. Picasso and the really
good artists thought him very talented and bought
his works, but the majority of people in the Quarter
thought of him only as a perfect nuisance and told
me that I was wasting my money. Whenever I had
any money to spare I would buy one of his drawings.
Sometimes they would come down to three francs.
Every morning he would come to the Rotonde with
his drawings and he generally collected five francs
before twelve o'clock. He was then quite happy
and able to work and drink all day. I had an introduction from a man in London to a Russian
woman painter called Marie Wassilieff; she had
been a pupil of Matisse and had now become a
Cubist. She had an Academy where Fernand
Léger was the professor. She lived in a large work-

shop in the Avenue du Maine. There worked Russians, Germans, and Scandinavians, but no English or Americans. There were very good models posed with draperies and mimosa. Every afternoon from five to seven there was a sketch class with poses lasting from five minutes to half an hour. On Fridays two models posed together. One day a large negro and his wife sat. They giggled all the time and another negro sat on a chair with a guitar and played a whistle through his nose as we drew.

Wassilieff and I became great friends. She did not speak any English and I learnt to speak fluent but bad French very quickly. Modigliani lived in the Boulevard Raspail in a studio with a garden; a watch was nailed on to a tree for him to see the time. He would often come home at two or three in the morning and start to carve stone. The neighbours, hearing the tap, tap of his chisel decided that he was " *louftingue.*" I only went there once, I was rather frightened of him. I went round one afternoon. At that time he did not paint, but drew and sculpted. There was a long head with a very long nose that was broken. Modigliani said, " *Un soir il a tombé et il a cassé son nez.*" What had really happened was that Modigliani came home feeling rather gay, bumped into it, and knocked it over. It is now in the Victoria and Albert Museum and its nose has been mended. One night he came home very drunk. He was very hot and he took off all his clothes and lay down in the garden on the flower-bed which was against the walls of the studio. In the early hours of the morning two cats

THE " FRIDAY " MODELS
AT WASSILIEFF'S

had a love affair on the roof, and during the howling period, slipped and dropped down on his naked body. He woke up with a scream and ran up the Boulevard Raspail into the arms of an astonished policeman. Every night he would come to the Rotonde and sit beside me. He drew all the time and I watched him. When he got too drunk to draw he would put his head on my shoulder and go to sleep. I was rather embarrassed and sat straight up feeling proud but rather foolish. One day I went to the Salon des Indépendants. This was the year that Arthur Craven—the nephew of Oscar Wilde's wife—edited a paper called *Maintenant*, and wrote a criticism of the Indépendants. He stood outside and sold it himself for thirty centimes. He was at one time a champion boxer and it tickled the French, who wrote columns about the "ex-champion of France" who sold art criticisms outside the "Exposition des Indépendants." The criticism was very funny and a great deal of it very true. He criticized celebrated female artists' figures and appearance rather than their talents. Of one lady he criticized her legs, which he did not approve of. Her lover, a distinguished critic, took exception to this and challenged him to a duel. He wrote in the next column of his paper, "*Si Monsieur —— continue de m'emmerder avec ses challenges je tordrai ses parties sexuelles.*" He would also write such things as, "*Nous sommes heureux d'entendre la mort de l'académicien Jules Lefèbvre.*" I never met him but I saw him often sparring with negro boxers at Van Dongen's studio on Thursday afternoons. Van Dongen lived near

the Boulevard St. Michel and all the critics came
and drank liqueurs on Thursdays. In one corner
boxing went on. One day they asked me to dance,
so I took off all my clothes and danced in a black
veil. Everyone seemed pleased, as I was very well-
made. I met Zadkine, the sculptor. In the evenings Zadkine would sit in the Rotonde and draw still
lives in pen-and-ink of glasses, packets of cigarettes,
and pipes, or anything else that was on the
table.

On Saturdays everyone stayed out nearly all
night. After the Rotonde closed at two we went to
the Boulevard St. Michel. One night Wassilieff,
Zadkine, Modigliani, myself and several others
walked to a café. The atmosphere of the Boul' Mich'
was very different to that of the Rotonde. There
were many painted ladies and dull students of the
Sorbonne, and sometimes business men who bought
everyone drinks. We drank cheap red wine, and
talked and laughed and sang. Zadkine and
Modigliani bought me a large bunch of roses; I
had a marvellous time and at seven-thirty a.m. they
accompanied me to my hotel.

I had a wonderful collection of stockings at that
time and wore flat-heeled shoes with straps on them
like children do. They made my feet look very
large. They cost five francs and were worn by
concierges. I had red stockings and yellow stockings
and some that looked like a chess board. Modigliani
would run after me up the Boulevard Raspail after
the Rotonde had closed. He could always see me
because of my loud stockings. One night he nearly

caught me so I climbed up a lamp-post and waited at the top till he had gone.

Zadkine had a studio in the Rue de Vaugirard. I said that my hair wanted cutting and he said, " I will borrow a pair of scissors from the *concierge* and will cut it for you." He cut my hair like a Russian peasant, the same way that he wore his own and I looked like one of his sculptures. The fourteenth of July came. Nobody goes to bed in France for three days. They start on the evening of the thirteenth and nothing closes until the evening of the fifteenth. I went to the Avenue du Maine and bought a pair of French workmen's peg-top trousers. I borrowed a blue jersey and corduroy coat from Modigliani and a check cap. I also bought a large butcher's knife made of cardboard and silver paper at the Bon Marché. This I put in the long pocket which was meant either for knives—as the Apaches wear them too—or rulers. I dressed myself up and went out alone. I met Modigliani at the corner of the Rue Delambre and the Boulevard Montparnasse. He did not recognize me and when I produced the knife he ran away. I went to the Rotonde, where the waiters did not know me, and to a fair outside the Closerie des Lilas. I returned to the Rotonde and we danced in the streets all night and kept it up for three days. Afterwards everyone retired to bed for at least a day. About every two or three weeks dances were given in a big café in the Avenue du Maine; they cost three francs, and everyone went. They were always fancy dress and were very amusing. I generally wore my Apache costume.

53

Once a woman friend of mine dressed herself up as a female Apache, with a black shawl and a red rose in her ear. She painted her face very much and we went round Montparnasse arm-in-arm. We looked so realistic that no one suspected that we were in fancy dress. Wassilieff gave her annual party. We collected Modigliani and the sculptor, Hunt Diederich, who had just had a great success at the Salon des Indépendants with his " *Levriers.*" Hunt went dressed as an Arab. He brought a huge copper kettle from his studio which he filled with beer, and we made Modigliani carry it. Guillaume Apollinaire was there. After a time Modigliani decided to undress. He wore a long red scarf round his waist like the French workmen. Everyone knew exactly when he was going to undress, as he usually attempted to after a certain hour. We seized him and tied up the red scarf and sat him down. Everyone danced and sang and enjoyed themselves till the morning.

I went to the Salon d'Automne. There I saw a portrait of a young man. It was not a very good portrait but the young man so impressed me that I stood for a long time before it. It was of a youth of about twenty with a long pale face and slanting eyes, with his coat-collar turned up. He looked sad and hungry. That night at the Rotonde he walked in. He did not seem to know anybody. For months I stared at him and when Modigliani slept on my shoulder I looked over his curly head at the young man's pale face. He fascinated me and disturbed my thoughts. I worked in the mornings at

54

Wassilieff's and visited Museums in the afternoons.
I drank café crème at the Rotonde. Life was so
exciting that I had no time to drink. Sometimes if
anyone was rich we drank champagne at fifty
centimes a glass.

One day Wyndham Lewis came from London in
order to arrange for the publication of his Vorticist
Magazine, *Blast*, in Paris. I had always got on very
well with him and regarded him as a great man. I
was delighted and flattered when he took my arm
and walked down the Boulevard Montparnasse with
me, explaining his ideas and the possibilities of the
future. He spoke in French and addressed me in the
second person singular, the only person who ever
had; I found it difficult to reply as my grammar
was very shaky.

I heard that Arthur Ransome was in Paris. He
introduced me to a very good-looking young man
who was an aristocrat. He wore very old clothes, a
large cloak, and a black hat, and wrote poetry.
His shoes were never cleaned; he said that he was
incapable of putting them outside the door at night.
After I got to know him we sent a postcard every
night addressed to him, " Dear Basil, please put out
your shoes in the morning." His name was not
Basil, but that is what I shall call him. We had
lunch at the Restaurant Leduc in the Boulevard
Raspail. When we were having coffee I said,
" Where does one find a bath here? I have not had
one for weeks." Ransome looked horrified and
they called a *fiacre* and told the driver to go to the
nearest public baths. The building was by the Gare

Montparnasse; it was of a circular pattern. Downstairs was for men and upstairs for women. Ransome bought me a piece of pink soap that floated, and
a towel. I was taken upstairs by an old woman and
Basil and Arthur remained downstairs. I scrubbed
and scrubbed till the skin nearly came off. I got
out and Ransome called from downstairs, "How
are you getting on?" I said, "I have finished washing." He said, "What! you can't possibly be clean,
go back and do some more scrubbing." So I went
back and splashed the water about until I was told
that I could come out. We then went and drank
some Vermouth Cassis, which is vermouth and a
syrup and is drunk by the work girls. Basil was very
good-looking and resembled Rupert Brooke, only
that he was shorter. He liked me very much. I
very nearly fell in love with him. He was a great
success with women, and was rather spoilt and conceited. I was told that he had treated a friend of
mine very badly. He had visited her daily and
implored her to marry him. She refused, but at the
end of six months, when she actually did fall in love
with him, he went off with a Frenchwoman. I
could not see myself being treated like that and I
rather despised him for being an aristocrat. I still
shared Henri's sentiments to a great extent.

In London the second Independant show was
being held, this time at the Holland Park Skating
Rink. I had sent a life-size nude painting of two
women. People thought it rather vulgar. I also
sent a portrait of Zadkine. Some of the critics liked
it. Henri wrote for *Blast*, Wyndham Lewis's paper,

56

and the *Egoist*. He sent me a postcard and on it was
" I liked your works at Holland Park very much as
you may have seen from my article in the *Egoist*."
He wrote this of me: " Miss Hamnett cares much
about representation. I was very interested to see
a portrait of Zadkine the wood-carver. In this
work there are great technical qualities of paste and
drawing—more amplified in the other portrait—
where carefully chosen blacks and violets create a
very distinguished effect. I see from the quality of
the ' Women composition ' that the affinities of this
artist are coming nearer to preference for abstract
design."

Henri did not like Zadkine. He knew him in
London before he had gone to Paris. Zadkine
carved trunks of trees into Apostles, and a large
group of figures. Henri despised people who did
not carve stone. This was not quite fair, as Zadkine
carved stone too. Basil came to see me nearly every
day. He asked me to marry him. I thought of my
unfortunate friend and said " No." The more I
refused the more persistent he became.

I was, in fact, in love with the pale young man
who sat at the Rotonde. Every evening Modigliani,
Wassilieff, Hunt Diederich, his wife and I dined at
Rosalie's. His wife, who was a Russian, designed
and herself carried out, very beautiful embroideries.
She drew at Wassilieff's Sketch Class. There were
forty or fifty people there every evening and Modigliani would come in and sit on the floor and draw.
There was a very long staircase leading up to the
workshop and we could hear him approaching if he

was drunk, and stumbling upstairs. If he was too far gone we would chase him out. Sometimes he would make terribles noises and frighten the old ladies in the class. Everyone suspected that I had a good figure and they asked me to take my clothes off and dance. I said that I did not know any dances but they said that it did not matter. I still had feelings of modesty but, being inordinately vain and proud of my figure, one day I took off all my clothes. Somebody played Debussy's " Golliwog's Cakewalk " on the piano and I improvised a dance. This was a great success and so was the figure. I danced for them two or three times a week. Everyone was charming and the old ladies brought me flowers. Zadkine and Modigliani drew as I danced. A German lady asked me to sit and carved a little statue in wood of me. I have forgotten her name, but she was quite talented in the Munich style. She did busts and painted them, including the eyes— rather like the archaic Greek sculptures.

Basil was a great friend of Isadora Duncan's. He told her about me. I did not want to dance and only pranced about for fun and to be admired. Wassilieff said that I was " Gothic." One day Hunt Diederich and his wife gave a party. They had some Russians who played balalaikas and sang. I danced to the balalaikas. I started by dancing in a veil and then took it off. A French millionaire was there and he wanted me to dance in a cabaret. I refused. I sat for Hunt and he did a frieze round a lampshade of me dancing round it in different attitudes. The millionaire consoled himself by buying it for a respectable sum of money. About midnight a disturbance was heard outside accompanied by loud bangings on the door. This was Modigliani, who always appeared if he heard that I was dancing anywhere. Hunt threw him out. I was rather sorry as we could have sat him down in a corner. Hunt and his wife were great friends of his; they bought his drawings and were very good to him. One day he sold a stone head for a hundred francs. He adored Picasso, who wore a blue serge suit and a yellowish-brown cap. Modigliani went out and bought a blue suit and a yellowish brown cap. He strutted up and down outside the Rotonde to be admired. Unfortunately towards the evening he got very drunk and fell into the gutter, covering the beautiful new suit with mud, and was very battered and sorry for himself the next morning.

Augustus John knew him very well and bought two of his sculptures, which are now at his house at Chelsea. He gave him several hundred francs for them. This was before I knew either of them. Modigliani said that he was tired of Paris and the vile existence that he lived, and pined for Italy. He asked John not to give him all the money but enough to get to Italy, where he could live very cheaply, and send him the money in small sums at a time. He went to Italy and, after, wrote to say that he was well and happy, enjoying the pure atmosphere and the sunlight, so far away from the temptations of Paris. John sent some more money and Modigliani took the next train back to France.

One day he was asked to the house of a very rich man who was having a reception. He was introduced to a woman with an exceptionally ugly but interesting face. He said, " *Madame, votre figure m'intéresse énormément: c'est la gueule la plus monstrueuse que je n'ai jamais vue mais intéressante,* admirrrable *du point de vue du dessin et je voudrais bien vous dessiner.*" The poor lady was very embarrassed, but later, I think, when she found out who he was, she sat for him. Modigliani always said "Admirrrable" when he saw something that pleased him. There was a very striking woman who came to the Rotonde, called Madame Bing. Her husband was Henry Bing, who worked on *Simplicissimus*, the German paper. She had a white face and short golden hair. She wore a long black cloak and a black hat. I asked her to sit for me and I painted a life-size portrait of her which was not bad (also mentioned by Henri in the *Egoist*). Wassilieff liked it. I did not paint Cubist pictures, although Léger had given me two lessons and I had succeeded in painting a life-sized nude torso; this certainly had a certain influence of Cubism.

I had a studio in a courtyard in the Boulevard Edgar Quinet. It cost fifty francs a month, which was at that time two pounds. It belonged to an American painter called Lionel Walden. He painted seascapes in the Hawaiian Islands, which were a great success at the Salon and in America. He had some plaster casts of legs and arms. I gave a party one evening after I had sold a painting. We dressed ourselves up in sheets and black draperies

MODIGLIANI

and held the arms and legs close to our bodies, so that they stuck out of the draperies. It had a curious effect and looked very *sur-réaliste*.

The gipsy I knew when I came to Paris was called Fenella. She had been discovered, sitting on a doorstep in London, by Ransome. She had posed for Augustus John and I had seen several drawings of her at his exhibition at the Carfax Galleries. She looked like a bird. She had a very long neck and large rather protruding eyes. She wore a tight dress with silver buttons down the front and shoes like I did, with straps. She had the prettiest legs and smallest feet that I have ever seen. She played a guitar and sang. She spoke about ten languages and sang in sixteen, including Japanese. She was supposed to be consumptive and drank soda-water and milk. She had a drawer-full of louis d'or, one of which she lent me one day and which I gave back. She came to my party and sang. We bought bottles of wine at fifty centimes a bottle and it was quite drinkable. At five a.m. we went to the Rotonde and sat there till nine o'clock.

Frederick Etchells, the painter, was living in Paris. He was a friend of Wyndham Lewis's.

There was a very amusing and clever painter called Charles Winzer and every evening we three would meet at the Rotonde. We wrote poems. I wrote the last words of the poems, four of which had to rhyme and a fifth that did not, and they wrote in the poems. They were very funny and we spent the whole evening laughing at them. My friend Basil, whom I quarrelled with periodically, was cut off by his parents every few weeks and had to return to England to pacify his Mother. My thirty pounds was melting away and I feared that I would have to return to England. One day he came back having got quite a lot of money. I said, " I shall have to go back to London." He said, " You must not go, I will buy two water-colours." So he gave me some money and I stayed on. One was a drawing I had done in 1912, when I stayed with a friend in Dorset. It was of a fair at Corfe Castle and was quite good. Basil left them at my place as he was going to Italy; he never collected them as he never had a place to put them in, so I kept them for him. He was afterwards killed in the War, and last year I had an Exhibition in Berkeley Street at the Galitzine Gallery and exhibited " the Fair." A strange man, whom I did not know, came and bought it for ten guineas.

Basil was going to Italy with a friend of his; he wanted me to go too. He said, " My friend, who is an elderly man, will chaperone you." His friend arrived in Paris and I met a most charming man who certainly was not over thirty. I did not go. They went and I received telegrams daily from Venice to join them. I think I was foolish not to have gone now, as I should have got into much less trouble than I did by staying in Paris. I did not realize at the time how genuinely fond of me he was and I still hankered after the pale creature at the Rotonde. I regretted very much when I heard in 1915 that he had been killed in Mesopotamia. I received a postcard from him, written the day before he died.

In the Quarter were two Japanese. They were known as "*Les Japonais*." They were a great success at parties. One was Foujita, who has since become world famous, and the other was Kavashima who is also a well-known painter and spends his life in Germany and America. They were pupils of Raymond Duncan. They wove the material that their clothes were made of and made their own sandals. They wore their hair in fringes with bands of ribbon round their heads, and Greek robes and sandals. They danced Greek dances and worked all day. Diego Rivera, the Mexican artist, did a Cubist painting of them both together with square faces. It was exactly like them, although far from realistic. It was what Jean Cocteau would describe as "*plus vrai que le vrai.*"

Kisling, the Polish painter, came each evening to the Rotonde. He wore his hair with a fringe too. He was thin and very good-looking. He had a dispute with a painter called Gottlieb and they arranged to fight a duel. Rivera was one of the seconds. They went out of Paris. A cinema man with a camera was there and we saw it on the pictures the same evening. Kisling came to the Rotonde with a cut on his nose and was considered a great hero. I think that if he had washed the blood off it would not have been visible. Very seldom we went to Montmartre. I went once to the Lapin Agile. Ghil (note the pun) was an old man who looked like the " old man of the sea." He wore a fur cap and had a long beard. This was the cabaret where Picasso and Max Jacob and all the famous painters and writers went years before, when the artists lived in Montmartre, and when it was really cheap and very gay. I took a violent dislike to the old man and could not go there without having a row with him. There was a life-size plaster cast of Christ, on which the students had carved their names; it was carved from head to foot with signatures and looked as if it was suffering from smallpox. I believe that I signed it too. We drank small plums in Kirsch and poets recited bad poems and Monsieur Ghil played a very fine guitar. I did not like the atmosphere of Montmartre, or the people, and I think only went there twice during my whole stay. I went to the Moulin Rouge once and saw elderly ladies in long skirts doing the can-can. That was fun as they looked just like the drawings of Toulouse Lautrec, and, in fact, I think were the same ladies having grown considerably older.

The Café du Dôme was opposite the Rotonde. It was filled with Germans and Americans. I very seldom went there. The Americans had a poker game every evening. This continued for about twenty years, and only broke up a few years ago. I did not know any Americans, but Basil used to play poker with them in the evenings, and sometimes made quite a lot of money which we would spend together. He would tell me funny stories about them. A large man with a red beard went out to the other side of the river to dine with his relations. He wore a dinner jacket. After he had disposed of his relatives he went to Montmartre and then to " Les Halles," where everyone ended

amongst the cabbages and onions. He returned
to Montparnasse in a very battered condition at
eight-thirty in the morning. Along the Boulevard
Montparnasse was a tramway, and the road between
the tram-lines was dug up for repairs, leaving a hole
about six feet deep. The red-bearded man felt
sleepy and got down the hole and went to sleep.

About an hour later the noise of the trams woke
him up and he appeared like " Venus rising from
the Ocean," and rose up in the middle of the street.
Many nice old ladies and their daughters, who were
studying Art, were having breakfast on the terrace
of the Rotonde and the Dôme and were shocked
and surprised at this strange sight.

Every Friday evening I went to Lavenue's, which

is opposite the Gare Montparnasse. I went with
Madame Bing and three other Germans. One was
a professor of mathematics. He did not like being
accosted by strange ladies in cafés, so he would sit
when he was alone, with a piece of paper stuck into
the ribbon of his bowler hat with "*Sourd-Muet*"
written on it. They talked of how the Germans
were going to kill all the English very soon. I pro-
tested, but they said, "You will see, and quite soon
too." Although they were very nice to me I think
they got great pleasure in trying to frighten me. I
knew nothing whatever about politics or the European situation and it did not worry me at all.
Occasionally we would go to the downstairs' bar at
the Café du Panthéon in the Boul' Mich'. There
were many students and very many painted prosti-
tutes there. Sprigs of white lilac were sold and
presented to the ladies. I was rather shocked and
thought that the white lilac was much too pure and
beautiful to be presented to such obvious harpies.

On Friday nights the literary people assembled at
the Closerie des Lilas. The great man there was
Paul Fort, and everybody sat round and listened to
him. He wore a large black hat and long hair and
certainly looked like a poet. Alexandre Mercereau
was there too; I knew him, but I never met Paul
Fort. The poets did not really like the artists coming there, but we sat in a corner and looked impressed, so they got used to us. I wore a jumper
made on the same pattern as those Henri and I wore
in London, only it was of a large cubist design in
blue, orange, and black. No one in Paris had seen

66

ETCHELLS MODIGLIANI

MYSELF

A FANCY DRESS DANCE IN THE AVENUE DE MAINE
1914

anything quite like it and although Sonia Delaunay was already designing scarves, this was more startling. It was made and designed for the Omega Workshops by Roger Fry. I have it on in the photograph of the dance in the Avenue du Maine, where Modigliani is standing in the background. In the Rue de la Gaîté is the Gaîté Montparnasse, a music hall rather like the " Old Bedford." At the back of the stalls are boxes. We used to go once a week. The gallery cost fifty centimes. Modigliani came with us, too. About twelve of us went one night and sat in a row on a very narrow and hard plank in the gallery. Modigliani sat on the end and pushed and pushed. We all pushed together and he fell off the end, so in disgust he left us and went to the bar. There were very funny and very vulgar revues with the usual bedroom scenes and simple-minded jokes that made the French workpeople roar with laughter. The last time I was in Paris I went there, but it had all been redecorated in horrible colours in an attempt to be very modern. One day I met Archipenko, the sculptor. He sculpted statues in tin and wood and exhibited at the Salon des Indépendants. He painted his statues in bright colours and had a very fine sense of colour. He was a tall man with a reddish beard and deep set eyes. I went to his studio with a sculptor whom I knew. He had a wonderful musical instrument with about twenty strings that looked like a harp. It was invented and made by a sailor and he had bought it and could play Russian tunes on it. Archipenko had pupils. There were two very beautiful German girls

67

who had come to study the abstract. They were very rich and the elder one kept a monkey and took a large studio. She drank ether and once went out for the evening leaving the bottle of ether by the stove. When she came home later she found one of the walls of the studio had been blown out.

I had sent the money that I had to a bank in England and received a money order once a fortnight. One day I went to the Post Office and found that the duplicate of the money order had not arrived and that I was penniless till Monday. A girl whom I knew said that she posed for an elderly American and would I take her job on for two days as she had to go to the country. He lived in the Boulevard Arago. He had a studio flat there. I was shown into the studio and the door was shut. I could hear the voices of rich-sounding women and felt like a housemaid who was looking for a situation. He put his head through the door and told me to undress. I took my clothes off and he eventually appeared. He grumbled at my figure and said there was not enough of it. I was furious and took a violent dislike to him. He made me sit in a most impossible pose which nearly broke my back, and did some dreadful drawings. He quite obviously disliked me as much as I disliked him. He then returned to his rich ladies and I dressed myself. He came back and gave me two francs-fifty. Two francs-fifty was half-a-crown in those days, and the usual fee. I sat for him the next day and then fortunately my money came. This was my first experience as a professional model. I had others later, but they were more agreeable.

Aleister Crowley was in Paris and I saw him from time to time. He always went out at midday to say a prayer to the sun. One day I met him in the Boulevard Montparnasse. Suddenly he stopped in the middle of the street and addressed the sun. I did not know the prayer in question, so respectfully stood behind him until he had finished. In the Quarter was a very celebrated artist's model. She was very beautiful and everyone had enjoyed her favours except Crowley. Someone said to A. C., " You really must take her out to supper and see what she is really like." The next morning everyone was having breakfast in the Dôme and Crowley appeared. They cried, " Hullo, A. C., what was it like? " and he said rather grimly, " It was rather like waving a flag in space."

One day Beatrice Hastings came to Paris. She had been a great friend of Katherine Mansfield's and was a very talented writer. She edited the *New Age* with Orage. It was about the most interesting and well-written paper in London before the War. She had an introduction to me. She was very amusing. I introduced her to Modigliani and we all spent the evening together at the Rotonde. They drank absinthe, as Beatrice had some money. They gave me one too, and I felt very daring, as I had never tasted it. After my first sip, which I thought horrible and reminded me of cough drops, Hunt Diederich appeared and threw the rest into the umbrella stand. I sat with Beatrice and Modigliani in the evenings, and one evening the young man with the pale face came in. I said to Beatrice,

" I think that young man looks very interesting and I should like to meet him." To my embarrassment she darted over to him and brought him across. He seemed very shy and did not say very much. Zadkine came in later and asked us all back to his studio. Beatrice, I, and the young man went along. Zadkine had a studio in the Rue Rousselet. The young man and I sat on the roof among the chimney-pots until the morning. I thought him very interesting and romantic. We afterwards went and sat in a café opposite the Gare Montparnasse. The young man said his name was Edgar. He would not disclose his surname. He said that he was a Norwegian and understood Scandinavian, but refused to speak it. He talked perfect French and German. I was very much intrigued with him. He appeared to be always broke and said that he lived in La Ruche, near the Porte de Versailles. He talked of the wonderful furniture and library that he had there. I was not asked to visit him. One evening he came back to my studio in the Boulevard Edgar Quinet. He stayed there with me. There was a small window very high up near the roof, and every night a black cat would jump up from the roof outside and sit there. When the moon was full it rose just behind the cat and silhouetted it. The evening he came the cat appeared, and seeing that I was not alone, vanished, and never came back again.

The young man appeared to be a complete mystery. I was by this time desperately in love with him. Whether he liked me or not I have never been able to discover. Basil was not at all pleased about it and it disturbed him a good deal.

Edgar stayed at my place sometimes and sometimes went to his mysterious residence. This was about the twenty-fifth of July 1914. One day I went to eat by myself in a small workmen's restaurant, opposite Wassilieff's studio, in the Avenue du Maine. I was suddenly seized with an indescribable feeling of horror. I turned cold and sick and laid down my knife and fork to stare at the blank wall opposite, unable to eat. I thought that something terrible was about to happen and imagined that it would take the form of a punishment for me for having had such a good time.

Little did I think that that punishment would wreck not only my life but the lives of millions of others during the four bitter years ahead.

CHAPTER VII   WAR

THERE was a feeling of agitation and unrest in the atmosphere. On the second of August War was declared on Germany. There was pandemonium. No one had any papers. I had no passport and Edgar had no papers at all except a mysterious birth certificate with a German name that I had not heard before. We had two weeks in which to get papers and register ourselves. My beautiful Russian friend went away and said that Edgar and I could live in the studio, which we did.

Nobody had any money. Paper money was refused everywhere. Only gold and silver were accepted.

On the third of August the mob stormed the Laiterie Maggi, which was a German firm. They killed several Germans and broke all the milk-shops. Everyone said that we would starve. Wassilieff started dinners at her studio at one franc-fifty, with one Caporal Bleu cigarette and one glass of wine thrown in. We all went every evening and Modigliani too. A Swiss painter did the cooking. Oddly enough, a few days before the declaration of War, all the Germans vanished from the Quarter. The last days of the time given for registry of ourselves were nearing their end. I implored Edgar to go to the police, but he refused; he appeared to think that he was superior to the police force. An American woman sculptor gave me sittings, and so I was able to earn enough money to live on.

People said that the War could not possibly last

more than two months and that we need not worry.

I had gone to the British Consul, who had given me a paper with which I could identify myself and get back to England. The time for registration had expired and one day two policemen appeared at my studio and took Edgar and me off to the police station. I was locked up for the afternoon and asked what I knew about him. He produced the birth certificate with the German name on it, and as they knew that he had known many Germans as we all did, they thought that he was a spy. They asked him to hand over his gun. He produced two dirty handkerchiefs and one sou. They let me out later on, but threw him into the Préfecture which was filled with all kinds of people who could not produce papers. They slept on straw, all together. There were millionaires with gold watches, and every kind of person, and there they waited till something happened. I was so unhappy that my American sculptress asked me to stay with her and her husband, and fed me, and they were very kind as I had no idea how long Edgar would be kept in prison, or what would happen afterwards. I collected enough money to get my fare to England. This was an appalling prospect as it meant returning home and I really began to think that my life was at an end. The future seemed completely without hope of any kind.

I took the train to Dieppe. When I got there I found that there were no boats going to England. I had about twenty francs. A porter took me to a

rather grand-looking hotel down a side street leading
to the sea. I took the cheapest and smallest room
that I could find. A whole girls' school was there.
They had come from a tour of Switzerland and were
in the same position as I was. I could not afford to
eat at the hotel, so I bought myself bread and cheese
and ate it on the seashore. I went to the old church,
which has a group of golden statues with Jesus
Christ in the Manger, surrounded by the Wise Men
and the Virgin Mary. I bought a candle and lit it
for Edgar. I also said a prayer, and afterwards
wondered if it would be registered in Heaven as I
was not a Roman Catholic.

For three days there were no boats and I was beginning to feel very hungry. On the third day a
boat sailed. I had a ticket as far as Newhaven.
During the daytime I sat on the quays. I had some
coloured chalks with me and did quite a lot of drawings. I just managed to pay the hotel bill and had
two pennies left. By this time nothing seemed to
matter. The boat did not go to Newhaven but to
Folkestone. When I got to Folkestone I went to the
station-master and said, "All I have is twopence
and I want to get to London." As a matter of fact
many people were in the same position. He was
very kind, and after I had given the name and
address of my parents he put me into a first-class
carriage. The railway company sent the bill in and
were kind enough to charge only the third-class
fare. I was extremely hungry, having had nothing
to eat for twenty-four hours. When I got to Victoria
I was able to take the Underground home, as two-

pence was just the fare. I was almost in rags when I arrived and the family were not any more pleased to see me than I was to see them.

Edgar wrote me postcards now and then. One I have never been able to understand. It was sent from the Prefecture of Police. As he always talked in parables I presumed it meant that he loved me. If I had decided that it did not I might have had the sense to stay in England and join the W.A.A.C.'s and have helped or hindered the Great War.

Basil was in London at the time and one day he introduced me to Augustus John. I never knew until then that he came from Tenby. We got on quite well and, of course, found that we knew everyone there.

One day I went to see Henri. He was very pleased to see me. We bought a bag of plums and walked to Richmond Park. We were both very gloomy and sat on the grass amongst the bracken. Henri knew the antelopes quite well and some of them came up to be patted. He did many drawings there. We sat silently and ate the plums. Henri said, " I shall have to go to France and fight and if I go I know quite well that I shall never come back," and I felt that he never would either. We walked silently back to his workshop under the arch and had tea and I went home.

This was the last time that I saw him as, when I came back from France, he had already left.

Everyone was very depressed at this time and no one knew what was going to happen. Basil was very kind to me and asked me what I proposed to do about the future. I said that I could not imagine, but that if Edgar got out of gaol, I should probably return to Paris and bring him back.

One day I got a letter from him to say that he was released and allowed to stay in Paris for the duration of hostilities. Basil gave me five pounds and said, that if I really loved him I had better go back and join him. Everyone said I was mad but I did not mind, and took a train to Folkestone. We arrived at Boulogne. There were two other English people on the train. The train took thirty hours to get to Paris. There was nothing to eat, and if the French peasants had not been at each station with food for the soldiers, and were kind enough to give us some bread and cheese, we would have had nothing. I was in a carriage with five French postmen who were going to Paris to join up. They had some bottles of wine and cider. I gave them two farthings to bring them luck. We arrived at Arras and had to get out as we heard that the Germans were somewhere in the neighbourhood. The station was filled with soldiers who had come from a battle. They were all bandaged up and covered with blood. I sat down with them and rather felt that to be taken a prisoner by the Germans would be the simplest way of getting out of it all. The train then went on and we got to another station.

A motor-car appeared with three French officers in it. They said to the engine-driver, " Go on at once, the Germans are three kilometres away." So we went on. The other two English people were old ladies, both married to Frenchmen. I spotted

76

the *sale bourgeois* at once by their faces and took a dislike to them. We got out at another station and sat on the platform. One sat on either side of me. They talked about religion, and the efficacy of prayer. I said I didn't think so highly of it and they said I was an atheist and left me. A train came in carrying more soldiers who had come from another battle. I found them more sympathetic. The train went on and we got to Paris.

I met Edgar at the Rotonde. He seemed pleased to see me. I had one hundred francs in five franc pieces, which I had tied up in a stocking. I took a room in the hotel where I had first stayed in Paris.

Every afternoon the Germans came in Taubes and dropped bombs. We all thought this very exciting and would lean out of the window of the hotel to watch the bombs dropping. The bombs did not kill people, but the shells that the French shot at them did. I was watching the fun one afternoon and something whizzed past my head. It was a bullet, and went through the hotel window downstairs. We found it on the floor with the end of it bent. As I only had a hundred francs Edgar said that I had better come and live in La Ruche, near the Porte de Versailles, his mysterious residence. I moved in. La Ruche was a large garden and in the middle was a circular building filled with studios. The studios were triangular and it was like a cake cut in pieces. His studio was in the garden and living there was a Russian admiral's daughter. There was a gallery which one had to climb a ladder to reach. Several rungs were missing from it. The Russian admiral's

77

daughter drank wine during the daytime and methylated spirits all night at my expense. She also stole my only night-dress, which was a calico relic and had originally belonged to my Grandmother. In the mornings we sent her to the soup kitchen to buy some stew, which we lived on. In the studio opposite lived an artist's model who brought us lobsters. She had been to the Bal des Quatz Arts and had brought a souvenir home. It was a model of the guillotine and we sat and admired it. There were no newspapers in Paris and every day we heard the German guns getting nearer and nearer.

Edgar found a large spider in the garden and did drawings of it every morning.

Wassilieff had her dinner parties every evening and her place was filled. A tall Russian from the Volga played the lute and sang to us and we tried to be as cheerful as possible.

Modigliani was living in the Rue St. Gothard and Edgar and I went to see him. He had a large studio which was very untidy and round the wall there were gouache drawings of caryatids. They were very beautiful and he said, " Choose one for yourself." The bed was unmade and had a copy of *Les Liaisons Dangereuses* and *Les Chants de Maldoror* upon it. Modigliani said that this book was the one that had ruined or made his life. Attached to the end of the bed was an enormous spider-web and in the middle an enormous spider. He explained that he could not make the bed as he had grown very much attached to the spider and was afraid of

78

disturbing it. This was the last time that I saw him as, soon afterwards, he went to Nice.

I was still sitting for the American sculptress and so we had enough money to live on.

The German guns were getting nearer and nearer and the Government had gone to Bordeaux. Outside the Gare Montparnasse were long queues of people going to Bordeaux with all their belongings. We went to see Brancusi, the sculptor, every afternoon. He lived in the Rue Montparnasse. He had two workshops and lived in a little room. He was very like a saint and played a guitar and sang Rumanian songs. He talked to us about life and cheered us up. Basil was in Paris again. He could not join the Army as he had a bad knee. He asked me what I was going to do. I said that I had better go back to England. I should, of course, have gone to Nice where many artists went and lived very cheaply.

One day Edgar and I went to the Cimetière Montparnasse. We used to go there sometimes and sit under the trees and read. It was very quiet. We would bring a bottle of cheap wine with us.

One afternoon Edgar said, " How much does it cost to get married in England? " and I said, " I think about seven-and-sixpence," and he said, " Let us get married! " I said that I didn't mind if I did. We had no money to get to England however, and I had been in Paris about six weeks. Basil lent or rather gave me some money and we took a train to Le Havre. Edgar had no papers except the birth certificate and when I got to Le Havre I had to see the British Consul. I told him that this was my *fiancé* and I was taking him to England to marry him and he passed us through. I took him home to my parents, who were not at all pleased that I was going to marry a foreigner, especially as he was completely penniless and knew no English. After three weeks we got married. My Father paid the wedding licence. Everyone was very gloomy, including myself. We took two attics in Camden Town. The rent was seven-and-sixpence a week. We had very little furniture. I took Edgar to the Omega Workshops and Mr. Fry gave us both some work.

Henri had already gone to France and Basil was trying to get into the Army. He finally persuaded a grand relation to use her influence and he got a commission in a Scottish regiment and appeared looking very magnificent in a kilt. He was very sorry that I had got married, and so was I. We went out and drank some drinks together and talked about the hopelessness of the future. He went to the War a few days later and was killed in Mesopotamia in 1915.

Edgar and I met many interesting people at the Omega. There were many Belgian refugees, musicians, and actors, and Madame Vandervelde, who was very good to them all and acted and recited in order to raise funds to help them. She also bought some of our pictures. Edgar decorated her flat for her and so we managed to live. She was a very brilliant and amusing woman and had extremely good taste in Art. Edgar suggested to Mr. Fry that

they should have a musical performance of Debussy's "*Boîte à Joujoux,*" and that he should make
and work the marionettes for it. This he did. We
all worked the marionettes. We lay on our stomachs
and pulled the wires. He cut them out of cardboard with a knife. We had a fine orchestra of
Belgians and a good audience and they made some
money.

After the arrival of the Belgians, Charlotte Street
became very gay. There were Bal Musettes all up
the street. A big Belgian played an accordion and
everyone danced and a hat was taken round after
for halfpennies, as they do in France and Belgium
in workpeople's dances. We worked at the Omega
for so many hours a day and often had lunch with
Roger Fry, who had a room in Fitzroy Street, where
he painted. He did several paintings of me, one of
which was at his last show in Bond Street. Vanessa
Bell and Duncan Grant worked sometimes at the
Omega Workshops. She was very beautiful and had
a wonderful deep voice. I used to go home and
attempt to lower my voice too. I think I succeeded
to a certain extent after some practice. They
painted batiks and boxes and turned out some fine
work. I was never very good at decorative work.
I met Edward Carpenter one day at lunch at Mr.
Fry's. He was a saintly old gentleman with a grey
beard and a grey shirt. Walter, now Richard,
Sickert lived in Fitzroy Street also, in fact he had
a number of mysterious rooms for miles around as
far as Camden Town. Edgar and I sat for him
together, on an iron bedstead, with a tea-pot and a

white basin on a table in front of us. We looked the picture of gloom.

We went every evening to the Café Royal and frequently walked home to Camden Town as we seldom had the 'bus fare. We could stay the whole evening there on a fourpenny coffee in those days.

Edgar had made friends with some people whom I considered dull, common, and boring, so he often went out with them and I stayed at home. He seemed to think that I should always be at home waiting for him and once, when I went out to dinner with an elderly man I had known for years, an awful argument took place and we threw sauce-pans at each other. I got so bored with this and being so poor, as there was not always work at the Omega, that I fell in love with a tall dark man whom I had met at the Café Royal. He talked about Greek Islands and black olives. He was a writer and had studied the piano and had most beautiful hands. He talked and talked about things which I did not understand at all. For three weeks I thought of nothing else but him, and would even walk up and down streets in which I thought I might get a glimpse of him. I would buy myself dinners at the "Sceptre," the restaurant behind the Café Royal, where I had gone with Henri. The tall man seemed rather amused at me. After about three weeks of thinking about him I saw him at the restaurant. He was alone, and asked me to have some coffee with him. My heart beat so rapidly that I shook all over. He told me that he was en-gaged to be married and I, with a choking feeling in

82

my throat, said that I would like to meet his *fiancée*. I went home and cried a good deal and a few days later met her. The passion immediately died, and she and I became great friends and I painted several portraits of her. It was trying, many years later, after he and his wife had parted and he was quite alone, when we had some drinks together in Paris and I told him of the great passion that I had had. He was very much surprised and said, seizing my hand, " Don't you think those things could ever be revived," and I said, " I am afraid they couldn't," and he was very sad. However we are still.friendly and he has become a very celebrated man and is now happily married.

I was getting more and more bored with Edgar who was daily becoming more soulful, and spoke in parables which I had long since given up attempting to understand. He bought some wooden blocks and did some woodcuts. These were very interesting and he sold a few. The painter, Benjamin Corea, lived in an attic in the next house. He was even poorer than we were. I would buy two pennyworth of bones twice a week and make a stew, and on this and porridge and margarine, we all three lived. One day someone bought a drawing so I bought some real butter. Edgar and I had a dispute about people with Victorian ideas, which I said he had, and he threw the plate and the butter at me. I was so upset about the butter that I forgot to throw anything back. I looked despairingly round and saw it sticking to the wall. It was still, fortunately, quite eatable. One day a rich aunt

83

appeared to see how we were getting on. She advised me to try a certain brand of margarine which cost ninepence. I said I only paid fivepence-halfpenny. She did not however leave the extra threepence-halfpenny behind. Soon after this my uncle, her husband, paid our rent, so that was a help. I am afraid that sometimes when we were very poor I spent the money on food and got into debt with the landlord. They were working-class people and, unlike many that I know, perfect beasts. We were naturally regarded with the greatest suspicion, having a German name.

I urged Edgar to go to the police and register himself. Everything was so unsettled that I think they had forgotten about him for the time being.

One day a District Visitor appeared and asked him what religion he belonged to. He said that he was a " Hedonist," so she went away. We met the painter, Foujita, one of *Les Japonais* in Paris; he was delighted to see us as he was just as poor as we were. He only became famous in Paris after the War. He still made his own clothes and wore his hair the same way, but without the Greek band. He wore strangely shaped baggy trousers and a black velvet jumper, which hung outside, and a leather belt. People called him the " Eskimo." He lived with some friends in Chelsea and did charming frescoes in their kitchen of antelopes and flowers. Someone afterwards took the house and said that they did not care for other people's decorations, and had them whitewashed. I think they are now sorry.

84

On Sundays, Foujita, Edgar, and I, went home
to my parents for lunch; this was frequently the
only decent meal we had during the week. My
Father became quite human, and in the afternoons
we all played " heads, bodies, and legs." That is the
game where everyone draws a head and leaves two
lines indicating where the next person should begin
the body. The pieces of paper were then passed to
the next person and then again until the legs were
done. The drawings were very funny and some of
them very good.

Foujita was a charming character and had the
most terrible struggles before he became famous.
I last saw him when I stepped off a boat on the
Ile de Bréhat, in Brittany. I had not seen him for
three or four years. He was sitting on the terrasse
of a café. His hair had turned very grey. He had
large gold earrings on and wore red horn-rimmed
spectacles. He was with his wife, who was very
chic and beautifully made up. There was another
Japanese with them. I waved to him and he said
" *Bonjourninahamnett,*" as if he had only seen me the
day before. We sat down and talked about the old
days. I was sorry that I had to go back to Paimpol
that day, where I was staying opposite, as I believe
they had wonderful parties every day with bathing,
singing, and drinking.

One day I went to dinner with a woman friend
of mine in Clifford's Inn. We had dinner and some
wine, and suddenly there was a strange whizzing
sound and she said, rather nervously, " What is
that? " I said, " That is only a motor-'bus." She

said, "Have another cigarette and some port," which I did. There was a terrific crash and we both went outside and in the sky was a thing that looked like a golden pencil. This was the first Zeppelin. We then heard several other crashes fairly near, but getting further away. I had to catch a 68 'bus to get to Chalk Farm. When I got to Chancery Lane it was about six inches deep in water. A bomb had hit a water main and a gas main, and the water was rushing down the street. I was annoyed as I had a pair of new shoes on and got them wet. The Strand was several inches deep in broken glass, as nearly all the windows had been broken. When I got to Wellington Street a huge green flame sprung up opposite the Gaiety Theatre. I thought that another bomb had dropped and sat down in the doorstep of a bank, thinking that death was rapidly approaching.

I thought of my wicked life, and of my Father and my Grandmother, with a certain sentimental regret. As nothing happened I got up and thought that I would go to the Café Royal. The people in the 'bus that I should have taken, if I had not had another cigarette and a drink, were sitting in the 'bus with their heads blown off, as a bomb had dropped outside. I took a 'bus to the Café Royal by the Savoy Hotel. In it were two Japanese. The evening cloak of one was torn to bits. He had been inside the Gaiety Theatre, but fortunately, his cloak had been hanging up in the cloak room. We all talked together of what had happened. In Paris in 1920 I met him. I said, " I have met you in London."

He did not remember me but did when I reminded him of the air raid. The café was in an uproar and everyone drank to celebrate their escape. Edgar and I saw the daylight air raid from our attic windows. It was a fine sight, and they were in wonderful formation, like a flock of birds surrounded by the little white puffs of smoke of the British guns.

One day I became so ill that I went home to my Father and Mother, who, although they disapproved of me, still liked to see me. My family lived at Acton and during the night I had a dream. I dreamt of noises which tapped and tapped. Suddenly I woke up and looked out of the window. I saw what I thought were fireworks, a big golden pencil diving to the earth. I came into my Father and Mother's room and said, " Please wake up, I think there must be a Zeppelin falling down." My Father said, " Go to sleep and don't disturb me." I said, " You must wake up and come into the garden," and he did and we saw it break in half and come down in a rain of golden showers. This was the Cuffley Zeppelin.

We visited the poetess, Anna Wickham, sometimes. She lived in a beautiful old house in Hampstead. It had an apple orchard and Dick Turpin had lived there once. There we met Richard Aldington and his wife. They were Imagist poets. Richard had known Henri very well and had some of his work.

In 1913, when I first met Anna Wickham, I had influenza very badly. I was living alone and did not want to go home to my family. She was kind enough to invite me to her house and to look after me. I stayed in bed and had a room overlooking the garden. Several times a week D. H. Lawrence, his wife, and Katharine Mansfield came to see Anna. Mrs. Lawrence and Katharine sat by my bedside and talked to me. D. H. Lawrence sang hymns for hours in the drawing-room. This was not awfully cheerful. I had never seen him and was told not to get out of bed on any account as my temperature was nearly a hundred and four. One day I heard voices in the garden. I heard Anna and a man's voice and got out of bed and saw a man with reddish hair walking amongst the apple trees, talking to Anna. That was the only time I ever saw Lawrence and never met him at all.

The Café Royal and other places closed early during the War and we found an Armenian café at the back of Shaftesbury Avenue. There everyone went. Epstein, Michael Arlen, John Cournos, in fact every inhabitant of the café. We drank Turkish coffee and ate Turkish delight and I think that the conversation, as the result of the Turkish coffee, was better than that of the *crème de menthe frappée*. There was an old man who spoke on soap boxes in Hyde Park who went there one day; he decided to take to painting. He used to buy old oil paintings from the Caledonian market and other places and touch them up and exhibit them in the Armenian café. He had a one-man show there. He also painted spirits. One day I saw him in Charlotte Street. He had a costermonger's barrow with him and it was loaded with the tops of old hansom cabs. I said to him, "My dear Arthur, what are you going to do with these?" He said, "You see, dear, I think they will be so useful to paint on."

He was reputed to have been found in the cellar, in which he lived, in bed with a policewoman; and her helmet and baton were hanging by a nail on the wall as a souvenir.

I saw him last in the Fitzroy Tavern. He came in looking just the same—this was about ten years later—his beard had grown nearly white; he had a sack on his back, and his coat was still fastened with safety pins. He bought a large jug of beer and filled everyone's glass. I hear that he is now respectably married.

One day someone took me to the studio of Lady Constance Stuart Richardson. She lived in an old Criminal Law Court near Sloane Square. There was a party and everyone brought bottles.

It was a huge place with many rooms. I stayed the night there in a large Greek bedstead. Several other people stayed in different places and we had breakfast in the morning. The others had to go to work at various offices, and Constance and I sat in front of the fire and talked and got on very well indeed. I had known a cousin of hers who had been killed. She was a most charming and interesting woman and my dreary existence was cheered up by her company. As Edgar neglected me a good deal I spent most of my time with her. She had a marvellous figure and danced with not much more on than a tiger skin before the War, and even then this was considered most shocking, and when she appeared at the Palace Theatre there was a terrible disturbance.

Neither of us had any money or, at least, very little and we ate often at a little restaurant in Soho where we got credit. We had often with us officers of all nationalities. Italians in blue cloaks, Frenchmen, Guardsmen, and so we did not always have to " Chalk it up." I painted a portrait of Constance. She had a black turban on and a red robe, rather like a burnous that the Arabs wear. It was a good painting and was bought by Sir Michael Sadler. I sent it to the National Portrait Society and it was accepted. On the day of the private view, Constance and I went. The place was full of all kinds of grand people. They all flocked to my portrait, expecting to see an almost nude woman. They were bitterly disappointed, and Constance and I laughed.

There were parties nearly every night, as all the time officers were returning on leave for a few days. This, I think, was the beginning of " gate crashing." Someone would arrive and say, " Let's have a party to-night, collect your friends and tell them to bring anyone they can," and, of course, they did. One week we went to five all-night parties and did not go to bed at all. The first one was in Chelsea, given by an artist who wore a Russian shirt and played the accordion. Constance and I went and brought two Italian officers with us who were much admired in their blue cloaks. The party was such a success that Constance decided to give one the

following night. That was a terrific affair. Some
of our friends had gone to the Ritz and the Berkeley
to see if they could find any more people to bring,
and they came back with a glorious creature in a
blue and gold uniform, covered in medals. They
said, "look what we have found." He was a
French Count. He had a very small motor, which he
called *Le Lapin*, and which he drove at terrific speed.

The third night Augustus John gave a party to
celebrate his going to France. He was a major in
the Canadian Army and was commissioned by them
to paint their part in the War. The party lasted all
night and in the morning we hung out of all the
windows and waved him " Good-bye." He looked
splendid in his uniform.

A beautiful woman, who was the wife of a Guards-
man, gave the parties on the two following nights.
Billie Carlton was there and all kinds of actresses
and Guardsmen and foreign officers in uniform.
Edgar came too. He made a scene because someone put his arm round me as I was walking upstairs to the ball room. I burst into tears and
everyone took my part and I told him to go home
I stayed the night there with Carrington, the girl
with the red and blue shoe, and another girl.

One morning two plain-clothes detectives came.
They were drunk and smelt of whisky. They wanted
to know why Edgar had not registered himself. I
said that I had frequently told him to do so. They
said that he had better hurry up as there would be
trouble. They were very unpleasant and familiar
and made me feel quite ill. Edgar still refused to do

anything. He used to stay with his friends in Chelsea for nights at a time. I never went to their house except once to a party. One day the police came there and arrested him in the kitchen for being an unregistered alien. My reputation amongst these friends of his was that I was a wicked woman who was ruining his bright young life and cramping his brilliant career. He did not come home that night. I did not worry as he never told me when he was returning.

Early in the morning the police came and told me that he was in a Police Court at Marylebone. I went to see him and the trial came on later. I did not go to it but his friends did. Later that morning when I was working at the Omega two young women came there, and with tears in their eyes told me that he had got three months' hard labour for not registering. I said " Oh! " and felt a sense of freedom at last. This sentence was passed under the Aliens' Act, which was enforced during the War.

I went to my attic and wondered how Edgar was feeling. I went to see him once; that was the only time I could. I think he rather enjoyed prison life. He had books to read and as he was of a ruminative disposition he was quite happy.

I was now able to go out and see my old friends. I sold drawings and paintings and was able to work in peace and began to be very bored with the attics in Camden Town. I made friends with a charming girl, Marie Beerbohm. She had been a friend of Edgar's and for that reason I hardly knew her.

We became great friends and I had a very good time.

Towards the end of Edgar's three months I wondered what would happen as I was very happy by myself and was very much disinclined to have him back. I knew I would have to. I asked the police and they said that he would not be allowed to stay in England but would be sent to France in the Belgian Army. I went to fetch him from the prison and, accompanied by detectives, took him to a camp, where he remained till he was taken to France. He seemed pleased to see me and sorry to go. I felt sentimental about the past and we both wept as we said good-bye at Waterloo. I have never seen him since. He wrote to me from France, and the last letter I had was just after the Armistice, when he asked me to send him five pounds, saying that he loved me as much as ever. I did not reply. Having made a little money and still having work at the Omega I decided to look for a studio in the neighbourhood of Fitzroy Square. I found one on a top floor in Fitzroy Street. It was quite large and had a bedroom and kitchen. I believe that at one time Augustus John had lived there, and later on Percy Wyndham Lewis. Walter Sickert lived opposite, that is to say he had a studio there, but he actually lived in Camden Town. I was happier there than I had been for three years. I heard that Sophie Gaudier Brzeska was living in Fulham and went to see her. She showed me a photograph of Henri at the Front. She was taking a cottage in Gloucestershire and asked me to stay with her.

We had a long correspondence, half in English and half in French. I went and stayed for a fortnight. She was certainly very eccentric. She agreed to pay for the food if I would provide the drinks—port and sherry she liked. She had a horror of the moon, and if we walked out in the evenings we had to walk either sideways or with our backs to it, as it might cast an evil influence upon us. She objected to the way I spoke and said one should speak like the working classes and not be snobbish. We had long arguments about this. In the evenings we drank our port and sherry and I did drawings of her. I slept in a top attic. There was no furniture except a rather short sofa in which my feet stuck out over the end, and one chair. Leading up to the room was a staircase. There was no door either to the room or at the bottom of the staircase, so at night she would stand at the bottom of the stairs and shout her views on philosophy and art and tell me to avoid looking in the direction of the moon, which came in through the window as there were no blinds. What with the moon and the owls hooting outside and Sophie's raucous voice holding forth on philosophy I felt sometimes rather unnerved. One morning, at about three a.m., Sophia screamed up the staircase, " If you had the chance would you have gone off with Henri? " And I screamed back, " Yes! " After a moment's hesitation, during which I felt rather frightened; she went back to bed. She talked extremely well. She suffered a good deal from ill-health and was rather nervous. She wore very old-fashioned clothes that she had had since about

94

1905, and a small hat. She always reminded me of Cézanne's portraits of his wife. One day she produced a nightdress, also very old-fashioned, it was very elaborate and had real lace on it. She said, " Would you like this, it might help you to attract men?" I said, "No, thank you, I can do that quite well without!" Sophia made pounds and pounds of jam, she had a mania for it. We picked blackberries and bought apples and when she rested in the afternoon I had to sit downstairs and see that it did not burn. Sophia was reading Casanova at that time, and from upstairs would make comments on his disreputable life, shouting down the staircase at me. I only intended to stay there a week, but as there were air-raids every day in London I thought I would stay on. Sophia had obtained from a park-keeper the permission to use an upstairs' room in the porter's lodge, belonging to a large estate. This she rested in at the end of her walks. It was very dirty and Sophia would lie on the floor and eat nuts and throw the shells all over the floor. She came there to contemplate, and I was only allowed in on the condition that I would not speak. The air-raids stopped a week later and I left. I had been invited by Roger Fry to stay at his country house in Guildford. I arrived there, rather shaken, after the weeks of Sophia. Roger said I was quite mad to stay with lunatics. Several members of the Strachey family were staying there. In the evening Lady Strachey would read us restoration plays and we would play games. Everyone would choose a book from the library and hide the cover. They read a passage from their books and the others had to guess who had written it. Someone read three lines and no one could guess who had written it. I had a sudden inspiration and said "Oscar Wilde," and, much to my astonishment, it proved to be right. It was from the pamphlet on Socialism; I had read it years before. That was naturally the only quotation that I ever did guess. Roger Fry one evening quoted a passage that no one could guess and it turned out to be from Baedeker. It was a wonderful week-end and I did not talk at all as everyone else talked so brilliantly. There was only one trouble, that a horrible bird arrived outside the library, sat on a small tree, and whistled three notes. This it did without ceasing. We went into the garden and collected pebbles with which we pelted it. This drove it away for a few minutes and then it came back again. When I left on Monday morning Roger was buying an air-rifle. I went back to Fitzroy Street and started work seriously.

I painted some artificial flowers in a white vase which Sickert bought. He still lived opposite and asked me to breakfast. He said, "You had better come every morning at nine, as I get up at six in Camden Town, swim for an hour, think for a bit, and have breakfast." At nine I crossed the road and had a large cup of coffee, two eggs, marmalade, and a large cigar. Breakfast lasted until about ten-thirty and then I was sent home to work. Sometimes I sat to him for a short time. Sickert was the kindest and one of the most intelligent and charming men I have ever met. He always seemed to know what one wanted to do next, and that is rare in any human being. He still had his Saturday afternoons. The studio was large and badly lighted after the daylight had gone, and he loved shocking the guests, who consisted of all kinds of people, from the very grand to the humble, but serious, art student. He had a life-sized lay figure and an iron bedstead in one corner, with a pink counterpane; he said it always reminded him of the "Camden Town Murder." One day he placed the lay figure on the bed in a rather compromising position, sat next it with his arm round its neck, and waited for the guests. They all looked rather startled when they saw this unusual group. I took Beverley Nichols there one day. He was seventeen and in the London Scottish. He was very good-looking and charming and played the piano marvellously; he was a great success at the Saturday afternoons. Later on I think I quarrelled with him. I forget why. I have always regretted it as I admired his work very much.

My friend, Marie Beerbohm, came often to Fitzroy Street. We all went in the evenings to the Eiffel Tower Restaurant and ate and drank afterwards. One morning Marie came to see me. She said, "An awful thing has happened; I was bringing with me half a bottle of champagne to cheer us up. I met Walter Sickert in the street. He saw it and said, 'Disgraceful that young girls like you should drink in the morning,' and he took it away from me." The next morning I saw it in the wine-bin, when I was having breakfast with him. It

remained there for about six months. One day I was
painting W. H. Davies, the poet. He said, " I don't
feel very well to-day, I had lunch with Sickert and
we had a bottle of champagne. He cooked the
lunch and afterwards said, ' Now what about
another half-bottle.' " I then realized what had
happened and sure enough the next morning, when
I went to his studio, it had gone!

Nancy Cunard, who was often at the Eiffel
Tower, started a magazine of poetry called *Wheels*.
Three young poets called Sitwell, wrote for it, and
there was a great deal of discussion as to their merits.
I met them one day with Ethelbert White. I
thought them most intelligent and charming, and it
was at their house that I met W. H. Davies. I was
told that he was very shy and difficult to talk to.
I had a golden evening-dress on, with a wreath of
autumn leaves round my head, and looked rather
like a dissipated Bacchante after a little champagne.
Davies was sitting on the floor and I sat down beside
him. I talked of the relative values of beer and
public-houses, and we got on admirably.

One evening Robert Ross was there, and St. John
Hutchinson, and they decided to act " Salome." I
had to play Salome whilst Robbie Ross acted Herod.
There were a lot of people present and I was
frightened to death, so much so, that when I had to
speak to him I made a dash for the door and hid in
the bathroom. The audience actually thought that
this was part of the play and I managed to get away
with it. Davies lived in two rooms in Great Russell
Street. They were filled with mice. He set a trap

W. H. DAVIES

for them, but was so sad when he found one dead that he made no further attempt to kill them but fed them instead. He said he always regretted the days when he was a tramp as, in New York, there were three or four of them who worked together every day, and in the morning they went out one by one. No one could come home until he had collected four dollars. He said that sometimes they would all be back by one o'clock. I asked what they did when they got home and he said," We smoked cigars and drank, and went to a music-hall." Augustus John did a very fine painting of him. Mine was a good likeness but not a very good painting. John and I both concentrated on his eyelashes. This amused me when I saw John's painting, which I had not seen before I started mine. One evening, Roger Fry asked me to come to his studio to have some coffee. I went and found there Robert Ross and Walter Sickert. We drank wine, and I think this was one of the most amusing evenings I have ever had. Sickert did his famous turn of reciting "Hamlet," imitating the voices of each character, Hamlet, the King, the Queen, etc. Robbie Ross told stories of Mr. Gladstone and Queen Victoria; I can only remember one. I think now how stupid I was not to have written down an account of that evening, but I was then too modest and self-conscious to do such a thing. The story I remember was of the funeral of Queen Victoria at Frogmore with Princess Louise and Princess Victoria.

With Constance Stuart Richardson I had met the " Kim," the Duke of Manchester. He said that he was giving a party at his house and as he only, as a rule, had theatrical people, he would like to invite for a change some painters; would I bring Walter Sickert *and* Augustus John? This seemed an almost impossible feat, but I promised to do my best. I found Augustus and he said that he would consider the matter. Sickert I asked at breakfast the next morning, and he was delighted as he had known Kim's father very well. The Sitwells asked me to dinner on the night of the party and Sickert and his wife were there. We had arranged to collect John at his house and take him with us. We arrived rather late and found a large motor-car outside. John was standing on the doorstep. We all three got in and went to the party. All kinds of stage stars were there who were famous at that time. The men were mostly in uniform. Melville Gideon played and sang. Luvaun, the Maori, was there with his Hawaiian guitar. Melville Gideon sang his famous song about the " Pussy Cat " and we drank champagne. I had my golden dress on with the wreath of autumn leaves, which got nearer and nearer my left ear as the evening wore on. Sickert walked home with me and left me on my doorstep in the early hours of the morning.

One day I got Spanish 'flu'. Everyone was dying. I went to bed in my studio. Sickert brought me milk in the morning and Adrian Allinson, the painter, cooked me onions in the afternoon. At other times I was quite alone. . . . I stayed in bed about a week without the assistance of a doctor and then recovered.

Mrs. Sickert was kind enough to ask me to stay at their house in Camden Town. When I got there I stayed in bed two or three days and then got up. She was a charming and wonderful woman and did beautiful embroidery. Every day I watched her and talked about myself, which seemed to amuse her. At the end of ten days I felt very strong indeed and returned to Fitzroy Street.

Living near me was a young Belgian who had been a soldier and suffered from time to time from shell-shock. He was very poor and I asked him to sit for me. This I enjoyed, as he sat very well, and I talked French to him, which reminded me of Paris. He had long hair and an interesting face. He painted also in a rather flamboyant Belgian style. I thought that the French were a much superior race to the Belgians, whose mentality seemed dreary and *bourgeois* in comparison. I painted a life-size portrait of him, which Sickert bought, and one seated at a table with all my books behind him on a bookshelf, which was good, and was bought by Walter Taylor. I saw it not long ago. I was pleased with it. Going to see a painting one did years ago is much the same as going to see an old friend whom you have not seen for a long time. One feels nervous and frightened that they may have become old and haggard and ugly and falling to bits. I had a pleasant surprise when I saw my painting.

The air-raids had not stopped but the barrage was doing its work and often chased them away before they got to London. During air-raid nights, if I had friends with me, we went down to the cellar.

Roger Fry came and joined us if he was alone, in fact everyone in the street generally visited each other on these occasions. We eventually got bored with sitting in the cellar and laid in a stock of wine for air-raid nights, and sat on the roof instead and watched the bombs dropping. The nearest escape from death, with the exception of the Clifford's Inn experience that I had, was when I was in a studio near the Eiffel Tower Restaurant with three young men, one of whom was half German and the other two naturalized Germans. They were playing in turn German music when we heard the whistles blowing for the alarm. They did not stop playing as we heard the bombs drop. Each one that dropped got nearer and nearer. Finally we heard a terrific whizzing noise, that sounded as if it were just over the roof, and then a crash quite near. The Germans had started throwing bombs the other side of Hampstead and had dropped one at almost regular intervals till they got to the West End. The last one dropped near Portland Street, on a hostel that the girls from some large shop lived in, but they had all gone away for a holiday. If it had dropped in a straight line as the others did, it would have been very near us. On another occasion I was at the Eiffel Tower with three young men. Mark Gertler and Geoffrey Nelson were two of them, and we were sitting near the large windows looking on to the street. We were amusing ourselves by playing "consequences." We heard the whistles blowing and then a loud crash. The bomb dropped outside Bourne and Hollingsworth's, which was not far away, so we had some more drinks and went home.

My painting still showed a good deal of French influence. At the Omega Workshops we thought and spoke only of modern French Art, Derain, Picasso, Matisse and others. Under the gloomy influence of London my colour, which had cheered up in France considerably, became duller and duller. J. M. Synge said that he had to live years in Paris before he could appreciate Ireland. I have found out that he was quite right. It was only much later, after ten years in France, that I could see any colour in London at all. Now I can see, but perhaps not yet express, colour everywhere, not so brilliant perhaps, but more subtle. My painting became more and more mechanical. Sickert said that I should not paint from life. "Make sketches and square them up, as the old Masters did." I tried this but failed. Whether this was from laziness or incompetence I do not know, anyway I could not paint at all like that.

I had already acquired quite a good library of rather an odd sort. Edgar and I visited the Charing Cross Road nearly every day. He found French books, including a small book of Jules Laforgue's poems. It was the first volume of poems that he ever published and Edgar paid sixpence for it. I sent his books to France to him later on and regret that I did not keep this one.

I met one day, Mrs. Ruby Lindsay, whom I had first seen before the War at a sketch class in Chelsea, where Henri and I went sometimes in the evenings to draw. She was the most beautiful person and always wore a chain round her neck to which was attached a little ball, covered in diamonds. I wondered what it was and stared at her and it in admiration when the model rested. I met her at one of Walter Sickert's Saturday afternoons. She was wearing it. I said, "Do you remember the sketch class in Chelsea?" And she did quite well. I said, "Do let me look at that wonderful sparkling ball that you have?" and when I did I saw it was a watch. She asked me to her house in Manchester Square, where she sometimes had models. One afternoon I went and she had a ballet girl posing in a pink ballet skirt. She had been a pupil of Sickert's and was doing a painting that had a great deal of talent. I sat in a corner and drew. I was very badly dressed and hid my shoes under the chair. Presently Lord Ribblesdale came in, and then Lady Curzon. They were charming and I hid my feet further under the chair, but they neither seemed to notice or to mind. We continued to draw and they talked about Art.

Osbert Sitwell and his brother were in the Grenadier Guards and looked imposing in their grey coats. I asked Osbert if he would sit for me. He came and sat in his uniform, but it was not a success. I painted another one of him in a small "John Bull" top-hat, a head and shoulders, and that was much better. He bought it, and I believe it is amongst their family portraits. I don't know what the family portraits think of it. I also painted Edith in a rainbow jacket that was exhibited at the

EDITH SITWELL
Drawing in the possession of Richard Sickert R A.

National Portrait Society's Exhibition at the Grosvenor Gallery. The *Tatler* criticized it and said, ". . . Finally was staggered by Nina Hamnett's, of ' Poetess Edith Sitwell ' and ' Poet Captain Osbert Sitwell '; sister in the funniest Futurist frock, with what someone called ' kaleidoscopic breasts,' and brother looking nice, in spite of all, in the pale, dreamy blue-grey and recherché high collar and waist of a Guard's overcoat." This I did not regard as very serious Art criticism. The *Times* said, " ' Miss Edith Sitwell ' is a serious work in the midst of much frivolity "; this was by Clutton Brock. People spoke of the Sitwells in the same way as they did in 1911 of the Post Impressionists. In 1911 a committee of doctors, who were experts in lunacy, were called, and the doctors assured everyone that they were all mad and within six months would be completely forgotten, but the Sitwells persisted in the same way as the Post Impressionists did and everyone was much disturbed. Every time the public thought that they had vanished from sight they cropped up again, new poems, new books, they were like corks floating; every time you tried to push them down they came up and floated on the surface. I was not considered very important, only rather a nuisance and so nobody minded much what I did. I was already beginning to think about France. I could not see any way of getting back there. I thought of Modigliani and the Rotonde and Wassilieff. I had occasional postcards, hearing that they were doing quite well.

A Polish poet had decided to become an art

dealer. Modigliani had come back from Nice and was very poor. They all said, " You must take up Modigliani and give him a contract." In Paris the dealers buy pictures by the inch; so much for so many inches, and so much money a month for so many metres of canvas. The dealer said, " He is no good, he is a *blagueur*." Finally, the art dealer was so pestered, that he had to give in and gave Modigliani so much a month. Modigliani was delighted and drank and worked more. The artists at the end of the War, in Paris, and shortly afterwards, did very well as all the army officers had money, and many liked pictures and bought them. They also gave incredible parties, much to the annoyance of the *concierges*, who never ceased to complain, but without any success. I began to think seriously of leaving for Paris. I did not know what to do about a passport. I was still rather frightened of the police and decided to wait. I saw Marie Beerbohm nearly every day. She used to go sometimes and stay in Oxford. One day she asked me to go too. I was delighted. We stayed at the Randolph. At that time there were many amusing people at the University; T. W. Earp, Aldous Huxley, and Roy Campbell, who was attending lectures, but was not actually an undergraduate. We sat on the lawn at Balliol under the mulberry tree with Aldous Huxley, who had grey flannel trousers, a corduroy coat, and a red tie. He was very tall and thin and snake-like. Marie was also very tall and thin and elegant. I sat and listened to them talk. J. B. S. Haldane was also at Oxford.

Everyone met at Tommy Earp's rooms, and from
there we went back to the Randolph and sat downstairs and talked and drank. Roy Campbell was
about seventeen and very beautiful indeed. He had
the most wonderful grey eyes with long black eyelashes. He spoke with an odd gruff voice and a
funny accent. He sang Kaffir songs. He gave me a
nice copy of the poems of Arthur Rimbaud; he
presented them to me at the Randolph, rather in the
manner of a headmaster presenting a prize to the
head of the class. He had just worked his way from
South Africa in a tramp steamer. Tommy Earp was
the President of the Union. He had wonderful hair,
which sometimes he allowed us to stroke. It grew
straight up like grass and felt like a doormat. We
dined at the George, the Mitre, and the Golden
Cross, and I was as nearly in Paradise as it was
possible to be. Tommy said extraordinary things.
One day someone said something about bunions,
and somebody else said, " What are bunions? " I
said, " Those things that grow on old ladies' toes."
After a bit Tommy said, " Bunions must rather
impede the Pilgrim's Progress! "

After two days we had to return to London as I
and everyone else had to work. Occasionally, when
I had time, I thought of love and wondered if
ever I would fall in love again. There seemed
so much to do and so many amusing people about,
one had no time to concentrate on such a serious
subject.

We still went to the Café Royal in the evenings
and then after to the Eiffel Tower. Horace Cole

was nearly always at the café. He had given up
ragging the Recruiting Offices. He was often with
Lilian Shelley, the girl who sang at the Cave of the
Golden Calf. She was the craziest and most
generous creature in the world. If she had a necklace
or a bracelet on and anyone said that they liked it,
she would say, " Have it! "

One day a tall young man appeared at my studio.
He said he was an art dealer and that he had bought
some of Augustus John's drawings. He bought
several of my paintings, for which he gave me a
small sum of money. This I did not mind, as
Sickert had always told me to sell things cheap
because, like that, one sold more. I asked him if he
knew Sickert and he did not, so the next day I took
him over to see him. The following day Sickert
asked him to lunch. I was not there. At that time
Sickert was by no means rich. Round his studio,
high upon the walls, was a shelf. On it were a quan-
tity of canvases, mostly small ones, with their faces
to the wall. During luncheon the art dealer looked
round the shelves and said, " I make you a sporting
offer for all the canvases on the shelf—fifty pounds! "
And Sickert said, " Done." He did not know himself what was on them. When he took them down he
found that on each canvas was a very very good painting. There were about fifty. The art dealer gave a
scream of delight, and on the strength of it, took a
gallery, and had an exhibition which was an enormous success, and everyone was delighted. One
day Sickert told me that he and his wife had taken
a house at Bath for the summer. He asked me to

come to Bath and stay there, not with them, as the house was very small, but for me to take a room in the town. I said that I had no money. Mrs. Sickert went first and Sickert remained in London to arrange some business. He took me out to lunch and to dinner. Sometimes we would walk up to Camden Town and round about Euston. We walked one evening to see a house that had been a school, kept by an old lady, and he had been to school there when he was six years' old. One morning when I arrived at the studio, he said, " I can't bother to cook the eggs this morning, we must have breakfast at the Euston Hotel," so we arrived there about nine o'clock. The breakfast was very good. I thought it rather a depressing place, but Sickert adored those kind of places. After a few days he went to Bath. He wrote to me asking me to come there and said that he had found a beautiful room for me, overlooking the whole town. I would have liked to have gone very much, but I remembered how dreadfully ill I always felt when I was at school. I wrote and told him that, but he answered by a letter containing fifteen pounds, and saying that he wanted to buy a portrait of a poet that I had done. There was nothing else to do but to go. Sickert met me at the station and took me to my room. It was a most enchanting place, in a row of workmen's cottages, half-way up a hill. The front door was higher than the back door, as the hill was quite steep. The landlady was the widow of a policeman. She wore a striped blue-and-white blouse with a belt, a large cameo brooch, and her

hair in a bun on the top of her head. I at once asked
her to sit for me and did a life-sized painting of her
with family photographs in suitable frames on the
table and a telescope. I forget why I put in the
telescope, I think it was a nice colour. Anyway
Roger Fry bought it and it was exhibited at the
London Group. I felt that I was behaving rather
badly, as Sickert had told me not to paint from the
model, but to do drawings and square them up.
He never came to my place so he did not know what
I was doing. I must say I was horribly bored and
I felt dreadfully ill and almost suicidal because of
the climate. I knew nobody at all. I went to
Sickert's rooms at five-thirty every day. He had
two rooms where he worked and we would go out
and I would watch him paint sketches of the river
and Pulteney Bridge. This was very interesting and
the paintings were really beautiful that he did from
his sketches. Afterwards I went back to my lodgings,
had some supper, and went to bed. I never have
been so bored in all my life. About twice a week I
dined with Sickert and his wife at their house; that
was very pleasant. On Sunday, Sickert did not go to
his painting rooms, and I had to spend the week-
end entirely alone. I thought sometimes that death
would be preferable; no one to talk to and feeling
ill and depressed. I stayed at Bath for five weeks.
One day I walked up Lansdowne and peered through
the gates of the Royal School for Officers' Daughters
of the Army. I saw two girls sitting on the grass
and longed to talk to them. I walked up to the
top of the hill and into a cemetery. The cemetery

had a strange tower and sort of folly, built by some old gentleman under the influence of a strange emotion. I sat on a tombstone and wished I were inside. Outside my window I could see a large, rather modern building. It was the C. B. Corset Manufactory, and had some trees beside it. I painted a picture of it from my room and sold it a few days later to the art dealer who had bought Walter Sickert's paintings from the shelf. I left Bath and returned to London.

Sickert was the Professor of Art at the Westminster Technical Institute. One day he decided to retire, and asked me if I would teach the evening-class there. He and Augustus John recommended me to the committee and I got the job. The class consisted of five students when I arrived. They were as much frightened of me as I was of them. I wore a large grey hat pulled over my eyes which I never took off. I had to engage the models. A small girl and her brother came and sat for me and also a large and very fat woman. After several weeks I had thirty students, including five tough Australian soldiers, who were very serious and always kept cigarettes behind their ears. I used to ask them to tea, two at a time. They were very simple-minded and unspoilt. I knew another Australian at that time and he used to meet me after the class was finished, in Victoria Street, and take me out to a meal. I did not introduce him to my students as I thought it might create a bad impression of frivolity. My Australian wrote plays. He took me out to dinner, sometimes to Frascati's and the

Monico. He never drank anything at all and I wondered why. One day I went to see a friend of mine whose hobby was collecting liqueurs. He had a hundred and fifty different bottles arranged on a shelf. I got to his flat about nine-thirty only to find my unfortunate Australian completely drunk. I asked him where he lived and took him out into the Strand to find a taxi. We found a horse cab and I took him home to his lodgings in Victoria where I put him to bed. This was not so easy as he was in uniform and had puttees on. I had never undone puttees before and this took some time. I eventually put him to bed and went home. I came the next morning and got him some whisky. He was one of those unfortunate people who, if they have one drink, cannot stop. I felt rather responsible about him. He knew hardly anyone in London. He got drunk again the next day and remained so for about a week. I told him that he had better come and stay at my place and sober up. He did, and remained drunk for several more days. I went to a friend of mine who had a collection of drugs of all kinds. I asked if he could give me anything to stop the Australian from drinking. He gave me a small tabloid and told me to put it into his tea. I did this the following morning and went out thinking that, later on in the day, I would come home and probably find a corpse. I came home in the afternoon and found my patient very well indeed. He refused to touch a drink of any kind and, shortly after the War, I saw him off at Waterloo for Australia. He said that he would come back in four years to fetch

MY CLASS AT THE WESTMINSTER TECHNICAL
INSTITUTE, 1919

me and to marry me. I believe he did come back
but I was, unfortunately, in Paris.

113

One day I was walking along Tottenham Court Road, and as I passed the National Cash Register Building, I stopped and read the news about the War. "Armistice" was written up in large letters. I was not sure what it meant, but I saw further on that hostilities would cease at 11.30. I thought that on such an occasion one must find someone to talk to. I went to my bank and got some money out and went to Shoolbreds, where I bought two bottles of champagne. I found Geoffrey Nelson, the painter, and we took a 'bus to Trafalgar Square. We then walked down the Strand where, out of every window, papers were being thrown. The street looked as if there had been a snowstorm. I went to lunch at the Eiffel Tower. There I found several people I knew, Aldous and Julian Huxley, Carrington, and the Sitwells. Before dinner I went to the Café Royal where everyone was drinking and celebrating. A friend of mine asked me to a party at his flat and I walked to the Adelphi. It was almost impossible to find a taxi or a 'bus. As I was walking down Whitehall I saw a crowd of people, and at the top of an arc-light, on a ladder, was a man who was taking the black paint off. We all watched him and were quite dazzled when the light shone out again with its pre-war glory. Everybody cheered loudly and I went on to my party. It was a very fine party indeed. Diaghilev was there, Massine, Lydia Lopokova, the Sitwells, Henry Mond, who became Lord Melchett, and many more people. There was a pianola and we danced and I was accompanied home by David Garnett.

CHAPTER VIII   PEACE

AT my Art Class I generally drew with the
students. I taught three evenings a week and for
two nights a week I joined the St. Martin's Art
School and drew from the nude. They had a com-
petition once a year for landscapes done in the
summer vacation and a Royal Academician came
and judged them. One evening I was drawing
and the Professor came to me and told me that
the R.A. could not turn up and would I judge
the paintings? This flattered me as I did not
realize that anybody knew who I was at all. The
work was not very good, but one picture I liked
very much; it was of a gipsy encampment and painted
in the style of the Douanier Rousseau. I gave it the
first prize. This I knew would cause some disturbance. I found that the young man who had painted
it was the nephew of Frank Brangwyn. I asked him
how much he wanted for it. He only asked a small
sum and I bought it from him. The St. Martin's
School gave dances from time to time. They were
very good and we brought bottles of whisky in suit-
cases. I have always had a passion for Art Schools,
I don't know why! One doesn't learn very much
at them unless one is lucky enough to find an interesting professor like John Swan or George Lambert.
There is an atmosphere of calm and seriousness that
I like and find inspiring. One day I decided to move
from Fitzroy Street; why, I can't imagine. I took
the top floor of a house in Great James Street,

Bloomsbury. It was very dark and depressing and I regretted very much that I had gone there.

Towards the end of 1919 the Polish picture-dealer, who had given a contract to Modigliani, came to London. He had a large room that had been used as a dancing-school and had an exhibition of the young painters in Montparnasse. The most important one was Modigliani. There were Soutine and Kremegne and Zavado and Ortiz and many others. The Modiglianis were not at all expensive and the one of the boy, now in the Tate Gallery was, I think, forty pounds. I found this exhibition very inspiring and exciting and longed for Paris. Modigliani had had consumption when he was eighteen and what with his hectic life was in a very bad way. The art dealer returned to Paris as news came that he was dying in the Hôpital de la Charité, where Alfred Jarry and so many other celebrated people have died. He died a few days later and telegrams were sent to London to put up the prices of his pictures. His wife, who was about to have a child, went to stay with her family, who were *sale bourgeoisie* and lived near the Panthéon. She slept in a room on the fifth floor. She was so despairing and miserable that, during the night, she jumped out of the window and was killed. Her family, who were religious, said that they could not have a suicide in the house. She was picked up by some workmen and brought to the studio in the Rue de la Grande Chaumière, in which I lived for several years afterwards. Two friends of Modigliani's sat with her body in case mice or rats were about the place;

they brought some wine and spent the night there. On the day that Modigliani died his cat jumped out of the studio window and was killed. Modigliani was given a fine funeral in Père Lachaise, and I believe an enormous crowd followed the hearse. His wife had always said that she would like to be buried in the same cemetery as he was. Her family would not allow this and she was buried in the Cimetière de Bagneux, where Oscar Wilde was originally buried. The friends of Modigliani and she went very early in the morning to the funeral and when the moment came when the funeral guests shake hands with the relations, they stood with their hands behind their backs as a protest. The art dealer's exhibition had finished in London by February. I don't think he sold many. He ought to have, as there were some interesting paintings.

The Southern Syncopated Orchestra had arrived in London. I went to hear them. I had never heard negro spirituals sung before and they sang very well indeed. I met Mrs. Reavis, who sang beautifully and looked rather like a painting by Gauguin. I asked her to sit for me and she came one morning. I knew that Epstein admired coloured people and I asked him if he would like to come and draw too. He came round and did several very beautiful drawings, which he left on the floor and I had framed. They were, of course, not signed, and a few years ago I sold them. The man I sold them to asked me if I thought that Epstein would sign them; I said that I could not possibly ask him as he would

probably be cross to think that I had kept them.
Apparently Epstein was asked to sign them by the
man to whom I sold them. He was quite pleased
to do so and said, " These are drawings that I must
have done about twenty years ago." I used to go
two or three times a week, to hear the Negro
Spirituals and talk to Mrs. Reavis, who was most
charming and very beautiful. One day she told me
that a coloured dance was being given, and that the
President of Liberia and his family would be there.
There was first of all a conference where speeches
were made and they talked about the troubles of the
coloured races. I went with a friend of mine and we
with one other woman were the only white people
present. The orchestra were aching to play and
dance, and were getting rather bored with the
speeches. It all ended in a great deal of dancing
and a terrible lot of noise. I was introduced to the
President of Liberia and his wife and family. They
were very dark indeed, and the daughter, who was
about nine or ten, had the funniest hair, there was
hardly any of it and it was very short and woolly.
What intrigued me was how she had managed to
attach a large white bow of ribbon to it.

I was beginning to be very bored with London
and thought of returning to Paris as soon as I got
paid by the Art School; this was once every six
weeks, so I only had a very little money unless I
sold some pictures. I made enquiries about getting
a passport and found that it was quite easy for me.
I had to have a Belgian one. I waited anxiously for
the term to finish and decided to go to Paris as soon

as I could. The Russian ballet was in London still. They were at the Coliseum. One evening I was walking up Whitehall after my class; the only person in sight was a short man in a khaki uniform. On his head he had a gold band to which was attached a sort of white curtain. He stared at me in rather an embarrassed way. I could not imagine who or what he was. I turned round and saw that he turned up Downing Street. I thought that I would go to the gallery of the Coliseum and see the ballet. When I got there, to my great surprise, in a box was the little man in khaki, surrounded by Arab chiefs. The little man was Colonel Lawrence of Arabia. The ballet was very good indeed. They played the " Good Humoured Ladies," which was more French than Russian, but the *décor* and Massine's choreography were very fine; although the dancing was good, very good in some places, none of it was up to the standard of the dancers before the War in Russia and Covent Garden.

I had met, a few months previously, a very nice man, who had been a prisoner of war in Germany. He painted pictures and spoke quite perfect French. He took me out quite often and was very kind to me. I often wondered why he ever had taken to painting. It was not because his painting was bad, it was very competent, but he seemed to have missed his vocation so completely. He was the most perfect type of soldier I have ever met and was quite obviously cut out to be a General instead of a painter.

The term at the Art School ended.

CHAPTER IX

TOWARDS the end of March I took the train to Newhaven. I got into a third-class carriage with a little dark man who looked like a foreigner. We were the only people in the train and we did not speak till we got to Lewes when he said, " Please, is the next station Newhaven? " And I said that it was. We talked quite a lot between Lewes and Newhaven. I said, " I am going second-class on the boat, but perhaps we will meet at Dieppe." He met me and bought me coffee and cigarettes and we got into the train. I asked him what he did. He was an Italian engineer who had been in the British Navy and said that he was on his way to Bombay. We were both half-reclining on the seats, one opposite the other. I said, " The women in Bombay must be very beautiful, aren't they? " He sat straight up on his seat and looking hard at me, said, " I don't care about 'em good-looking," at which speech I felt highly flattered. When we got to Paris we shook each other warmly by the hand and said that we hoped we would meet again.

I took a taxi and drove to the hotel that I stayed in when I arrived there in 1914. I looked out of the window and saw the lights of the Rotonde. It had not changed. I went to the Rotonde and asked a strange-looking young man where Zadkine and Wassilieff were. I heard that they were both in Paris. I went to Wassilieff's studio and it was just the same. Wassilieff asked how my figure looked so I took off all my clothes and she said, " *Oui, la même chose*," so I put them on again, seeing that she was satisfied that I had not dropped to pieces. In a small cot, beside Wassilieff's bed, was a child. I asked where it came from. Wassilieff said that during the War, one day she was sitting in the Rotonde and opposite to her she saw a most glorious looking creature. He was very dark and wore the uniform of a French officer. He had the Legion of Honour and many medals. She called for the waiter to bring some paper and did a drawing of him. The officer called a waiter and sent a message asking if he could buy the drawing. Wassilieff spoke to him but refused to sell it; she invited him to her studio. He came to see her and Wassilieff found that he was an Arab of Persian origin. She said that they at once fell in love and that he always ate grapes in bed during the night. One day he had to return to his regiment. Some months later, Wassilieff, looking at herself in the mirror, noticed that she was getting rather stout. She remembered that her Mother had grown fat at quite an early age. As she got fatter and fatter she decided to visit a doctor who informed her that in four months' time she would, if all went well, produce young. The Arab had completely disappeared, but Wassilieff, being a very courageous woman, was not unduly upset. She gave birth to a small brown son, who had a very loud voice indeed, and very nearly drove the poor lady mad. She told me of all her troubles during the War. In 1914, as I have already explained, she had a canteen where Modigliani, Edgar,

myself and all the poor artists and writers dined for
one franc-fifty, which included a glass of wine and
one cigarette. Trotsky was in Paris. He had sold
newspapers in the streets and was quite penniless.
He ate every evening at the canteen, free of charge,
as Wassilieff was extremely kind and hospitable,
especially towards her own countrymen. The
troubles in Russia took place and Trotsky became a
great man. Someone said that Wassilieff had been
Trotsky's mistress. She was immediately arrested
and taken away from her son, who was only a few
months old. Ferdinand Léger, and Jeanne his wife,
took care of him, and poor Wassilieff was nearly
distracted. There was a great trial and all Paris
came to the Court to see the mistress of the great
man. They expected to see a great beauty and
when Wassilieff appeared they were very much
astonished to see a very small woman who looked
like a peasant. Wassilieff rose to her full height,
which was just under five feet, and made a speech.
She said that it was perfectly true that Trotsky had
dined at her canteen every night for many months,
as he was quite penniless, and she said, " And now
you imprison me. I, who have given birth to a
Frenchman who will fight for you. Look at my
hands, they are scarred with work and I have even
got a skin disease." She made such an impressive
speech that she was immediately allowed to go free.
Later on that evening I found Zadkine, who still
had the same studio in the Rue Rousselet. He had
then married the painter, Valentine Prax. She was
a pretty, fair girl, who had been brought up in

Morocco and had a great deal of talent. She worked in the same building as Zadkine did and, as she had to go away to the country, asked me if I would like to take her studio, which I did. I was so pleased to be back in Paris that, during the daytime, I walked about by myself, visiting all the places I had been to before the War. I went to La Ruche and saw the studio that Edgar and I had lived in. I wore out a pair of shoes in three weeks.

The Rotonde closed at 10.30 as the war-time regulations were still enforced, so we went to people's studios afterwards, if we did not want to go to bed, and brought bottles with us. I found Brancusi, who had moved to the Impasse Ronsin, and lived in a large workshop opposite the studio, where Madame Steinheil had lived and the tragedy had taken place. He was pleased to see me and was just the same as he had been before the War. He had sculpted a bronze bird that was very beautiful. It was highly polished and shone in the corner of the studio. The only table was made of white plaster. It was a solid lump, round, and about four feet in diameter. He asked me to come to dinner with him. As he was very fond of cooking he said, " *Moi je déteste les restaurants, je mange chez moi, je visite le boucher le matin et j'achète les bifsteaks par le mètre.*" When one dined with him one had to eat and drink at the same time. He had marvellous burgundy and one started with some apéritifs. As the evening went on one got into almost a state of coma, as the " bifsteaks " were certainly measured by metres, and the Pommard was rather potent. I had heard that he had done a statue of a princess. I had seen one that he did about fourteen years before in marble, of a very beautiful woman with her head slightly leaning on one side and nude to the waist. He had worked and worked on it until it was almost completely abstract and resembled the same object that Gaudier Brzeska's head of Ezra Pound did. He had apparently sent it to the Salon d'Automne. It was also made of polished bronze, the same material that the bird was made of. It was placed in the Salon in the middle of a large room. One day the President arrived and sent for the police. He explained to them that it was an indecent object. The policeman said, " *Je ne vois rien d'indécent; ça a l'apparence d'un escargot.*" Brancusi was sent for and the President said, " It is disgraceful to exhibit such a thing in the same place as Monsieur Rodin exhibited." Brancusi said, " *Mais Monsieur Rodin n'a pas pris la place pour perpétuité.*" All the same he had to remove it. The night I dined with him I asked to see the portrait of the Princess. In the corner of the studio I saw something wrapped up in a white sheet. Brancusi uncovered it and said, " There it is! " I did not like it as much as some of his things and Brancusi said, " *Voilà le portrait de la Princesse!* " And I said, " And a remarkably handsome woman," and he covered it up again.

Wassilieff I saw every day. She was not painting much at that time but making the most amusing dolls, portraits of people. They were made of kid and the eyelashes and eyebrows were sewn in silk. She went to a shop where they stuffed birds and chose different coloured glass eyes to suit her clients. She made two of Evan Morgan in evening dress, with a white shirt and every detail of his clothes, cuff links, buttons, shoes, all imitated in an extraordinarily ingenious way. She also sometimes did naked *portraits-poupées* of people who rather admired themselves with nothing on. She painted the kid to match their skins. Sometimes she would use smooth white kid and sometimes chamois leather. She did a wonderful head of Paul Poiret, the dressmaker, and made his beard of orange wool, as he had red hair. One day at the Rotonde I saw a young man with long fair hair; he was badly dressed. I was with Beatrice Hastings at the time. She had been sensible enough to stay in Paris during the War. It was a repetition of Edgar. She said, " He is a very talented Polish artist; would you like to meet him? " I rashly said, " Yes." After the Rotonde closed we all went to someone's studio in the Rue de la Grande Chaumière. He was then very drunk. I had an awful presentiment that at any minute I should fall in love with him. He had a guitar with him and sang Polish songs. He was so unlike any of the people in England and reminded me so much of Paris before the War, that I asked him to come to my studio. He brought some of his paintings with him, which were mostly of flowers and of a very beautiful colour. I was delighted with him and we sang to his guitar and drank white wine all the afternoon. He told me that he had had a dreadful love tragedy the year before, that he had loved a beautiful girl, who was also Polish, and that she had died. He showed me a photograph of her lying on her death-bed, covered in lilies. As the white wine and the songs had rather gone to our heads we both burst into tears. I found out later on that it was not really such a tragic story and that he had behaved very badly to her and that the description of his tragic feelings and great sorrow was really only put on for my benefit. The young men of the Quarter always made a point of cultivating English and American women, as they were convinced that they had money. I was glad to realize later on that they were quite frequently disappointed. My money, which was not very much, was beginning to give out. I had been in Paris for three weeks and had decided that I could not possibly live in England any more. I had to go back and send in my resignation to my Art School, which I quite well realized was disgusting behaviour. I went back to London, sent in my resignation, borrowed five pounds from a friend of mine, and returned to Paris and the abominable Pole. He met me at the Gare St. Lazare, looking quite clean. He said, " Do not spend your money on lodgings, come and stay in the hotel that I do. It is near the Cimetière Mont-parnasse, and costs very little." I took a room there. I met with him an extremely nice Pole, who lived in Modigliani's studio. The first night I stayed in a little hotel near the Avenue d'Orléans, where I was eaten up by bugs. I had met them before in Grafton Street, and they certainly could bite. The next morning E. suggested that I should paint a picture out of the hotel window. The window overlooked some roofs. As I had already done several roof scenes in London, I was interested to see some new roofs of a different colour. I found that these were much more gay and I sat at home most of the day painting. I gave him all the money that I had as he would take me out in the evenings to a workmen's restaurant, near by, in the Avenue du Maine, and we had a good dinner and a small bottle of red wine for almost nothing. What he did during the day I did not know and never took the trouble to enquire. One day I introduced him to a friend of mine, whom I had known in London. She was very good-looking and well dressed and had some money, about eight hundred a year. I saw that she liked him (she had a passion for stealing other people's men), and that he liked her was obvious. She had much more money than I had. I had written to some friends of mine in London, and as they knew that I was working, and that it was cheaper for me to live in Paris, they sent me thirty pounds.

This was in June 1920. I knew only two or three people and those not very well. One of them was Zborowski the picture-dealer who gave the contract to Modigliani. I gave the Pole most of my money to look after. One day he said, " I love your friend and I am going away with her to-night." He disappeared, leaving me almost penniless. This of course, was my own fault for being so stupid, but, I thought, thinking of my past experiences, " One has to pay for all one's stupidities, and they are very expensive, so perhaps that one day I will learn some sense." I went and wept on Wassilieff's chest. She, knowing the young man very well, rather took it as a joke. I didn't, as, in about two days' time, I was completely penniless. I went to see Zborowski, who was kind enough to lend me a hundred francs. I got thinner and thinner and wondered what would happen to me. I met a very nice Arab and also the other Pole whom I had met with my friend. They knew what had happened to me and were very kind. Wassilieff allowed me to stay in her studio, and I wept for about a week. Finally, she got very bored and threw me out, so I went back to my dreary and dirty hotel. In Montparnasse there was a Russian Jew, whom I had met before the War. He had come to Paris quite penniless, with the idea of studying painting, but was very poor, and, having a good figure, he posed in the Academies. He was a terrific *blagueur*, and really very stupid and simple-minded. He also thought that my friend, who had gone off with E., was rich and told me that they had gone to Fontainebleau—he had been to see them; he said that they were going to get married and that he had engaged himself as their chauffeur. The art dealer was delighted and came and told me that E. was marrying a rich girl and that she would buy many pictures. This girl, whose name I can't mention, I knew very well, and knew that she, being British, adored *La chasse*. The moment that she had stolen anyone's man away she got tired of him. As soon as E. stepped into the train

for Fontainebleau, she couldn't bear him any
more. Bored and fed up as I was, I had already
realized this would happen and waited for the time
that he would return. One day an Englishman
whom I had known before arrived in Paris. I told
him this idiotic story of my stupidity; and, having
some money, he gave me a few hundred francs. I
was beginning to work again and take a new interest
in life. I was still in the same abominable and dirty
hotel. One day E. returned from Fontainebleau
and explained that my friend had to return to
London and after three months she would come
back to Paris and they would get married. During
the three months he would live with me platonically!
I said, " Come out to lunch with me and we will
discuss the matter." He was completely penniless
and he had lunch at my expense in a restaurant near
the Avenue d'Orléans, near the church where the
funeral had taken place of his dead *fiancée*. I told
him in French what I thought of him. I had a fine
vocabulary, which I had learnt from Modigliani,
and I should think that if anyone who had not
been such a complete monster had been spoken
to in the way that I did to him, I should have
been strangled. After lunch I paid the bill and gave
him ten francs. He didn't believe that I really
meant what I said and he would pursue me from
café to café. I have never spoken to him again, and
although he still sends me his love, I never will. Of
course my friend never came back to marry him,
and I am glad to say that he became the laughing
stock of Montparnasse. I did not speak to my friend

for eighteen months after this affair, but we ended by being as good friends as ever and were able to laugh at the whole incident. This annoyed E. as he used to see us sitting together and talking and laughing at the Café du Dôme and the Rotonde. The other Pole who lived in Modigliani's studio and the Arab were extremely kind to me, and used to sit with me in the evenings. I knew that they thought I had been very stupid about the affair with E., but they were kind and tactful enough never to mention it at all.

The Russian Ballet was in Paris at the time, and one evening I was taken out to dinner and afterwards to a box at the Opera, where they were performing. I was taken by a painter called Charles Winzer, the man who, before the War, had spent the evenings in the Rotonde with Frederick Etchells and myself, inventing silly poems. He was a great friend of the Princesse Eugénie Murat's and I was introduced to her. We made friends and she asked him to bring me to her house. I had never been to the Opera House before and was much impressed at the *chic* of the French women. They were very much made up, but the only grand and aristocratic woman that I could see was sitting in a box opposite to us with some friends, and I asked who she could be. My friend, Winzer, who knew nearly everyone there, told me that it was Lady Juliet Duff. I met her some years afterwards at the Princess Murat's. During the intervals we went to the promenade and talked to Diaghilev and the Princess.

In London I had met André Gide. One day he

came up to the Café Parnasse, which has now become part of the Rotonde. This was at that time much the most amusing café in Montparnasse. He was delighted to see me and had with him a young man called Marc Allegri, who, a year or two ago, went to the Congo with Gide and made a wonderful film of the natives there. Several English officers who had been at the Peace Conference were still in Paris and used to come to the Parnasse in the evenings. They knew many songs and we found an American who sang too, and we would spend the evenings singing. André Gide would come up and listen. He spoke English almost perfectly and I think enjoyed our singing, although it got very loud and noisy as the evening wore on. I had left the Hotel Victor and was living in a hotel opposite the Gare Montparnasse. Marc Allegri said that he would like to see some of my work, some of which I had at my hotel. He had seen it at Cambridge and had come with Gide to my studio in Fitzroy Street on one occasion. I arranged to meet him on the terrasse of the Café Parnasse and waited for some time. Presently I saw Gide by himself walking by. He waved to me and came and sat beside me. I said, " Where is Marc? " He said that he did not know, but as he had nothing to do for an hour or two, could he come himself and see my pictures. We went back to my room and he liked some of my drawings very much. Seeing my guitar hanging on the wall he asked me to sing some English songs, and I spent the whole afternoon singing to him. He was a charming man, elderly, very good-looking and very amusing. I was very pleased that a man whose works I admired so much should spend the afternoon listening to my silly songs and enjoy himself.

I found a girl whom I had known in London, in fact she had been at Brangwyns with me and had married a very nice man who was in some government service in Paris. I had known him in London slightly. She did coloured dry points of people and made a lot of money. She had to go to England for a few days to see her children who were at school. She said, " Take my husband out and keep him from being bored." This, I think, was the time of Mardi Gras, and there were several holidays. We spent Sunday at the Rotonde drinking Vouvray with some friends, and he asked me to meet him there again on Monday and we would go to Fontainebleau, have lunch there, and then walk to Moret, where there was a little inn where Arnold Bennett had lived for some years. We decided that we would drink to his health when we got there and have dinner. I had never been to Fontainebleau before and we went to a very nice restaurant and had lunch and some white wine and started out to walk through the forest. It was a very hot day and there was nothing but four or five miles of forest. We rested by the road-side from time to time and about six o'clock we got to the inn, very hot and thirsty. It was about half a mile from Moret itself and a most charming looking little place. The café had a garden in front of it with some tables and we sat down and ordered bottles of beer. We were so

MYSELF
1920

ONE OF EDGAR'S
MARIONETTES
(*cf. p* 81)

thirsty that we drank eight or nine bottles which, one by one, as we finished them we placed under the table. We ordered dinner with a whole duck, chose the wine, and then went for a walk whilst they cooked it. We sat on the edge of the forest near a peasant's hut. It was rather damp and marshy. I had never met mosquitoes before and did not realize what they were capable of. I began to scratch my legs, so did my companion. We went back to the inn and had a magnificent dinner and drank Arnold Bennett's health again in white and red wine, then walked to the station at Moret, got into a train packed with French *bourgeois*, and, being very tired, slept one on each seat, packed like sardines between the French, until we reached Paris. The next day my legs were swollen to about twice their natural size and my friend telephoned to me at the Rotonde to say that he had to stay in bed as he couldn't walk at all. I have since been careful of damp and marshy ground.

The nice Pole who lived in Modigliani's studio said that I could come and work there if I liked. The studio consisted of two long workshops, up many flights of stairs. Gauguin had lived on the floor below. It was next to the Académie Colorossi. The house looked as if it were going to fall down at any moment and one could see the sunlight shining through a part of the wall. There was a fire-escape on the wall on the inside of the window. It was a rope ladder with wooden rungs attached with an iron hook. No one ever dared to go down it as we thought that the wall and the house

would probably come down too. I believe Modigliani climbed down on one occasion. The studio
was exactly as he had left it, and parts of the
walls had been painted different colours to make
different backgrounds. The staircase was lopsided,
as it had already slipped about two inches from the
wall. I was rather nervous at first about going up
and downstairs, but it seemed to be quite safe. In
the studio underneath lived Ortiz de Zarate, the
South American painter. The Pole and the Arab
sat with me in the evenings at the Café Parnasse.
There were many Polish painters there at that time
and they were unanimous in their hatred of E.
who had gone away with my friend and my money.
There was one particularly amusing painter called
Rubézack, who drank wine, sang songs, and made
jokes all day and half the night. The Arab had
a mistress who was a Frenchwoman and was
very jealous of him. I thought him most charming and very good-looking; he seemed to like me
too. Rubézack had a son and had one day to
go out of Paris to a country place to inspect the
school. He came to the café and found the Arab and
myself drinking coffee and asked us if we would
accompany him for the afternoon. We took the train
and came to a charming place with a large house,
which was the school. Afterwards we sat in the garden of a café and drank Vermouth Cassis, a drink
which eventually goes to the head and is mostly
drunk in France by work-girls and *concierges*.
There was a swing in the garden and we took turns
on it and behaved in a ridiculously childish way.

We then walked across some fields, took the tram, and came back to the café to find the Arab's mistress, not looking too pleased, and the Pole who lived in Modigliani's studio.

Underneath the Hôtel de la Haute Loire, which was the hotel I stayed at in 1914, was the Restaurant Baty. Outside were baskets of oysters stacked up. Inside, the floor was tiled and covered in sawdust. Rosalie was still in the Rue Campagne Première, in her restaurant, and wept when Modigliani's name was mentioned, although, when he was alive, she threw him out several times a week. This was not really surprising as he caused a dreadful disturbance at times. One day I met Blaise Cendras at the Parnasse. He had only one arm, the other he had lost in the War. I had read his poetry and admired his work very much. He was a great friend of Ferdinand Léger, and they and many more amusing people ate every day at Baty's. Sometimes they would sing whilst they ate. They sang snatches from the Russian Ballets. They were particularly fond of snatches from "Schéherazade" and "Petrouska." One day, after lunch, an elderly Baroness came to the restaurant and they decided to go and see Brancusi, bringing some wine with them. They took the Baroness with them. She must have been very beautiful when she was young. She wore a yellow wig, which she twined round her head. She still had a fine figure. She asked me to dinner at her flat. She had several pictures of Henri Rousseau, the Douanier. She had the "Wedding," a large picture with the bride in white in the middle and

135

the one with the horse-trap and the black dog. I
was thirty at that time and she must have been very
much older. She asked me how old I was and I
said, " Thirty." She said, " How funny, I am only
three years older than you." I had never met
anyone who lied quite to that extent before and was
rather disturbed. I thought that conversation
under those circumstances was going to be difficult,
if not impossible. Evan Morgan came to see her
with me one evening. She told us that we were
both vulgar and common and it nearly ended in a
battle. The day that they all went to Brancusi's
they danced and sang and the Baroness, feeling tired,
asked if she could go upstairs and lie down for a
short time. She did, and then went home. When
Brancusi went to bed he was horrified to find the
Baroness's yellow wig. It was an embarrassing
moment for him. The next day she wrote and
explained that it belonged to her; she said that she
did not, as a rule, wear it, and would he send it back
at once.

I worked at Modigliani's studio with the Pole and
drew at the Academy. I felt rather a fool about my
painting as all the Poles and, in fact, all the painters
painted in very bright colours, and mine still looked
like London fog. I was very happy and felt very well
as I always did in Paris. The Pole liked me very
much. He painted portraits and flowers. He was
small and well-built and looked rather like Charlie
Chaplin, whom he imitated very well as he wore a
pair of very baggy corduroy trousers.

"THE POLE"

137

CHAPTER X   THE SOUTH OF FRANCE

THE Pole asked me if I would go to the South of France, but, he said, " We must get married first." I had to confess that I already had a husband. After thinking for a time he decided that it really did not matter very much. It had never occurred to me that it did. I had to pretend that it was a sacrifice on my part. The same dealer, who had been induced to give Modigliani money, bought my Pole's pictures from time to time. We went to see him and his wife. I felt like a *jeune fille* with her *fiancé*. They were pleased and congratulated us both. The dealer bought some of his pictures and gave him some money. I sold some drawings for a few hundred francs, very much less than the money that he had and we took a third-class train for the South. I did not ask where we were going to, as I was so thrilled with the idea of going South that I did not mind. Two South Americans came with us, too. One of them was going to Collioure to stay with Foujita and his wife. The train was very uncomfortable. The seats were made of strips of wood which, when one tried to lie on them, made holes in one's body. We slept uncomfortably and I leant against my Pole, who put his arm affectionately round my waist. When we started from Paris it was cold and pouring with rain; as we got further South it got warmer and warmer. The South Americans and the Pole spoke Spanish. My Pole had lived for five years in Spain and spoke Spanish like

138

a Spaniard. I spoke to them in French. We stopped
for ten minutes at Lyons and went into the station
café, drank coffee and ate ham sandwiches.
The train got hotter and hotter and the sun shone
from a cloudless blue sky. We saw olive trees and
flowers of all colours, and finally the Pyrenees in the
distance. I thought that I was approaching Paradise, and began to wonder if I had not died during
the night and had really arrived there. I ached all
over and was getting very hungry. We decided to
stay at Collioure, if we liked the place, and to find
some rooms. In order to get to Collioure we had to
get off the train at Port Vendres, the place where
the boats sail for Algiers and Morocco. We arrived
there at eight in the morning, and dragged our
weary bodies to a little café on the quays. I had
never seen such blue water and such beautiful fishing-
boats with curved sails. The boats were painted the
brightest of blues, greens, and reds. I looked at
them and wondered however I should paint them;
they were so perfect in themselves that it seemed
impossible to do anything that would not resemble
a coloured photograph. The café had melons piled
up outside. We had a bottle of red wine to revive
us, some coarse bread, and butter and cheese. From
Port Vendres we had to walk to Collioure along the
cliffs for about four miles. There were high mountains behind us and as we walked we saw an Arab
castle on the top of a hill. It looked like something
out of the *Arabian Nights*. At last we turned a corner
and saw a bay, the other side of which was Collioure.
There were pink, green, and white houses and an

Arab tower on the sea-shore. We walked round the bay and got down to the shore. There was a stone path at the foot of the old fort and the sea came right up to the path. The Foujitas had the best house in Collioure. It was practically on the sea. There was only a road and a small stretch of seashore in front of it. Matisse had lived there for many summers. It had a balcony and several large rooms. At this time Foujita was living with his first wife, whom I had not met before. She was French and had most beautiful legs, but her body was shapeless and enormous. She had the most terrifying face I have ever seen and I was frightened of her. She screamed at Foujita most of the time. They were very kind and pleased to see us and found us a charming place in a very narrow street near the sea. It cost a hundred and fifty francs a month. It had a large room, with two windows looking on to the street, and an alcove at the back which contained a bed. There was also another small alcove. In the front room was a primitive stove which burnt charcoal. The old lady who rented it to us was very ugly and had long teeth like a horse. Apparently in this part of the world, there is something in the water which makes people's teeth drop out, and even the quite young women had teeth missing.

There were no sanitary arrangements of any kind and a bucket was placed in the smaller alcove for my use. The gentlemen of the town walked every morning up a hill to the moat of the fort. The old lady and most of her family earned their living by packing and salting fish, principally sardines.

Under each of the houses in the street were large cellars in which they packed the fish. The women dressed in black with black handkerchiefs over their heads. Our landlady's sister kept a little shop. She sold everything, including tobacco. She had one of the most beautiful faces that I have ever seen. She must have been nearly fifty and wore the black dress that all the women wore; she moved her hands most gracefully. She had a beautiful voice and looked like the Virgin Mary. I asked the landlady if there were not any photographs of her when she was young. She said that they never troubled about anything like that, and that the people for miles around came to Collioure to look at her and admire her.

The evening of our arrival Foujita and his wife asked us to dinner. Foujita was a marvellous cook, and we all went to the kitchen and helped. It ended by us all being chased out, as Foujita explained in Japanese, rather forcibly, that " too many cooks spoilt the broth." We had breakfast in a café the next morning, and afterwards I wandered round the town with a string bag to visit the shops. I bought some meat, and some potatoes and onions, and the Pole and I cooked it. He cooked very well indeed, and I knew how to do several things quite well. We had lunch and then went out to view the landscape to see what we could paint. I was frightened of beginning anything, as he painted much better than I did, but he was very kind and sympathetic, and said that it did not matter much what I painted, but " *Il faut travailler.*" He had been a great friend of

141

Modigliani's, and knew many stories about him, so
I was never bored for a minute. We went to the
sea-shore every morning with the Foujitas and the
South American. There were bathing-boxes, and
Madame Foujita and I shared one and the men had
another. Foujita swam like a fish and dived
beautifully. I could not swim at all, the result of
my having been " ducked " when I was a child, but
they all decided to teach me. We all made a great
effort and finally after a week, I managed to swim
five metres, and after a scream of triumph, sank.
We went in the evening to a café where they had, on
Friday nights, Café Concerts. The songs they sang
shocked even me, they were of an unbelievable
indecency, but the population were delighted, and
cheered loudly. I drew at the café during the daytime, as we sometimes went there after lunch.
There were Senegalese working near by, digging a
trench. They never appeared to be doing any work,
they just posed in attitudes, resting on their pickaxes
and their shovels, standing in very well composed
groups, never moving at all. We stayed at Collioure
for three months and even then the trench was not
completed. One day my Pole said to one of them,
" How do you like the women here? " And he replied, " Not at all, they smell too much." Apparently the white girls smelt as badly to them as
the black men did to the white girls, and so no one
had any success at all.

We had brought metres of canvas with us and
some stretchers, and a few days later I found a
motif. It was up a hill; one saw roofs in the fore-

ground and the Arab tower with the sea behind and a few fishing-boats with white sails, and in the background a green hill with white waves washing against the rocks. I saw the painting again the other day. It is in the collection of Mary Anders. The white waves were very well painted and so was the Arab tower. The roofs and the sea I did not think so highly of, and thought how much better I could have painted them now. The Pole was very sweet and encouraging. The Foujitas suggested that we should take our supper and some wine to the Arab castle that we had seen on our way to Collioure. We started off about four p.m. and climbed the hill. There had been a drawbridge, with quite a narrow and small drop, only about two yards wide and six feet deep. It was quite easy to jump across it, which I and the Pole did at once, without a thought. When it came to Mrs. Foujita she screamed with terror. The Pole and I jumped back and made her jump, she was in a fainting condition by the time she got to the other side. I made a few sinister remarks in bad taste about education at the Royal School of Officers' Daughters of the Army, the British Empire, cricket, sport, courage, etc., which I don't think the poor creature was in a condition to hear. We revived her with some wine and walked up the steps inside the castle. The castle was square outside, but inside there was a round hole, surrounded by a path. On the stone floor, at intervals of a few yards, were holes, and underneath was water, into which enemies were pushed. We got on to the roof, which was large and flat. The view was magnificent. We sat down and had our supper of wine, bread, olives and sardines: one could never escape at any meal from the eternal sardine—it appeared in every form—salted, fresh, boiled and fried. Madame Foujita spoke in a gruff and angry voice, even when she was not annoyed, but that was not often. Foujita was angelic and never answered back or said a word. I don't think that she had ever seen or met an English person before, and she would sit and gaze at me in astonishment for hours. The South American had apparently been very rich once and was an ex-amour of Madame Foujita's. He had a face like a hawk and a long thin body that was rather beautiful and resembled an old ivory Spanish crucifix. He was very Spanish and talked about poetry, life, hope, and the soul. The Pole knew a good deal about Spaniards and laughed at him sometimes. Madame Foujita suspected me of laughing at her too, but she was, I am thankful to say, not quite sure. Foujita painted at home during the afternoons. He did not use an easel, but placed a canvas against a chair and sat on the floor with his legs crossed. He worked with a tiny brush, very rapidly. The South American sat in the sun, drank wine, and blinked his eyes.

My Pole and I went out every day to find new *motifs* to paint. After a week we saw so many subjects that we thought that we would have to stay there for about seventy years in order to accomplish them. I tried to paint olive trees. I found them almost impossible. One day we found a beautiful

motif on a hill. It was very windy, so we attached
our easels to a string and a large stone, so that they
could not move. I was painting furiously, and
suddenly, behind an olive tree, appeared a Japanese.
He said, " *Bon jour, Nina*," and I looked at him for
a moment and recognized him as the friend of
Foujita—Kavashima. This was quite fantastic as
one does not expect to see people one has not seen
for ten years on a Pyrenee.

One day we decided to have a picnic in the
woods. We bought sardines, bread, cheese and
some wine. We found a place with very green
grass. I thought at once of mosquitoes—we
spread out some paper on the grass. After lunch
the paper was strewn all over the place. I said,
thinking of Hampstead Heath, " We must clean
the paper up." Madame Foujita said, " *Pourquoi!* "
And I said, " It spoils the landscape," and so I
dug a hole in the ground and buried all the paper
and sardine bones. After lunch Foujita saw a
large tree. It had a big trunk and no branches at
all. He said, " I will climb this tree." I wondered
how he was going to do it. He took the trunk of the
tree with one hand on each side and climbed up
like a monkey. We all looked at him with astonishment and admiration. He could use his toes in the
same way that he could use his fingers. To enter
Spain one had to have a *visa*. None of us had one,
but we wanted very much to get to Port Bou, which
is the first Port in Spain. Madame Foujita, although
tiresome at times, was a woman of determined
character, and if she made up her mind to do some-

thing, nothing, not even the police force, or the customs officials, could thwart her. We heard that there was a fête day in Spain. She had a brilliant idea.

We would take the train to Cerbère, the last station before Spain, and walk over the Pyrenees into Spain. Madame Foujita dressed herself up in her best clothes, with a pair of very high-heeled patent leather shoes, not forgetting to put in Foujita's pocket a pair of rope-soled shoes. This I did not know about when we started and wondered how she would climb the mountain, which was of a respectable height. I wore a corduroy land girl's coat and skirt, with pockets all over it, and looked extremely British. We got to Cerbère and arrived at the foot of the mountain. Madame F. took off the high-heeled shoes, which Foujita put in his pocket, and put on the rope-soled shoes and we began to climb the mountain. About a quarter of the way up we were stopped by the Customs, who asked to see our passports. Madame F. took the situation in hand, and explained in forcible language that we were not climbing the mountain with a view to descending the other side into Spain, but only to admire, from the top, the Spanish scenery. I think they were so terrified of her that they let us continue. When we got to the top of the mountain we could see thirty or forty miles of Spain. This mountain was not nearly so high as the one that we had climbed before; so we saw the view much more clearly. We saw a square hole in the ground, which had some steps leading downwards. We all walked down and

found a cellar with Spaniards drinking wine out of
bottles with long spouts. They held the spouts to
their lips, opened their throats, and down went the
wine. We ordered a bottle of wine and some glasses.
The Pole and the South American drank out of the
bottles. The French, who were entering Spain,
drank to the health of the Spaniards, and the
Spaniards who were about to enter France, drank
to the health of the French. We drank to everybody's health, including our own, and the Customs
House Officers. We then descended the other side
of the mountain and entered Port Bou. The cafés
were filled. The Spanish men wore black hats and
smoked cigars. When they saw me they screamed,
" *Inglese! Inglese!* " This, I realized, was regrettable,
but could not be helped. The Spaniards had little
fans, which they flapped all the time. We found a
restaurant and ordered a large lunch with a *litre* of
Spanish wine. It cost us a good deal of money, as
we had to change our francs into pesetas. The wine
was so strong that even five of us dared not finish the
bottle, which we left only three-quarters empty.
After lunch we visited the fête. There were re-
gattas, and dances, and guitars, and what was described as pigeon-shooting. This rather horrified
me as the unfortunate pigeons were tied to posts
by their legs. The Spaniards shot at them. There
was a whole row of pigeons and if one was wounded
—they very rarely killed one outright—it flapped its
wings and frightened the other birds. It was then
time to return, as we had our train to catch at
Cerbère. We passed the Customs, who were tactful

enough not to ask us any questions, and returned to Collioure.

After two weeks Foujita and his wife had to return to Paris. We had a letter from a Pole, R., and his wife, to say that they were coming to Collioure. They had found an apartment near the port. Madame R. was very fat and very *bourgeoise*, and I thought rather kind. My Pole did not like her very much. I think the same kind of person, if she had been English, would have been quite impossible, but we, being females, and of such different races, got on very well. At least she was a change from Madame Foujita. She was always suffering from a different malady, she had indigestion, rheumatism, change of life, stomach troubles, headaches, feet that would not walk, and all kinds of other things. One day we went to the seashore to bathe. R. very seldom bathed, because he said that his figure looked like a " *sac de merde*," which indeed it did. His wife had the good sense not to bathe at all. My Pole bathed with a pair of bathing-drawers, not the regulation kind that covers the chest. When he walked out of his bathing box Madame R. gave a scream of horror and said, " *C'est indécent!* " I then gave another lecture about England and told her what I thought about her views of morality in very forcible language. One evening we were sitting in our café, which had a terrasse in front and each side a small wall about two feet high. It was about six p.m. and quite light. Suddenly, on the other side of the wall, a strange figure appeared; he had a black beard, a cap, and scarf round his neck. He said something in Spanish and my Pole said, of course, in French, as he did not speak English, " He speaks fifteenth-century Spanish." My Pole knew Spanish literature very well indeed, and answered him, and they had a conversation. We asked him to have a drink, but he disappeared behind the wall in the same way that he had appeared. We never saw him again. My Pole said to me that it was a *drôle de chose*, and I agreed with him.

One morning I went out with my string bag to buy the food for the day. I saw outside the butcher's a cart full of pigs that had come to be killed. I thought that perhaps they would kill them in a slaughter-house and went for a walk to buy butter and bread. When I came back I saw one pig sitting outside the butcher's shop with its head on its front paws, and large tears streaming out of its eyes. I was told that its brother had been killed in the street before its eyes and that it was crying. This sounds a fantastic story. I walked away and told my Pole. He said that it was true and that pigs were so like human beings that they wept when they were unhappy. An hour later I went back to buy some pork and they gave it to me and it was warm and I cried too. R., my Pole, and I went for walks together. Madame R. could not and would not. We were all glad about this as her only topics of conversation were her diseases and her troubles. We walked sometimes to Port Vendres. I sat in the café on the front. There was a very high mountain behind Collioure. We wanted to climb it, but heard that it was very much further away

and higher than it looked. I was determined
to do some mountaineering, so we found a nearer
mountain that was only seven hundred metres
high and from the top of which one could see
Spain. We started one afternoon. The first part
was easy, but as we got higher up we had to climb
over rocks, sometimes having to cling on to the
grass and shrubs. We got hot and thirsty and
found a spring. We wished that we had brought
some beer with us. When we reached the top the
view was wonderful. Spain was so entirely different
from France. The whole character of the landscape
was different. On the horizon was a small black
cloud. My Pole said that we must descend as
quickly as possible as, in a very short time, there
would be a terrific storm. Just as we reached the
foot of the mountain the storm broke. I had never
seen such lightning before and we had to take re-
fuge in a shop. It was like a large cellar and the
whole floor was stacked with melons. We sat on
the melons, which were very uncomfortable, and
the old lady gave us some wine. The storm went on
for so long that we got bored with waiting and went
home. We had to take the path at the foot of the
fortress, where we had walked on the day we
arrived. The rain came down in torrents and within
a few seconds we were all dripping. The lightning
struck the sea a few feet from us and I never expected
to get home alive. Our street was a pool of water.
We lit the charcoal fire and were not dry till the
next day.

At least every two weeks there was a fête, when

nobody did any work. A comic band appeared. They played in a little square. There were four of them in Catalan costume and they sat on four barrels. Three of them played curious instruments like clarionets, but they made an odd noise, almost like bagpipes, and the fourth one played a trumpet. They played one particular tune over and over again and the peasants danced Catalan dances. I think that, during one week, there were three fête days. As we lived near the square and as the band played till after midnight we found it rather tiresome. We painted one *motif* in the morning and another in the afternoon. I found a wonderful scene with trees and houses. After I had painted the usual blue sky for two afternoons a storm arose and the sky became dark blue I painted as hard as I could and the painting was getting better and better and then the downpour started and I had to run for shelter. Of course, I never finished the painting as there was not another storm. I always think that it might have been a masterpiece. I think one thinks that about every picture one has not finished. We had painted about fourteen pictures and the money was getting rather low. We had only about three weeks' money left.

There was a curious old lady who paraded up and down the streets. She was a beggar and moved from place to place according to the seasons. She spent the winter months in Paris. Everyone hated her because she sang or rather croaked in a loud and raucous voice. When she walked down our street all the inhabitants put their heads out of their windows and aimed at her with the contents of their *pots de chambre*.

The grapes were now ripe and the time had come for the wine to be made. In the street in front of our door a wine-press was put up. One had to step over a part of it in order to get out. This continued for about a week and the wine-press was removed. One morning I went out with my string bag to buy the lunch and was hailed by our landlady. She asked me to come and taste the newly-made wine. I went into her cellar where she packed the fish. I met her beautiful sister coming up the stairs smelling very strongly of sardines. It seemed to me odd to find a woman, who looked so like the Virgin Mary, smelling of fish. I went into the cellar, where I found my landlady, who had lost another tooth, surrounded by all her relatives, tasting the new wine. I joined them. It was rather raw, but gave one a pleasant feeling of amiability. When I left I met, in the street, another neighbour, who also invited me to taste her wine. I could not possibly refuse and had some white wine. On emerging I found still another neighbour and had to repeat the process. I then arrived home without any lunch at all and fell sound asleep. My Pole was very kind and sympathetic and forgave my abominable behaviour.

The patron of the café we frequented was a charming man and now and then bought us drinks. (Madame R. had already left for Paris.) When he heard we were leaving he asked us to have a Catalan breakfast. He said that we must arrive at eight a.m. Breakfast consisted of a huge dish of anchovies, swimming in oil and garlic, sausages, olives, black and white bread, and first white wine and then red. There were three bottles of white wine and three of red and four of us to drink them. At nine-thirty we left. My Pole, R., and I decided that the only thing for us to do was to take a long walk. We walked silently for about three miles when we came to the sea-shore where we lay down in a row on the pebbles and slept. There was, of course, no question of the tide coming in or going out as there is practically no tide at all in the Mediterranean and some hours later we woke up feeling rather worse and smelling horribly of garlic. I have never since really appreciated either anchovies or garlic and hope that I shall not again have to experience a Catalan breakfast. We had by now just the railway fare back to Paris.

CHAPTER XI   BACK TO PARIS AND TO CELEBRITIES

I WENT to Modigliani's studio and stayed with the Pole. It was very uncomfortable but I did not mind as I was quite used to discomfort. My Pole sold some pictures to the dealer and a collector, so we had a little money to live on. We had a large coke stove on which we cooked. There was no gas or electric light, so we had an oil lamp. In the mornings the Pole cleaned and filled the lamp, and in the evenings we read the French classics, sitting one each side of Modigliani's old and scarred table. The picture-dealer had a spare copy of Modigliani's death mask. There were, I think, four taken. It was rather horrible as his mouth had not been bound up and his jaw dropped. It looked terrifying through the door of the first workshop in the shadow. We felt that we had to keep it with us, because if we put it out or gave it away it would be a breach of friendship. The Arab came and spent the evenings with us. Sometimes we got a bottle of cheap wine and talked about Montparnasse before the War. The painter who lived downstairs came to see us sometimes too. In the summer he became very eccentric and did the most odd things. The first thing he would do was to break the lock of his studio door. One night we came home from the Café Parnasse about midnight and found his door wide open. In front of the door, on an easel, was a painting of an enormous eye. It was done in great detail and was about two feet wide and a foot high.

154

He was not in. We did not know what to do, so we closed the door. We were quite certain that Modigliani was still with us and fancied at night that we could hear his footsteps walking through the studio. It was certainly a most sinister place.

We worked during the daytime. I painted Still Life and worked at the Academy from the nude in the afternoon. We did a great deal of work. We had a tabby cat. Once we were all very broke, myself, the Pole, and the Arab. For three days we could not find a penny, we did not mind much about ourselves, but we were so sorry for the cat, who had to starve also. We had a lot of Modigliani's books and in despair the Pole took one on philosophy and read it to us. As he turned over the pages he suddenly came to a HUNDRED FRANC NOTE. Modigliani's wife used to hide money away from him and this was one of his notes. We were so delighted that we rushed into the nearest workmen's restaurant, taking the cat with us, and ate and drank to Modigliani's health the whole evening. The poor cat ended in a very tragic way. One evening we were reading and the cat began to run round in circles. We realized that it had gone mad so we locked it up in the lavatory and went out. We dared not come home until the next morning. We sat in cafés all night and at eight in the morning came home to find an apparently dead cat. We went to bed as we were very tired and suddenly heard a most dreadful howl. We opened the door of the lavatory and found that the cat was really dead. The next thing to do was to dispose of the body. We

decided that we could not put our poor friend in
the dustbin so we sat down and thought. In the
gutters of the streets of Paris are, at intervals,
small slits about a foot and a half long and about
six inches high. These lead to the sewers of Paris,
which lead to the Seine. We decided that at
night we would wrap our cat's body up and drop
him down, and he might eventually float down to
the sea. I thought of Alfred Jarry's remark about
dead people. I think it is in the *Docteur Faustrol*; I
can't quote it in French, but when he asks, " What
is the difference between live people and the dead? "
the answer is, " The live ones can swim both up
and down the river, but the dead ones can only
swim down." We stretched our cat out straight and
wrapped him in two layers of paper and tied him up
with string. We made a handle of the string and he
looked rather like a parcel containing a long bottle.
At nine in the evening we went out, the Pole holding
the parcel by the string handle. We crept round
the neighbourhood, looking for a quiet spot. We
walked for some time round the Luxembourg
gardens and finally found a suitable place in the
Rue d'Assas. Both crying bitterly, we popped him
in and then went to the Café Parnasse, and had
some drinks. Everyone asked why we were so sad,
but we did not tell them, and went home to bed.

The Pole knew many Spaniards and they came
to our studio and played and sang. . . . They were
much the same as the South American. I liked the
Spaniards. They seemed to spend their lives playing
guitars. Even so they really did a great deal of work.

That is what I admired so much about them. There was a Spanish hairdresser in the Rue Delambre. I had my hair cut there. There was not a ladies' place and I had to sit with the French workmen, who were being shaved. The Spaniard was a little man with a turned up moustache, who danced on his toes as he was shaving the workmen. One day his wife came in with a large bunch of flowers. The Spaniard was delighted, and the Frenchman whom he was shaving, said, " Why do you buy flowers? I should prefer to buy bifsteak," and the Spaniard stood on his toes, waved the razor, and said, " *Pour nourrir l'esprit*," and after that I appreciated the Spaniards even more.

There was a strange old Spanish gipsy called Fabian. He had been in England with Augustus John and Horace Cole. He was at one time one of the finest guitarists in Spain. He had taken to painting and painted rather bad El Grecos. He spoke frequently of *Le Dessin* and I went to his studio, more to induce him to play the guitar than to see his pictures. On an easel was an enormous canvas with a crucifixion on it. It had a red curtain in front of it and Fabian drew it aside with great reverence. I finally induced him to take down his guitar from the wall. He began to tune it. Guitarists are very difficult people—I can accompany songs of a rather questionable nature myself—and I have a good deal of sympathy for them. Fabian being a Spaniard, and a gipsy at that, was extremely difficult and tuned and tuned for nearly an hour. At last he got it tuned and played

157

gipsy tunes and dances, which made one want to dance. A Spaniard one day became very angry with him and wanted revenge. It was not a very serious quarrel and the Spaniard decided to have a little fun and a quiet revenge at the same time. He explained to Fabian that his eyesight was weak and that he ought to see an oculist. They went off together and found one. The oculist showed Fabian some printed words in quite small print and said, " Can you read that? " And Fabian said, " No." He then showed him some larger print and Fabian again said, " No! " After showing him some larger and larger print poor Fabian had to confess that he could neither read nor write. This, of course, the Spaniard knew already and went home quite satisfied. There was another Spaniard who came often, before the War, to Hunt Diederich's studio. He was the laziest man I had ever met. He did admirable woodcuts. I think he had done about three in ten years. One day he was sitting in the studio with his guitar and Hunt gave him some money to go out and buy a bottle of wine. He was so lazy that he could not even do that. He was painted by Modigliani, a very fine portrait and likeness. He was trying to sell it in 1920 for four hundred francs. Alas! I could not find the four hundred francs.

At this time, 1920, Nancy Cunard, Marie Beerbohm, T. W. Earp, Iris Tree and Evan Morgan, and several other English people were in Paris and we had wonderful parties at Charlie Winzer's flat. Some more English arrived and found that the

French drinks were not strong enough. After some serious research work a drink was concocted that satisfied them. It was named " Pernod (Susie) Suze Fine," imitation absinthe, gentian, and brandy. The cheap French brandy is very much like methylated spirits. I tried the mixture but found it impossible to get down. This kept them happy for some weeks, until a day came when one member of the party, whilst attempting to cross a street in Montmartre, became suddenly transfixed in the middle of the street. He was rigid like a waxwork and as immovable. His companion had, with the aid of a friendly taxi-driver, to lift him bodily into a taxi. After this incident the English satisfied themselves with milder forms of alcohol. One day I bought Odilon Redon's Journal, called, "*à soi même*," and, whilst reading it, came upon the following passage, which I thought rather beautiful: "*J'ai passé dans les allées froides et silencieuses du cimetière et près des tombes désertes. Et j'ai connu le calme d'esprit.*" I thought that I would visit the Cimetière Montparnasse. It gave me a curious feeling of gloom as I thought of Edgar. I walked down the avenue of trees and came across a large section which is set apart for Jews. Further on I found a most curious tomb. It was the tomb of some *sale bourgeois*. It consisted of a large bronze French bedstead. At the top was a bronze angel and at the foot a bronze india-rubber plant. In the bed, on a bronze counterpane, lay Monsieur and Madame Pigeon. Monsieur lay on his side in a bronze frock coat, and Madame lay beside him

159

in dark bronze bombazine. Her hair was done in
a bun on the top of her head, in the same manner as
the ladies in the drawings of Forain and Steinlen.
In the middle of the bed, between them, was a dip
in the counterpane, which, when it rains, becomes a
large puddle. Further on, on the same side of the
cemetery, in the corner is a small grave covered in
ivy, with China jam-jars, filled with daffodils. The
tombstone was sculptured by Brancusi. It represents two crouching figures glued together. A man
and a woman. The female is to be distinguished
only by her long hair and a slight indication of one
breast. The rest of her anatomy is shared by her
partner. This, I found out afterwards, was most
unsuitable, as the body in the grave—the inscription
was carved in Russian, so I could not read it—was
that of a young Russian girl of seventeen who was
infatuated with an elderly doctor who was married and did not love her. She committed suicide
and died a virgin. I crossed the road, as a road
runs through the cemetery and found the tomb of
Baudelaire. He lies on his tomb in a winding
sheet. At the head, looming over him, is a sinister
figure, the model of which, I believe, was Monsieur
de Max. A Frenchman whom I knew had a whole
nest of ancestors buried somewhere in the cemetery,
and on the anniversary of any one of their deaths
arrived with some friends and bottles of wine and
they drank to the health of the Oncle Augustin or
the Tante Emilienne. I found also Ste. Beuve,
who sits in front of a stone bookcase, containing all
his books, and these are quite enough to fill the

whole bookcase. Further on I found an obelisk, about twenty feet high. This is in memory of the Admiral Dumont d'Urville who discovered the Venus de Milo. Encircling it are his three *tours du monde*. In the last one you can see the Admiral in full uniform in a small boat, lifting from the ocean the nude and stony corpse of the Venus de Milo. By this time I had arrived at the part of the cemetery which is near the Avenue du Maine. I found the tomb of the Famille Guillotine and further on an enormous and important-looking tomb. On each side sat two lions, rather like those in Trafalgar Square. On the tombstone, in the middle, are the names of a Greek prince and a French countess, with no explanation. I thought that this was very romantic. I hoped that they had loved one another, but thought afterwards that, perhaps, they had only had business relations. I have never discovered the truth about them. After this I returned to the Café Parnasse where I had found that some English friends had arrived. They asked me out to dinner. I had known them slightly before the War. We ate oysters and dined at Baty's, did all the cafés, found some pre-war friends, and ended up in the markets, Les Halles, amongst the cabbages. When one visited the markets one always arrived back at the Dôme or the Parnasse laden with flowers and cabbages, which were very cheap. One day someone arrived back with a sack of potatoes !

The English, at this time, were going very strong indeed, they all had money and had not been back to Paris since the War. My Pole did not really approve of them as they were only too glad to lead me astray and, as almost every day one found someone whom one had not seen for years, it was difficult not to celebrate. On another occasion an old friend of mine, after dinner, found a cellar near the Place St. Michel called the "*Bol de cidre.*" One entered a café through a large door, which was down a little passage. The patron was an enormous Norman in a white apron. There were large barrels of cider on the floor, and at the back a smaller room. On the walls was a list of celebrities who had visited the place. Paul Verlaine, Laurent Tailhade, Oscar Wilde, and so many others that I have forgotten their names. We drank cider out of a bowl and had a calvados to cheer it up. Downstairs was a cellar with Norman arches dated 1145 This place had been the stable of Francis I. The street next to it is called "*La rue où gît le coeur.*" I always thought that that meant, "The street where the heart lodged," but I was told afterwards that it meant something different. Down a side street, at the corner, was the river. There was a large house which had belonged to Francis I, at the corner of the street on the quays. In the time of Francis I the river came right up to the house. At the other corner of the street was a smaller house. Here had lived his mistress and high up over the street was a footbridge connecting the two houses. In the front room of the *Bol* was a counter at which were standing a collection of ruffians of both sexes. We went downstairs to the cellar. There were wooden tables and chairs and a small platform with a man playing an accordion.

We sat down and ordered some cider mixed with calvados—calvados is made from apples and tastes very agreeable. A singer got up on the platform and sang vulgar songs. Having learnt my French in the University of Montparnasse I could understand every word; at times I rather wished I couldn't. The songs were what Evelyn Waugh would have called, " Blush-making." Sometimes there were very unpleasant battles in the cellar, and as the staircase was narrow and winding, it was not easy to get out in time. One evening a man and a woman were there who spoke English and tried to pick a quarrel with us with a view to blackmail. Having visited this kind of place before, the man was rapidly disposed of.

One day I was sitting on the terrasse of the Rotonde, at about nine in the morning, reading the *Continental Daily Mail*—a deplorable habit—and a figure appeared, having leapt over three tables. This was Evan Morgan, who had just arrived back from Marseilles; he was dressed in black and looked very smart. He said, " How do you like my clothes? " I said, " How smart! " He said, " Oh, no, a sailors' shop in Marseilles. To-day is my birthday, let us have a dinner-party and you must be the hostess." We walked down the Boulevard Montparnasse in the direction of the station. Opposite the station is a very good restaurant called the Trianon, where James Joyce always dines. I had not met him at this time. It had *Plats régionaux*, a different dish each day from a different part of France. We decided to ask twelve people, fourteen including ourselves. I had discovered in Montparnasse an artist's model who was the image of Evan. He was much amused and said that we must invite her too. We hired a private room and ordered the dinner. We invited Curtis Moffat, who had a passion for *écrevisses*. *Ecrevisses* are like very small lobsters and repose on a large dish covered in a very beautiful sauce. We ordered fifty. We ordered hors d'oeuvres, soup, chickens, a colossal dinner with cocktails, red and white wine, champagne and coffee and liqueurs. The patron gave us an estimate of eight hundred francs, which was very cheap indeed. Ivan Opfer, the cartoonist, came. He is a Dane and had lived in America and talks with an accent that is a mixture of Danish and American. He looks like a Viking, and tells stories better than anyone I have ever met. He is the only person I know who can take a long time to tell a story, and he is such an admirable actor that he can make every word interesting. Curtis came and was delighted with the *écrevisses*. Eating them is a long and messy business, because one has to use one's fingers. Harrison Dowd was there and played the piano to us. The artist's model turned up and bored us so much that we regretted having asked her. I must say that I behaved very well. I was so flattered to find myself in the important rôle of hostess that I was extremely occupied the whole evening dealing with the needs of the guests, and did not drink too much. Fortunately, the artist's model, having decided that there was not much chance of getting money for the honour of her presence, re-

membered that she had an important engagement
with a rich man. We breathed a sigh of relief and
settled down to the coffee and liqueurs and to listen
to Ivan's stories. After a few liqueurs everyone else
remembered some stories, including myself, and the
party continued till the early hours of the morning.

I decided to do a series of water-colours of cafés
and street scenes, and have an exhibition in London.
Every day I did a drawing which I took home and
painted from memory. I was astonished to find how
quickly one can train one's memory and after a few
weeks I could do them with perfect ease. I was
thinking of the pictures that I had done at Collioure.
I had about fifteen of them and decided that I ought
to go to London and try and make some money.
Walter Sickert had a house near Dieppe and I wrote
to him telling him that I was going to London by
Dieppe-Newhaven. He wrote asking me to stay
with him. I packed my pictures up and Sickert
met me at Dieppe. I did not recognize him at first
as he wore a sailor's peaked cap, oilskins, and a red
spotted handkerchief round his neck. He was
always difficult to recognize if one had not seen him
for some time. He might appear with an enormous
beard like a Crimean veteran or he would dress
himself in very loud checks and a bowler hat and
look like something off a race-course. We took a
taxi to Envermeu, where he had a house; it was
some miles away from Dieppe. We drove through
the forest of Arques, where there was a battle in
about 1600. The forest looked very beautiful, as it
was autumn, and the roads and the ground of the

forest were covered with red and yellow leaves.
Sickert had bought a house that was once a Police
Station. It was on the main street. As a matter of
fact there was only one street. It was a long, narrow
house, and the rooms were in a straight line and all
numbered. These had been cells. My room was
"numéro 3." We ate in a large kitchen. The cook
and the gardener sat at one table and we sat at a
larger one in the middle of the room. Sickert talked
to the servants throughout lunch and dinner and
made them laugh a great deal. They drank red
wine and cider and we drank red wine and calvados.
Envermeu is a dull, flat place, and I never knew
why Sickert had chosen it. I don't think he painted
much there but went into Dieppe, where he painted
some of his best pictures. These are very different
from his Camden Town period. The Camden Town
ones are in a very low key of blacks, greys, and
Indian reds, whereas the Dieppe pictures were
painted in the most brilliant greens, blues, yellows
and reds. I think that it is quite impossible to com-
pare their merits and that it is really a question of
personal taste. On the evening of my arrival I
showed him my pictures, hoping that he would like
them. He was, unfortunately, horrified and hated
them. This filled me with gloom. I rather admired
them myself at that time, but, having seen some of
them recently, am inclined to think that he was
right. I have come to the conclusion that the South
of France and I have nothing in common. Brittany
I can deal with, as it is more like England, but the
South, with its hard purple shadows, white houses,

and perpetually blue sky is not a part of my " make up." We went into Dieppe to look at the Channel and found it so appallingly rough that I waited another day and then took the boat for Newhaven.

I arrived in London and went to the Eiffel Tower, where I got a small room near the roof. The next day a friend of mine bought a picture. I had not enough pictures for an exhibition, but Mr. Turner, of the Independent Gallery, said that he was having a mixed show of English painters and that I could exhibit four or five. I sold another small painting and decided to return to Paris and to my Pole. I was glad to be back. I was in no better position than if I had not gone at all and felt that my life was a failure and damned the South of France. I continued my water-colours. I went daily to the Luxembourg Gardens where I did some really good work, I think. There is a statue there that I always admired. It is of a lady standing up, with her feet crossed, in a very short skirt indeed, and a strange little hat like an inverted soup plate. I did a drawing of her. Some years later I went to the Bal Julien dressed as her. I wore a pink silk accordion pleated garment, that really was a pair of knickers. They had no legs, but only a ribbon to divide them. I borrowed them from a rich American woman and cut the ribbon so that it looked exactly like the skirt of the statue. They had garlands of blue silk forget-me-nots embroidered on them. I wore a short blue, tight-fitting jacket that I had bought at the " Flea market " at Caulincourt and a very small blue hat that looked like a comedian's bowler. It was almost flat and looked very like the one worn by the statue. I had a great success at the ball, especially when I explained whom I represented.

My friend, with whom I had gone to Russia in 1909, returned to Paris with her husband. They were both very bright and cheerful and had met Ferdinand Tuohy. Tuohy was a large, good-looking and cheerful Irishman, who laughed perpetually and wrote the most beautiful English. B., my friend's husband, was a very amusing man and did extremely funny caricatures. One day Tuohy had been celebrating. I forget whether it was the finish of a love affair, or the beginning of another, as he was generally in love with someone. He arrived at the Dôme about breakfast time. I was with B. and his wife. Tuohy ordered what he described as " Turk's blood "; this was stout and champagne mixed. We realized that any idea of spending a serious day was out of the question. About 12 a.m. several other people had joined us and there were a considerable number of stout and champagne bottles. It suddenly occurred to Tuohy and B. that they looked like soldiers and they proceeded to divide them into regiments, the champagne bottles representing officers, large and small, and the stout bottles ordinary soldiers. This kept them occupied for hours. Finally they took them out on the terrasse and were joined by some workmen and taxi-drivers who were much entertained and described Tuohy and B. as " *très rigolo*," which indeed, they were. The English were still in search

168

of new forms of alcohol and one day B. discovered Mandarin Curaçao. It is extremely powerful stuff and, I think, must have some kind of dope in it as, at any rate, one evening B. drank a great deal of it and wandered off by himself. No one knows what actually happened to him, but he returned home the next morning, very early, so badly damaged that he was hardly recognizable, and said that he had tried to fight the French Army, that the French Army had won, and that he would never touch Mandarin Curaçao again.

We met another Irishman in the Quarter. He was a journalist and spoke French as much like a Frenchman as any Irishman can who already speaks with a strong Irish accent. He had absorbed so much absinthe before the War that he had become completely paralysed. He went into a home and had to be taught, by slow degrees, how to use his limbs. He frequently went out to Montmartre and Les Halles. One morning he arrived at the Café Parnasse, about eight a.m., with a friend of his. They had been out all night and had just come from the markets. They had some dice with them and decided to toss up for the possession of the next person who entered the café. The Irishman won and they sat and waited. There were only very few people who came in so early and they had to wait for some time, meanwhile, consoling themselves with a few Pernod Susie *fines*. After a time the door opened and a dark respectable-looking man entered. The Irishman jumped at him and screamed, " I've won you! I've won you! You're mine! " The man turned out to be a Spaniard and, when the situation was explained to him, he quite appreciated the joke and they all continued to drink together. I remained with them for a short time, but realized that if I stayed very long an ambulance would have to be sent for to carry me home to my Pole, who did not appreciate the eccentric behaviour of the Anglo-Saxons. The Irishman was very strange and secretive about himself. He often hinted at the unusual way in which he earned his living. We knew that he was a journalist, but nothing at all about the paper or papers he worked for. One day I was with the War correspondent, Donohue, who is now dead, and two other men. The Irishman hurried past us. I said afterwards to him, " Why on earth did you run away from us like that." He said, " Those men know all about me." Eventually we discovered that his great and terrible secret was that he was on the advertising staff of a very well known English newspaper. He was extremely good at his job, and went all over Europe interviewing Lord Mayors and important business men. When he found out that nobody except himself seemed to consider it a bore, and an undignified way of earning one's living, he became quite calm. As far as we could make out he got the sack regularly once a week but, being apparently indispensable, was taken back the following day.

One day when I was sitting in the Parnasse, two strange females appeared. I was sitting with Harrison Dowd, one of the few Americans whom I knew in Paris. One was Jewish and the other was one of the most extraordinary looking creatures I have ever seen. She had a whitish green face and ginger hair, cut short like a boy's, with a fringe. During the War, for a short period, I cut my hair in the same way in London and everyone stared. It was no wonder, as I looked really terrible. This girl had very large blue eyes, which were rather beautiful. She had a very long body and rather short fat legs. They were both Americans, and the strange-looking one had arrived from New York with six dollars, which was all that she had in the world. Dowd knew them and I was introduced. The strange one's name was Bernice Abbot. She was very shy and seemed to be only half conscious. She drew extremely well and wanted to become a sculptress. That seems to be the ambition of every young American girl. She took, later on, to photography and, I think, has taken some of the finest photographs—especially of men—that I have ever seen. I saw her last in Paris. I did not recognize her at first, she looked so beautiful and well-dressed. She was driving a smart motor-car and had had a tremendous success in New York.

It was now December and we were wondering how and where we should spend Christmas. Christmas Eve is the great evening, and all the cafés and restaurants keep open all night. The beautiful Russian, who had been in Finland with us, had returned to Paris with her husband. She had married an American theosophist, a devotee of Rudolph Steiner, and I had met him with Arthur

Ransome in London. He had a very good job in Paris as the European correspondent of one of the largest American newspapers. She had two charming children. The Dôme and the Rotonde advertised Christmas dinners at midnight on Christmas Eve. My Pole and I were very broke, and were delighted when my Russian friend and her husband asked us to dine with them at the Dôme. It was freezing during Christmas week. Our studio had a large coke stove in the back room but, as it was not one of the kind that burns all night, we had to break the ice in the sink and the icicles from the tap each morning. One's toothbrush also had an unpleasant habit of freezing, and had to be thawed before use. On Christmas Day I received a little money from England. We went to the Café Parnasse, in the evening, and waited till twelve p.m. when we crossed over to the Dôme. The whole of the back part of the café was converted into a dining-room with two long tables. It looked very gay and bright with festoons of coloured paper, and we ate through an enormous dinner. We got home about four a.m.

New Year's Eve is a much more lively and serious festivity than Christmas, as Christmas is a religious celebration, and the New Year purely enjoyment. We celebrated the New Year by visiting all the cafés for miles around with B. and his wife. B. conducted, with Ortiz, a bull fight at the Parnasse. B. was the bull and Ortiz the picador. They very nearly wrecked the place and all the Spaniards joined in with professional interest. The ladies

Hammett
Dome 1924

AT THE DÔME

stood up on seats as the floor was entirely occupied. At twelve, the lights were turned off for a second and one kissed or was kissed by one's neighbour. In order to avoid disturbance it was better to be found at twelve p.m. sitting next to the person that one was supposed to be kissing. I was sitting in the wrong place and got into trouble because I was embraced by quite the wrong person.

I had met once in London, at the Eiffel Tower, a few months before, a very good-looking young man, who had been at Oxford. He had told me that he was coming to Paris, and hoped to get into the Diplomatic Service. He spoke French, German, and Italian extremely well, and suddenly arrived in Paris from Italy. He had a charming voice and sang in all three languages. He visited exhibitions with me, and took to wearing a large black hat, corduroy trousers, and black sand shoes. This I strongly disapproved of, as they did not suit him at all, and finally induced him to abandon them and wear his ordinary clothes. By this time I had had quite enough of artistic-looking people, long hair and shabby clothes, and was only too thankful to be seen about with a presentable person. Evan Morgan was still in Paris and knew him well. Aleister Crowley was there and they were very anxious to be introduced to him, having heard the most dreadful stories of his wickedness. Crowley had a temple in Cefalu in Sicily. He was supposed to practise Black Magic there, and one day a baby was said to have disappeared mysteriously. There was also a goat there. This all pointed to Black Magic, so people said, and the inhabitants of the village were frightened of him. When he came to Paris he stayed in the Rue Vavin at the Hôtel de Blois. I asked him if I could bring some friends to see him and he asked us to come in one day before dinner and have some cocktails. He said that he had invented a beautiful cocktail called Kubla Khan No. 2. He would not say what it was made of. I told Evan and he, I, and two young men went to try it out one evening. Crowley had only a small bedroom with a large cupboard. He opened the cupboard and took out a bottle of gin, a bottle of vermouth, and two other bottles. The last one was a small black bottle with an orange label on it, on which was written "POISON." He poured some liquid from the large bottles, and then from the black bottle he poured a few drops and shook the mixture up. The "POISON" I found out afterwards, was laudanum. I believe that it is supposed to be an aphrodisiac but it had no effect at all on any of us except Cecil Maitland, who was there also. After we left he rushed into the street, and in and out of all the cafés behaving in a most strange manner, accosting everyone he came into contact with. I introduced J. W. N. Sullivan to Crowley. They got on very well together, as they both were very good chess-players and very good mathematicians as well. I don't think that Sullivan was much interested in magic, but they found plenty to talk about. Crowley had taken to painting, and painted the most fantastic pictures in very bright colours. He painted a picture about a foot and a half wide, and nine inches high, of a man on a white horse chasing a lion. It was very interesting, a little like the Douanier Rousseau; it had a great deal of life and action. I would have liked to have bought it, but I was very broke, and he wanted a high price for it. He gave me a painting, on a mahogany panel, of a purple negress, with a yellow and red spotted handkerchief round her head, and a purple rhinoceros surrounded by oriental vegetation. The rhinoceros had got rather mixed up with the vegetation, and it was rather difficult to distinguish between the trunks of the trees and the animal's anatomy; it was quite a beautiful colour however. His wife arrived from Cefalu. She was a tall, gaunt Jewess, very thin and bony, with a strangely-attractive face and wild eyes. She had been a schoolmistress in New York. She had had a child by Crowley which had died, and Crowley was very much upset about it. He showed me a photograph of himself and her and some children standing up to their knees in the sea, with no clothes on. I got on very well with them. They were very anxious for me to go to Cefalu. I did not care for the type of person who clung round Crowley. They seemed so very inferior to him and so dull and boring that I could never understand how he could put up with them.

Betty May, whom I had known in London in 1914, with Basil, arrived in Paris one day. She had been one of Epstein's models and one of the principal supports, with Lilian Shelley, of the Crab Tree Club, which was started in 1913. I only went

175

to it once with Basil in 1914. Betty had married
recently her fourth husband, a most brilliant young
man called Raoul Loveday, who was only twenty
and had got a first in history at Oxford. He was
very good-looking, but looked half dead. She was
delighted to meet me and we all sat in the Dôme
and drank. They were on their way to Cefalu as
Crowley had offered him a job as his secretary. He
was very much intrigued with Crowley's views on
magic. He had been very ill the year before and
had had a serious operation. I had heard that the
climate at Cefalu was terrible; heat, mosquitoes,
and very bad food. The magical training I already
knew was very arduous. I urged them not to go.
I succeeded in keeping them in Paris two days
longer than they intended, but they were determined to go and I was powerless to prevent them.
I told Raoul that if he went he would die, and really
felt a horrible feeling of gloom when I said " Good-
bye " to them. After five months I had a postcard
from Betty on which was written, " My husband
died last Friday; meet me at the Gare de Lyon."
I could not meet her as I got the postcard a day too
late and she went straight through to London. He
died of fever. There were no doctors at Cefalu and
one had to be got from Palermo, but it was too late
when he arrived. There is a long and very interesting description of life in Cefalu in *Tiger Woman*,
Betty May's life story, but not half so good as the
way in which she told me the story herself.

Cecil Maitland and Mary Butts were very much
interested in Crowley and went to Cefalu. Everyone

176

in the temple had to write their diary every day and everyone else was allowed to read it. The climate and the bad food nearly killed Cecil and Mary, and when they came back to Paris they looked like two ghosts and were hardly recognizable.

Crowley came to Paris from time to time. He gave the appearance of being quite bald, with the exception of a small bunch of hairs on top of his head, which he twiddled into a point. He shaved the back of his head and appeared entirely bald. One fête day I was sitting at the Rotonde and a most extraordinary spectacle appeared. It wore a magnificent and very expensive grey velours hat. Underneath, sticking out on each side was a mop of black frizzy hair and the face was heavily and very badly painted. This I recognized as Crowley. He said, " I am going to Montmartre and I don't know of any suitable cafés to visit." I could not think of any where he would not cause a sensation, but I suspected that that was exactly what he wanted. I told him the names of a few suitable places and he disappeared. I never saw him in this disguise again and did not dare enquire whether he had a successful evening or not. He appeared sometimes in a kilt and got howled down by the Americans, who were rude enough to sing Harry Lauder's songs at him. He had a passion for dressing up. One day the Countess A., a Frenchwoman, asked me to lunch. I had been to her home several times before and we were becoming very friendly. She spoke excellent English and had heard about Crowley. She was most anxious to meet him. I

refused to introduce him to her as she had been very
kind to me and I knew how fond Crowley was of
pulling the legs of people whom he suspected of
being rich and influential. It was a curious kink that
he had which had lost him many opportunities and
people that would have been useful and friendly
to him. It was a kind of schoolboy perversity. A
friend of mine introduced him to her and she asked
him to her house to lunch to meet some distinguished and rich women who were longing to have
their horoscopes read. I was not at the luncheon
party, but Crowley, I heard, had a great success and
told them all kinds of things about themselves that
they were dying to hear. He looked at the Countess
and said, " I have met you in another life." She
was naturally very intrigued and asked him when
and where, and he said that, in fact, he had written a
story about her that had been published and that he
would send her a copy. This he eventually did and
to her horror when she read it, it was a perfectly
monstrous story, about a perfectly monstrous and
disreputable old woman bearing, of course, no resemblance to her. She was naturally furious and
refused to see him again. One evening, before the
unfortunate incident took place, a man whom we all
knew, asked us to come to his flat and try a little
hashish. I had never tried any, but only a few days
before, the Irish journalist whom I knew, had told
me about his experiences when he had tried some.
It is not a habit-forming drug and does not do anyone much harm. The Irishman went to see some
friends one day and they gave him some. I believe

that one loses all sense of time and space. It takes about a hundred years to cross quite a narrow street and, as Maurice Richardson pointed out when I told him the story, probably a hundred years to order a drink. The first effect is a violent attack of giggles. One screams with laughter for no reason whatever, even at a fly walking on the ceiling. The Irishman went through all the stages and finally decided to go home. He had to walk across Paris and cross the river by Notre Dame When he reached it he found that it was at least a mile high, and, giving it one despairing look, sat down on the quays to wait till its size had diminished. He had to wait for some time, but finally he decided that it had grown small enough for him to continue his walk home. The Countess had asked Crowley to dinner, and he appeared in what he considered to be suitable evening clothes. He wore black silk knee breeches, a tight-fitting black coat, black silk stockings, and shoes with buckles on them. The coat had a high black collar with a narrow white strip at the top. On his chest he wore a jewelled order and at his side he carried a sword. I asked him what the order was. He said, " The Order of the Holy Ghost, my dear." We went to our friend's flat after dinner. He had a large pot on the floor which contained hashish in the form of jam. On the table were some pipes, as one smoked or ate it, or did both. I tasted a spoonful, swallowed it, and waited, but nothing happened. The others got to work seriously and smoked and ate the jam. I felt no effect except that I was very happy, much more happy than if I had

179

drunk anything. I sat on a chair and grinned. The others entered the giggling stage. This was for me a most awful bore as I could not say a word of any kind without them roaring with laughter. I got so bored that I went home to my Pole. Crowley eventually returned to Cefalu, taking his wife with him, and so we had no more Kubla Khan No. 2.

There was a charming Frenchman who visited the quarter. He wore a black hat and had curly black hair which was going grey. He was a very important person at the Prefecture of Police. He was a great friend of all the artists in Montparnasse and bought many pictures from the Polish picture-dealer. He had several very fine Modiglianis. He sang old French songs very beautifully, including one which had been the favourite song of Henry the Fourth. It was a most charming song and I wish that I had learnt it. One day I had to visit the Prefecture of Police about my *carte d'identité*. He had told me that if I wanted any help to come and see him in his office. I went one morning and mentioned his name. I was shown to the office by several policemen, who were very polite. The door was opened and, sitting at a desk, was Monsieur S. looking very unlike a Chief of Police. The walls were covered from top to bottom with modern paintings— very good ones indeed—and for the moment I completely forgot why I had come. I had no wish to remember either, as I was much too interested in the pictures. Unfortunately he was a very busy man and I had to explain my difficulties and go away. I tried to know as few English and

Americans as possible, as an evening spent with the French or the foreign artists, who had known Montparnasse for years, was very much more entertaining. There was a big man called Ceria, with a large beard. He was a Frenchman from Savoy. I always called him François Premier, which pleased him. He painted very well, in fact I found some pictures of his at the Leicester Galleries the other day.

Each year the Académie Colorossi gave a fancy dress ball. In 1920 I did not go. The result was that neither the Pole nor I had any sleep at all that night. The Academy was only divided from our studio by a small garden and the din was awful. I decided that the next party I should be there. Although we worked at the sketch class, and at the *Cours libre*, we rather despised the art students, who consisted mostly of silly Americans, French *bourgeois*, and imbecile English. Oddly enough the ball was entirely run by the French, in fact by the Professor, Bernard Naudin, a funny little man, who is a very famous illustrator and a great friend of the Fratellinis', the three famous clowns from the Cirque Medrano. He was an admirable clown himself and came to the dance dressed as a comedian. He brought with him a wooden horse on wheels, which he dragged behind him on a string. Ceria came dressed as Edouard Manet, and he looked exactly like him. He wore a brown square bowler hat and had grown his beard in the same shape as Manet had worn his; he had sponge bag trousers and white spats. He was acting as barman and mixing the

most deadly cocktails. The French still think that
it is very " chic " to spend the whole night drinking
cocktails. I knew only too well what that might
lead to and stuck to wine. I wore my workman's
blue trousers that Basil and I had bought for six
francs in the Avenue du Maine in 1914, a sailor's
jersey, and espadrilles. We danced and danced,
every kind of dance, jigs, polkas, old-fashioned
waltzes and jazz. I met a most charming woman
whom I had met once before. She was Polish and
a very talented sculptress. She was very ugly, but
with that kind of ugliness which is attractive. I sat
on her lap and told her how much I liked her works.
She was delighted, and we became great friends
afterwards. She had, a few years later, a success in
the Salon d'Automne. Naudin did some stunts
with one of the Fratellinis, whom he had brought
with him. We successfully chased any boring
English or Americans away. I was permitted to
join in the fun, as I was of the pre-War brand, and
my Montparnasse and Apache French amused them.
As the night wore on, I remembered more and more
French and finally went home about five-thirty a.m.
feeling very tired.

One day Rupert Doone, the ballet dancer, came
to Paris. He was then just beginning to dance. He
was very poor and had posed for Cedric Morris and
Dobson. He had a very fine head. He sat for the
Academies to make a little money. I wanted to
paint him. I did some drawings of him in my
studio for which I paid him a little, but I could not
afford to give him longer sittings. I introduced him

THE ACADEMY COLOROSSI

183

to the Professor of Colorossi, and he gave him a month's sitting in the portrait class. The portrait class had not got a *cours libre* and one had to have criticisms from the professor. This amused me as I had not been taught in an art class for years. I started a small head which went very well. On Friday the Professor arrived. I have forgotten his name, but he is a well known exhibitor at the Spring Salon. He was a sweet little man with a grey beard; he stared at me a good deal and gave me a very good and true criticism. I took his advice and it turned into, I think, one of my best portraits. It was bought in 1926 at my Exhibition in London by Mr. Edward Marsh and is now in his collection.

I had met at the Sitwells' house in London, a most charming South American. He had a large flat in Paris and one day came to Montparnasse, where he found me. He had with him Christopher Wood, who was staying in his flat. He was a very promising young painter and had been originally discovered by Alphonse Kahn. I found him a most charming young man. He had a studio near the Boulevard St. Germain. I dined with him and we danced at the Café de Versailles. He knew many people whom I had known in London and we had a very entertaining evening. He had models in his studio and asked me if I knew of any good ones. I recommended Rupert Doone and brought him with me. We all had lunch at the studio and afterwards drew. I am afraid we were very cruel as we wanted a kneeling position from the back and Kit tied the unfortunate model to the gallery of the studio with a

184

table napkin, and although the balcony was not very much higher than the model's throne, the strain on his wrists nearly killed him. We were, however, very satisfied with our drawings. I often went to the studio and drew and did some good work, and also had some very good food and drinks, which more often than not, I badly needed. The Pole knew a certain number of very respectable French and Polish *bourgeois* friends who came occasionally to have coffee at the Dôme and at the Rotonde. One day, things were very bad indeed, and I went to the municipal pawnshop with a ring. There are no pawnshops like those in London, but only the State ones. I entered an enormous building in the Boulevard Raspail, that looked like a bank and waited in a queue. I was given a number and shown into a large room, where, to my surprise, and to their embarrassment, I found several of the French *bourgeois* that I knew. Conversation at moments like this is a little awkward, and even I was at a loss to know what to say. I thought that the situation was rather funny, but the poor things were only disturbed. We all sat on benches and, at a little office at the side, our numbers were called out, and at the same time an offer of the price that they were prepared to give. This really was most humiliating and nearly always disappointing. I waited my turn and suddenly my number was called out, " Number 12, thirty francs." Everyone's head turned in my direction and, with a strange feeling in my throat, I said " *Oui.*" On another occasion my Pole and another Pole went to pawn a piece of jewellery which had been in before for seventy francs. It had been redeemed and had to go back again. They were given a number and waited their turn. Suddenly the man in the office called their number: " Number 5, eighty francs," and they were so delighted and astonished that they both screamed " *Oui* " together in such a loud voice that everyone stared.

One day I received a letter from my elderly Canadian cousin, the one who had lived at my Grandmother's flat and thought that I had gone to the devil, when I abandoned corsets at the age of seventeen. I had not seen her for some years. She was living with another elderly lady in a *pension* near the Luxembourg Gardens. I went to lunch with them. The *pension* was one of the dreariest that I have ever entered. It reminded me of Balzac's *Eugénie Grandet*. We sat at a long table. My cousin and her friend drank water. Bottles, with table napkins tied round their necks, and names on the labels, were placed on the table belonging to the French. I drank water and had an abominable lunch. After lunch my cousin handed me two one pound notes. I was getting very bored with the ladies and had an inspiration. I said that I had just remembered an important engagement at three p.m. at my studio with a picture-dealer. I arranged to meet them at a teashop in Montparnasse later. I took a taxi and went to the nearest exchange, which was in Montparnasse, where I received quite a respectable number of francs. I went to the Parnasse Café, where I bought the boys and girls drinks, much to their astonishment and delight. I had some also, and arrived at the teashop in very good form. In Paris teashops wine is sold and generally spirits. It was a very cold day and I told my cousin and her friend that rum was a very good thing to prevent people from catching cold. I ordered them two hot rums, and they were so pleased that I ordered them two more. They were quite lively and almost human, and I sent them back to their dreary *pension* feeling very happy. They had a curious existence, these women, they refused to learn a word of French, and became furious with the French servants because they could not understand what they were talking about. Their whole lives consisted of economizing. They had apparently no ambitions of any kind. They had wasted all their youth, having been taught when young that it was only necessary to behave like ladies and wait till a suitable, and preferably rich husband, turned up. Of course, the husband never did turn up. I often wondered what would become of them if they were suddenly to lose all their money. They toured Europe and wintered at Hyères, Beaulieu, and Bordighera, where they stayed in *pensions,* with elderly Colonels, Generals, and old women, who were as bored with life and each other as they were. Everyone that I know has at least three or four relatives exactly like mine. They reminded me of my Grandmother, who, for quite thirty years, had patiently awaited death. Anyway, they had given me two pounds and my feelings towards them were of the kindliest.

I met, about this time, Ford Madox Ford. I had read his books and admired them very much. He talked a great deal and so well that nobody else wanted to, or felt that they could, say anything interesting. He told stories very well indeed. He had most amusing stories about the time that he was in the Welsh Regiment. He learnt to speak Welsh, as many of the soldiers could not speak English. He and Stella bought some of my drawings and were very kind to me. I met Gertrude Stein at his house. I had been taken to her studio once in 1914 by Charles Winzer to see her pictures. She was one of the first people to discover Picasso and had a fine collection of his early blue-and-pink pictures. She had a magnificent portrait of herself by him. She was, when I met her again, writing her book, the *Making of Americans*. I never read the whole of it, but read parts of it in the *Transatlantic Review*, which Ford published later in Paris. I read one chapter on marriage, which I thought a very remarkable piece of writing, and hope to read the whole book one day. I spent in Paris, afterwards, every Christmas Day, with Ford and Stella. We had Christmas lunch in the Boulevard Montparnasse, at a restaurant called, "*Le Nègre de Toulouse.*" Ford had a small daughter, and in the afternoon there was a children's tea-party, with a Christmas tree and a real Father Christmas. Ford dressed up as *le père Noël.* He looked magnificent as he was very tall. He wore a red cloak with cotton wool representing fur, and a red hood, and large white beard. He appeared with a large sack and spoke French, as nearly all the children spoke French better than they spoke English, and Ford's child did not speak English at all. Gertrude Stein nearly always came. These occasions were the only ones when I ever had a chance of talking to her; she was very interesting to listen to, but I always ended by getting into an awful state of nerves. She wore in the winter thick grey woollen stockings and Greek sandals. The stockings had a separate place for the big toe, as the sandals had a piece of leather which went between the big toe and the other four toes. She sat with her legs crossed, and the sandal on the crossed leg dangled and swung from her big toe, to and fro; it never stopped swinging for an instant and ended by nearly driving me mad. The grown-up people drank punch and vermouth, and played snapdragon with the children. I did not like children very much, so sat by the punch-bowl and talked to Gertrude Stein. She used to drive about Paris in a very small and old-fashioned motor-car with a woman friend of hers. Ford gave me a copy of his book, *Some Do Not*, with an inscription inside, on Christmas Day in 1925. Stella painted very well in a very precise and accomplished manner. She did an excellent portrait of Ford asleep. Ford was not too pleased, because she caught him when he had fallen asleep and was snoring with his mouth open. She said that he posed much better when he was asleep.

One day Osbert and Sacheverell Sitwell came to see me. I asked them if they would like to come to Brancusi's studio. We went in the after-

189

noon and knocked on the door. Inside we heard a
noise of approaching footsteps and Brancusi, dressed
in overalls, with wooden sabots on, opened the door.
He showed us all his work and his photographs,
including the Princess.. We left after about an hour,
all covered in dust, as one cannot sit down in a
sculptor's studio without getting covered in plaster
and clay. Willie Walton was also in Paris, and we
all dined together that evening. Osbert said that
he would like me to meet a friend of his, Sir Coleridge
Kennard, who would like to meet Cocteau and
Radiguet. Sir Coleridge had a Rolls-Royce, and
Osbert said that if I arranged a day they would
come to the studio and fetch me. I put on my
best clothes and waited, hoping to impress the
neighbours, and especially my *concièrge*. I waited
behind the front door, but to my bitter disappoint-
ment they came in an old and very shaky taxi.
We went to the Rue d'Anjou, the house of Madame
Cocteau, Jean's Mother, where he had some rooms
to himself. We were shown into a very large room
which was filled with all kinds of amusing and
wonderful things. On the wall was a portrait of
him by Marie Laurencin. A bust of Radiguet, by
Jacques Lipschitz, which was very good. A portrait
of Cocteau by Jacques Emile Blanche, one by Derain,
drawings of Picasso, a glass ship in a case, and on
the wall by the fireplace, a most wonderful photograph of Arthur Rimbaud, looking like an angel,
that I had never seen before. Cocteau went to a
cupboard that was filled with drawers and, out of
each drawer, produced a drawing or a painting of

himself by, I think, nearly every celebrated artist in France. We had tea and everyone talked a great deal. I had been taken by Marie Beerbohm to a restaurant in the Rue Duphot, called, La Cigogne, and was kept by Moïse, an Alsatian, and specialized in *foie gras de Strasbourg* and hock. Lady Cunard, Stravinsky and all "*Les Six*" went there very often and, after dinner, they played the piano and danced. I did not know Lady Cunard at this time but I knew her daughter Nancy, whom I had met in London. Jean Cocteau and Raymond Radiguet dined there every night. It was a very nice, warm, and comfortable place and the *foie gras* was perfect. One day I met a friend of B.'s, who had been at Oxford. He introduced me to a tall and very good-looking young man, who was a great athlete, and had been the champion long-jumper of Oxford. He was six feet-four and asked me out to dinner. He spoke French very well, which is always a great help in Paris, and saved me the trouble of talking to the waiters. I suggested that we should eat at the Cigogne. As we got out of our taxi we saw Jean Cocteau also getting out of a taxi. I said, " I would like you to meet my friend, who is an athlete." Cocteau said, " *Enchanté; j'adore les athlètes.*" My friend and I had dinner and Cocteau joined us afterwards for coffee. We had a very amusing conversation, as Cocteau can talk marvellously and is not at all a snob and will talk brilliantly to anyone whom he finds sympathetic. I asked the athlete if I could paint his portrait. He lived in a very small

room behind the Panthéon. It was in the next
street to a street filled with Bal Musettes and in a
very low quarter. This I thought very chic and also
very economical. I went to his place and painted
his portrait. He sat every morning at a table with
his hand on a book and a pipe beside him. I liked
him very much but found him rather boring after a
time. I went out with him and danced. He danced
beautifully and was nice and tall. He made great
friends with Cocteau, who adored Englishmen.
The English are still very highly considered by the
French. Principally, I think, because of what
Baudelaire said about their clothes. I saw Radiguet
often with Cocteau. He was a most charming boy
and spoke the most beautiful French that I have ever
heard spoken. He also spoke very slowly and distinctly. He had white, regular teeth and greenish-
grey eyes, which were of a very fine shape. His
father was a very good draughtsman and worked
for a French paper. The best draughtsmen in
France, and there are many good ones, are very
badly paid and he was very poor. He had three
other children and Raymond was the eldest.
Cocteau had met him and thought that he was very
talented and Radiguet had become a protégé of his.
I think, at the time I met him, he was nineteen or
twenty. I met also, about this time, for my memory
is not quite exact about dates, Georges Duthuit,
who afterwards married the daughter of Henri
Matisse. Georges was very tall and very good-
looking and had lived at Oxford. He spoke extremely
good English and had large blue eyes.

Cocteau told me that he and Moïse were opening a new night club and café in the Rue Boissy d'Anglas, near the Rond Point. I saw Cocteau quite often and met Erik Satie with him. Satie was a divine old gentleman with a most malicious tongue and diabolic face. We got on very well and I saw him almost every day at the Dôme. He lived at Arcueuil, not far from Paris. No one had ever been to see him except, I think, on one occasion, Jean Cocteau. I liked him very much as he was quite old, and when I was with him I always felt rather young and girlish. I was at this time beginning to feel rather old and wondered if I should not take on an attitude of middle age. Now and then, when feeling really depressed about my age, I would remember what my Catholic convert aunt would say to me, " Those that the Gods love always die young." She carefully explained, I was eighteen at the time, that this saying did not mean that one died at a youthful age but that one's spirit remained young when in years one was old. This I have found out is true as a most divine lady, Lady H., died not long ago at the age of eighty-four, much younger in spirit than many of the young things of to-day, who, as far as I can see, have never been young at all. She had a most wonderful figure, the figure of a girl of twenty. Her face, it is true, was lined. I never, alas, met her, but I have seen her dancing until the early hours of the morning with all the best looking young men in London. Satie had been a contemporary of Debussy's and of Alphonse Allais, whose works nobody in England has, as far as I can make out, ever heard of. Allais was the first man to start the fun and nonsense school of French literature and was the man who said that " *Mont Blanc a l'air très vieux pour son âge*." He also visited a French landlady with a view of hiring a room. The landlady showed him over her hotel, and, after having visited all the rooms he said, " *Madame est-ce que il y a des punaises?* " The landlady was horrified and said, " *Mais non, Monsieur, mon hôtel est tout à fait propre!* " And Allais said, " *Madame, quel dommage, autrement j'aurais pris une chambre toute de suite.*" Satie always carried an umbrella, it was known as *Le parapluie célèbre*. I never saw him open it, but he always carried it. After his funeral, to which I went and which I will describe later, there was a sale of his possessions, and I met Sauguet, the composer of the Russian ballet, *The Cat*, in London. He told me that he had been to the sale and I asked him who bought the umbrella. He said that there were twenty umbrellas and that he had bought fifteen.

Moise and Cocteau told me that they had arranged the date for the opening of their new café and restaurant, which was to be called, " *Le Boeuf sur le Toit.*" Marie Beerbohm saw Cocteau and Radiguet quite often, and I was generally there too. Radiguet adored Marie. Cocteau made us laugh the whole time. We were talking of ghosts one evening and Cocteau told us a beautiful ghost story. There was a man one day waiting at the Gare du Nord for a train and a man walked past him whom he had not seen for years. He said to the man, " Hullo, M., I thought you were

194

dead," and M. said, " Do you believe in ghosts? " And the man who was waiting for the train said, " Of course not." And M. said, " Well, I do," and vanished into space! Some years afterwards I met a ghost at Juan les Pins, and a very unpleasant one too. I will describe this later.

I made friends with a young French lawyer. He did not speak any English and as a result of talking to him my French improved. I introduced him to Raymond Radiguet and he asked us both to dine with him. The lawyer was only twenty-two and quite amusing to talk to. At the age of fifteen he had apparently become a cocaine fiend, but had broken himself of the habit. We had a long and complicated dinner, cocktails, red and white wine, and ended by each smoking a very large cigar, to the astonishment of the other diners, who looked at us as if they thought we might all suddenly be sick.

A friend of mine, a very nice Spaniard, came to Paris. He had been at Oxford and spoke perfect English. He took me out to dinner at the Ritz, and we told each other our adventures during the past two or three years. He was one of those very pleasant people who take the trouble to entertain their guests. So many people expect to be entertained the whole time. We both had a great deal to talk about and had a very amusing evening. I asked him if he would care to come with me one evening to the Boeuf. Cocteau had told me that one evening, some days before the official opening he and some friends would be there. I dined with the Spaniard at the Swedish Restaurant in Montparnasse and we went to the Rue Boissy d'Anglas about eleven o'clock. We found there Marie Beerbohm, Picasso, Madame Picasso, Marie Laurencin, Cocteau, Moïse, Radiguet and Brancusi. They were drinking champagne and we joined them. In front of the entrance was a wooden screen, one of the kind that will roll up, and everyone was much intrigued with, and decided to experiment with it. The Spaniard put it on the floor and rolled himself up in it, much to the delight of the company. He rolled and rolled on the floor. Sometimes we caught glimpses of him and sometimes he was entirely entwined with the screen. The evening was an enormous success and I left for Montparnasse with Brancusi and Radiguet, who had on a dinner-jacket. Brancusi lived near Montparnasse and said that he would see me home. We arrived at the Dôme at five minutes to two, just in time to buy some cigarettes. Brancusi had an inspiration. He said to Radiguet and me, " Let us go to Marseilles now." I, being very stupid, said that I must go home. I did not really think that he meant it and went home to my Pole. Brancusi and Radiguet, the latter still in his dinner-jacket, took a train for Marseilles a few hours later, without baggage, just as they were. On the way to Marseilles they decided that, being once started, they might as well go on to Corsica. When they arrived at Marseilles Radiguet bought some clothes from a sailor's shop and they took the boat for Corsica. They remained there for two weeks. I have never regretted anything so much in my life as not having gone with them. The only other thing that I regret was having married Edgar. Anything else that I have done does not seem to matter.

Some nights after was the official opening of the Boeuf sur le Toit. I was taken by the athlete. We dined at a restaurant near the Madeleine and went there about eleven-thirty. Cocteau, whom I had last seen at the unofficial opening, showed me a telegram which was from Corsica and from Brancusi and Radiguet. It said that they were having a splendid time and would return to Paris perhaps soon and perhaps not. Cocteau was much disturbed at the complete disappearance of Radiguet. We talked about it for a short time and came to the conclusion that he would be quite safe in Brancusi's care. They returned a few days later, having had a wonderful time with the peasants and the Corsican brandy. When members of the pre-War School of Montparnasse went out " on the bust " they did things in the pre-War style. It is a much better way, I think, than going out for two or three evenings a week. When once they started and that was not very often, as they usually worked very hard, they continued for days, and sometimes, if the money held out—for weeks. On one occasion, during the fourteenth of July celebrations, Brancusi and Braque, the Cubist, painted their faces in Cubist designs, in red, blue, and white. I did, alas, not see them, but I am told that they looked really fantastic. They began by walking up the Boulevard St. Michel. Everyone was so startled at their odd appearance that they ran away in terror. They

197

stayed out three days and three nights and finally ended in Les Halles. That is what I was told, and it is quite possible that, after Les Halles, they took the train to Chartres. The cathedral of Chartres and the Palace of Versailles were two very popular places for people who had been out for some days. They seemed to have, especially Chartres, a curious calming and soothing influence on them. I dined often at the Boeuf sur le Toit, with Marie. It was quite a small place with one room only. The walls were quite plain with one or two photographs of Stravinsky, Picasso, and Cocteau. At the end of the room was a high bar with chairs where the drinks were a little cheaper and were produced more rapidly than if one was sitting down. All kinds of celebrities were to be found there and, at any rate, the first year it was a most amusing and interesting place. Moïse was a most charming man. He was, of course, Jewish, but was very tall and fair and I would not have known it if I had not known his name. It was here that I met Erik Satie. He did not stay often in Paris for the evening, but when he did he brightened up any place that he was in and was most witty and amusing. *Les Six* had published a small pink paper. It was not in the form of a book but a large sheet which folded up. In this were published various remarks of Satie; for instance, written sideways round the edge of the paper was " *Monsieur Ravel a refusé la légion d'honneur, mais toute sa musique l'accepte.*" Ravel had been offered the Legion of Honour and had refused it. Satie simply could not resist an opportunity to be witty and, more often than not, very "catty." There was another remark of his that I thought very funny: " *Quand j'étais jeune tout le monde m'a dit, ' Quand vous aurez cinquante ans, vous verrez, maintenant j'ai cinquante ans et je n'ai rien vu.' * " I had some copies of this paper which, unfortunately, I have lost. At the beginning of the Boeuf there were hardly any English or Americans. Moïse, I, Nancy Cunard, Iris Tree, Evan Morgan, Tommy Earp and a few others, but no tourists at all. Later on it became filled with dreary and rich Americans, who simply got drunk and either fought or fell asleep.

Tommy Earp was still rich and gave us a wonderful time. He seldom said, "Will you dine on Friday, or lunch on Wednesday," but would arrive at the Parnasse and suddenly ask, " Will you have a small dinner with me? " The dinner nearly always ended at seven-thirty a m. in the markets. On one occasion we took a taxi to Montmartre to a restaurant in the Rue des Martyrs called *L'Ane Rouge*. It is a very expensive restaurant and frequented almost entirely by French people. A band played special tunes that Tommy called for and we had a really stupendous dinner with white wine, not champagne, but much better and nicer. Tommy said that the night was too young to start on champagne. After dinner we started out to " do " Montmartre. We went to the Savoy and ordered a bottle of champagne. This one has to do in any case. The champagne in these night clubs is mostly sweet and horribly expensive. The sweet kind is really more drinkable than the *sec*, which

199

tastes like vinegar. There were lady dance partners of all ages and sizes. There was one very fat lady, far from young, dressed, or rather "upholstered " in red velvet. As I was very thin, Tommy thought it would look very funny to see her dancing with me and called her over. The lady was delighted and, much to my embarrassment seized me round the waist and whirled me round and round. Tommy handed her twenty francs and insisted on her repeating the process. I was becoming really exhausted and we asked her to join us in some wine. She sat down and entertained us with the story of her life, which was much the same as that of any other lady in any other night club. We then went to La Pigalle, which is, I think, the gayest and most lively of all the *Boîtes*. There people seem to be really enjoying themselves and, at most of the other places, the gaiety seems to be forced. Paper streamers were being thrown about, and little muslin bags, containing coloured cotton-wool balls, were handed to us to throw at our neighbours. In the middle of the room was a table, and, sitting at it, I recognized Little Tich. I was thrilled, as I had seen him on the stage but never in real life. It was impossible not to recognize him. In front of him was a bottle of champagne in a bucket, and Tommy and I pelted him with our stock of ammunition. I hit him on the head twice, which I don't think he liked much. I was a very good shot as I had learnt the accomplishment of throwing straight from the bathing-machine boys in Tenby. The third time I hit the bottle of champagne, which was apparently empty, as it rolled round the ice bucket and made a clattering noise. We thought that Little Tich had had enough attention and devoted our time to trying to hit a fat blonde. After a time we got tired of Pigalle's and decided to move on. Tommy's pet place was *La Perle*, in the Rue Pigalle, quite close to the Pigalle. We went to see Angèle, an incredible old woman, who must have been a great beauty in her youth. At the door was a small page-boy dressed in red with brass buttons. We found Angèle, who was dressed in a magnificent evening dress of corded purple silk. She was very fat and the dress was very low. When she leant over the table the front displayed to view a very fat paunch. She was delighted to see us and bought us a bottle of champagne. Suddenly a row started between one of the ladies, a very tall, fat one, and the page-boy. They had a battle and finally fell on to the floor and rolled over and over. This was a really funny sight and I wish I had been able to do a drawing of it. It was now about two a.m. and we thought that we would see if the " Boeuf " was still open. We wandered down a side street in search of a taxi. The street was very dark, there appeared to be no street lamps at all. We saw a dark shadow which turned out to be a taxi, and, standing beside it, was an upright form, completely black. On our approaching it we found that it was a negro chauffeur. At this time " Batouala " was having an enormous success and we had the brilliant idea of hiring the chauffeur and bringing him to the Boeuf and introducing him as Batouala himself. We took his taxi, but unfortunately lost our nerve when we arrived. The Boeuf was very lively indeed and I danced and Tommy talked for some hours. We then went to Les Halles and had supper or breakfast or both, and some white wine, and returned to Montparnasse about eight a.m. At the Dôme, having breakfast, was Sisley Huddleston, who Tommy introduced me to. He was perfectly charming. I think I fell asleep shortly after, but no one seemed to mind. I eventually woke up feeling rather ill and went home·to bed.

I had done a good many water-colours and thought that it was time that I had an exhibition in London. I wrote to Mr. Turner of the Independent Galleries, and he said that I might have one in the autumn. As it was the middle of summer I decided to go to London almost at once. Tommy had already gone back and was living in his flat in Regent Square. My friend, who wanted to get into the Diplomatic Service and who sat for me, was going back to England and said that if I cared to go back the same day on which he did, he would pay the extra fare for me to go first-class Calais-Dover, rather than third-class Dieppe-Newhaven, the way that I always went. I was delighted. The train was packed. On the boat was a French Diplomatic Mission, I think, with Monsieur Briand; any way, there were glorious creatures in uniforms and covered in medals. The boat was packed and we had to sit on the deck on some life-buoy boxes and dangle our legs. Suddenly the most handsome and magnificent officer came up and shook my friend

by the hand. He was some important diplomat's
aide-de-camp, and was covered with medals of all

"THE PLOUGH," MUSEUM STREET

kinds and gold braid. I was introduced to him and
we became the centre of interest of all the old ladies
and gentlemen. My friends still had my flat in

203

Great James Street and I thought that I would stay
there. When I got there I found that they had gone
away and had taken the key with them. I went to
the Eiffel Tower where I found Tommy Earp.
Tommy said that he had a spare room at Regent
Square and I could stay there until I could get my
key from my friends. I had dinner at the Eiffel and
we decided to call on the way back to Regent
Square, on a friend of ours who lived in Bedford
Square. We rang her up and she asked us to come
and see her. When we arrived she unfolded a tragic
story. Her father had gone away that morning
leaving a very old mahogany box in the drawing-
room, containing bottles of brandy and wine, but
the key could not be found. We all gazed at this
very solid looking box, with its iron lock and enormous keyhole. Silently Tommy took the poker, I
took a corkscrew, our hostess took a nail file, and
another girl took a fork and got seriously to work on
the box. We wrenched and dug and poked furiously
for about ten minutes with no success at all. Finally,
Tommy attacked the hinge with the poker and it
showed signs of opening but, alas! the box lifted
from the ground and then dropped down with a
thud and a dreadful noise of smashing glass. Out
of it poured a long river of red liquid. Tommy, with
great presence of mind, seized a tumbler and held
it between the lid and the box. He filled the glass.
From another portion of the box a small stream
trickled along the parquet floor and made rivulets,
which formed into a small lake. This was all very
disheartening. We shared the glass. It tasted like

brandy, red wine, and mahogany. Later on our friend went out to replace the bottles. She bought whisky and red wine. Next morning she found the key of the box in an envelope addressed to her brother in the hall. The bottles did not contain whisky but brandy. After this disaster we went to Regent Square. Some time before, the flat had been shared by Aldous Huxley and his wife. Upstairs lived two elderly ladies. They made, sometimes in the evenings, a great deal of noise. The landlord was a retired vicar. Aldous wrote a letter complaining of the noise and asked him if he would be kind enough to ask the ladies to stop their nocturnal " bombinations "; the French slang for raising hell and disturbing everyone is to *faire la bombe*, and this word was an invention of his. The Vicar wrote a pained letter back and said that he was quite certain that the Misses A. were quite incapable of committing any kind of abomination. The flat was, at this time, shared by Russell Green and his wife. Russell had been a contemporary of Tommy's at Oxford. Facing the Square was a large room with two windows and book-cases with very fine books. First editions of Restoration Plays and all kinds of rare and interesting works. By the window was a telephone and in front of the fire was a large wicker " Oxford " armchair. Near the door was a divan on which Tommy slept. As I had travelled all day and was tired I said that I would like to go to bed. Tommy gave me a bottle of Bass to drink, if I was thirsty during the night, and went into the kitchen, saying that he was going to cook some onions. He showed me my room, which was at the back and facing some roofs. I had been foolish enough to register my luggage only as far as Calais and had no clothes at all except what I had on. I had to sleep in a very old, short, and ragged chemise. About five a.m. I woke up choking. The room was full of smoke and smelt as if something was burning. I did not take this very seriously as I thought that Tommy had probably burnt the onions. I tried to sleep and suddenly there was a banging on the door and I heard Tommy say, "Don't you think that you had better get up, you know the house is on fire." I jumped out of bed and opened the door. In burst flames and smoke. The smoke was so thick in the passage that I could not breathe, and I seized a towel, which I stuffed into my mouth, and held my nose. I found my way downstairs, still in the very short chemise and, standing at the bottom of the staircase, was the vicar with his hat on. I found out afterwards that the reason that he wore his hat was that he usually wore a wig and during the excitement was unable to lay his hand on it. I felt slightly embarrassed and so, I think, did the Vicar. I saw an umbrella-stand and hat-rack and on it hung a clergyman's top coat. I grabbed it and put it on as, after the fiery furnace upstairs, I felt rather cold. Russell Green had gone to the nearest fire alarm and sent for the Fire Brigade. He came back and he and his wife and I took some of the clergyman's chairs and sat in a row just inside the front door waiting for the firemen. They arrived in a few minutes and laid on the hose.

We still sat on our chairs and rested our feet on the hose pipe. Tommy never came down at all. He was upstairs in the kitchen handing the firemen beer. We asked them if they considered that it was a good fire and one fireman said, " Not 'arf, burnt the 'ole bloomin' floor out." We asked Tommy afterwards why he did not come downstairs, and pointed out to him the risk he was taking of being burnt to death. He had, apparently, not thought of that and explained that he objected to " Personal injury." I suppose he meant fighting his way through the flames and smoke. The fire, fortunately, did not get as far as the kitchen, although it raged outside. Suddenly, Russell Green remembered that he had left the manuscript of his novel upstairs and I realized that my passport was in my room. We took each other by the hand and went upstairs through the flames and smoke. He found his manuscript and I snatched my passport from the dressing-table, which I was able to feel my way to. It was impossible to even open one's eyes, the smoke was so thick. To have one's lungs filled with smoke is a most disagreeable feeling and I hope that I shall never be in another fire. Apparently it started by Tommy having gone to sleep, probably having left a lighted cigarette end on the floor. The whole of the floor of his room was burnt out before he woke up. It was only when the sleeve of his pyjamas became singed that he woke up. He was very ill for days afterwards. A great many of the books were destroyed, but fortunately he was insured. I felt awful and arrived at a friend's flat at about eight a.m. She said, " Where on earth have you been to, you smell like a smoked herring? " I said, " I am." I had a bath and was regaled with brandy as I felt very sick.

The next day I found my friends who had my flat and got the latch-key and stayed there. I had to arrange about my show and get my water-colours framed. I had hardly any money and felt very gloomy. I could not pay for the frames so decided to visit a kind uncle who had a business in the city. He was the brother of my terrifying aunt. I explained my troubles and he was kind enough to lend me the money (I have never paid him back, I am ashamed to say, but I will some day) to pay for them. My luck was in a very bad way as the day my exhibition opened there was a coal strike. I had a good private view, that is to say, all kinds of people came, but all I sold during the whole show was one drawing for seven guineas. Nancy Cunard was in London. She asked me to a luncheon party that her mother was giving in Carlton House Terrace. During the morning I had arranged to do a drawing of Stulik, the proprietor of the Eiffel Tower Restaurant. I worked for several hours and did a drawing in pencil which, although I don't think a good drawing, is, at any rate, an excellent likeness. It occurred to me that I might as well take it to the luncheon party and show it to Nancy, as she knew Stulik so well. I arrived, feeling rather nervous, and left the drawing in the hall with my coat. The footman showed me into a drawing-room. I had never seen Lady Cunard before, but,

of course, knew her at once by her resemblance to
Nancy. She was perfectly charming and I felt at
once at my ease. I met Lord Inchcape and Lady
Cynthia Asquith and then Aldous Huxley, the Sitwells and several other people came in. I sat next
Lord Inchcape at luncheon and was rather frightened, but Lady Cunard is such a wonderful hostess
that no one could possibly feel nervous for more
than a second. After luncheon she sat beside me
and asked me what work I had been doing. I said
that I had spent the morning drawing Stulik and
she said how much she would like to see it. I said
that I had got it with me. I fetched it from the hall
and they all liked it very much. Lady Cunard
asked me if I would do a drawing of Nancy, and
how much would I charge? I said boldly, " Ten
guineas," and I arranged a sitting a few days later.
I did, I think, quite a good drawing and got my
cheque the next morning. If only more patrons of
art would treat artists in this way we would not be
so frequently " in the soup."

I visited my exhibition every day and felt gloomier
and gloomier. In the evening I went to the Eiffel
Tower and wondered if I should ever get back to
Paris. After the show closed, some kind person
bought a small picture and I took the first train
back to Paris. During this visit to London I had
looked with interest at the river and the dirty streets,
and began to think that I might be able, some day,
to paint them. I felt, however, that I had not yet
got all that I could from Paris and that I should
have to stay there for still some years. I had my

water-colours sent back to France. It is impossible
to find out the reasons for people buying pictures.
I had excellent criticisms and the pictures were very
bright and gay. I have since sold them nearly all
and destroyed a few that I did not like. It is really
the greatest mistake to destroy one's drawings or
paintings. The last time I was in Paris, three and
a half years ago, I went to the studio where the
Pole still was, bought a bottle of wine, and burnt
about fifteen oil paintings and two hundred drawings
in a fit of rage. I have learnt a lesson since, as, not
so very long ago, a man turned up and said that he
would like to buy some drawings. He looked
through dozens of drawings and finally asked me if
I had any oil paintings. I looked in cupboards and
in corners and found some, and at last came to a
still-life, that I had very nearly put into the dustbin.
I took it out and showed it to him. He gazed at it
for some time and asked me how much I wanted for
it. I said " twenty guineas." He thought for some
time and said, " I will give you fifteen guineas
down." I said, " Yes." Having not seen it for
some years I realized that it was not so bad as I had
thought.

I still lived in Modigliani's studio and painted
portraits of any kind of odd-looking person that I
could find. A friend of my Pole's had been to
Marseilles and there had found a Tunisian who was
a very tough character. He had brought him back
to Paris to be his cook, valet, and general servant.
He had very black eyes, in one of which was a cast.
He wore a check cap and a blue linen suit, no collar

and espadrilles. He would suddenly appear late at night at the Parnasse to fetch his master home. One suddenly turned round on the terrasse and saw him standing like a statue. I asked him if he would come and sit for me and one afternoon I heard a knock on the door. The staircase was very long and, as a rule, one could hear people pounding and groaning up the staircase. He sat without moving. He was quite terrifying, as, like Landru, he never blinked his eyelids. I became almost hypnotized and had to ask him to rest about every quarter of an hour. I did a good painting of him, which was eventually accepted by the Salon d'Automne. I sold it the other day to Miss Ruth Baldwin, and it now hangs near the cocktail bar in her house in Chelsea. If one paints a good picture it is a little sad to think that one will never see it again. I am not actually speaking of that one, but some of mine have gone to America and Africa and some have been bought by people that I do not even know. I think writers are so much luckier than painters. In the first place it costs them nothing to write. To paint costs money. If one paints a good picture, even a very good one, it may have a success at an exhibition and be sold, and it is never heard of again until one is dead, or, perhaps not even then. If a writer writes a book its reputation, if it is a good one, goes on for years and the writer continues to get money for it.

An extraordinary man came daily to the Café Parnasse. He was very tall and frequently wore a top-hat, a tail coat, and white spats, and carried

over his shoulders a pair of field-glasses, and he wore
an eyeglass. He did not seem to know anyone.
We could not make out what his nationality was.
He appeared to be so conceited that the Arab and
the Pole nick-named him " Mézigue "; this is the
argot for " I," " me." " Sézigue " is the argot for
" he," " him," just as " tézigue " is for " thou,"
" thee." One day Ortiz spoke to him and found that
he came from Chili. His father was a merchant from
Lancashire, who had gone to Chili and married
there a Chilian lady. We picked him up and found
him quite mad but very funny. He had come to Paris
to study opera singing. We pointed out to him that
Paris was not the place to study and that he ought
to go to Milan. This had not occurred to him before. Later on in the evening he sang; he had a
most wonderful voice of a very beautiful quality and
most awfully loud. It shook the whole café. He
sang us " Pagliacci " and other operas. He was, apparently, quite broke and had only one other suit
of clothes besides the top-hat. He confessed shame-
facedly to us that he earned his living by accompanying Cook's tourists round Paris in a char-a-banc.
He spoke English very well, but not so well as
Spanish, and I asked him if he would come and sit
for me in his top-hat. He was delighted and I
bought a large canvas in order to paint him life-
size. I arranged him sitting down with his legs
crossed and holding his stick and the top-hat. In
the background I put a Moroccan rug, which was a
very beautiful colour; reds and blues. This rug I
bought from one of the carpet-sellers who infest all

continental cafés, and who will walk up and down
in front of the terrasse selling rugs. We had one
particular carpet-seller who also sold coats and
necklaces and sometimes had really beautiful things
for almost nothing. One day he was pestering a
very drunken American and the American said,
" Go away, I don't want any of your goddam
stinking carpets," and our Moroccan answered, in
a deeply pained voice, " Sir, it is not the carpets that
stink, it is me." In the background of my portrait
I put my guitar and a pot of red flowers on the
floor. The white pot, his white collar, and the
spats were the only white spots in the picture. The
canvas was over five feet high, and I had to work
like the devil, even to cover it up. My Pole was
painting in the next room and now and then came
and gave me criticisms. He was an extremely intelligent man and knew a great deal more about
painting than I did. The top-hat was indescribably
difficult, not only the drawing, but the shadows,
they were so intensely black. I used no black at all
in my palette but only dark blue, and had to paint
the rest of him in a much higher key than I would
otherwise have done. He was a splendid model
and very vain, and it was almost impossible to
stop him posing when he had once begun. One
day his Father arrived and I was asked to meet
him. He was a charming old gentleman of seventy-
six, but he did not look as old. He had long
fair whiskers and dressed in a dark blue-serge suit.
He had rather a nautical appearance. He could
not understand why I wanted to paint his son,

213

whose face certainly was not what the English workman would describe as an " oil painting." He said, "I have seven sons, this one is the best, you can imagine what the other six are like." I very much wanted to know but I did not like to ask him. I sent his portrait and four others to the Salon d'Automne. I saw Othon Friesz, whom I knew quite well and who liked my work and, knowing that he was on the committee, asked him to look out for them. This is done in Paris as elsewhere. I received a notice, to my astonishment, to hear that they had all been accepted. I went to the Varnishing Day and found, to my surprise, that they were not in Friesz's room at all. Each member of the committee has a special room, where he can hang the paintings of the people that he approves of. I looked round the Salon and found that all mine were very well placed in a group " On the line," in the Salle of Andre Lhôte. This was very odd, as apparently Friesz had not been able to find my pictures on the day that the committee had judged them, but they had been discovered by Lhôte, who was not on speaking terms with Friesz at the time and he had placed them in his *salle*. I had met Lhôte one day in 1920 at the Rotonde with Wassilieff, but I don't think he had even seen my work and certainly did not know my name, so that I considered that it was a great compliment. I had a few press notices in the French papers and one in Polish that was very complimentary. I decided to have a " One man show." I had met Monsieur Lucien Vogel at the Boeuf sur le Toit. He had a very nice

MADAME WALTER DURANTY

Gallery in the Rue St. Florentin, just behind the Place de la Concorde. I showed all my water-colours that had been in London, the ones from the Salon, the paintings of Collioure, and some drawings. It really looked quite nice. In Paris artists nearly always get a well-known critic to write a notice. I had made the acquaintance of a prominent critic-editor who said that he would be delighted to write one for me. He came up to my studio. The Pole hated him, he had a dreadful voice. He wrote to me asking me to visit his office—he was the editor of an important art paper—I arrived one day in the Boulevard Raspail to see his article. I think it mentioned my name once. It was a long discourse on English painting and nearly all about Roger Fry and P. Wyndham Lewis. He then demanded two thousand francs. I was furious and told him what I thought about him. He then told me what he thought of me and opened the door, pushed me out, and kicked the door to with his foot, so I had no notice. Cocteau and Radiguet came to the show and were most awfully nice. Cocteau said, as he said about anything that he appreciated, that the drawings were, " *Plus vrai que le vrai.*" And Radiguet said the most charming things: I think he had the best manners of anyone I have ever met. Brancusi came also and was very sweet. I think he thought they were too realistic, which, of course, they were. I sold very few, as it is very difficult to sell pictures in Paris if you are not French, and have not got a picture-dealer to back you. As, however, it often happens one sells more pictures after a show than during it, and during the few weeks after I did quite well.

I visited the home of my friend the Countess quite often. She was very kind to me. One day she invited me to a dance. I had some quite good evening dresses that Marie and Nancy had given me and so, fortunately, I could go out looking quite respectable. I arrived about eleven p.m. There were mostly French people there, very *chic* women, and Miss Elsa Maxwell was playing the piano with great vigour. I danced a lot and when the people began to leave, the Countess said to me, " Don't leave but stay on, we will get rid of the dull respectable people and have some fun, *avec des amis.* Leading out of the ball-room was a small room where supper was laid. There were only about ten people remaining. Lady Michelham who, alas! is now dead, the Marquis de Ségur, Cécile Sorel, Madame M., a beautiful Russian, and several others whose names I do not remember. I wore a most beautiful dress that the Countess had given me. It was long and straight and was covered all over with golden spangles, which looked like fishes' scales. . . . It fitted quite tight and exposed the lines of the figure to view and I was very much pleased with myself. The Marquis de Ségur played the piano. He played very loudly and we pelted him with oranges, Cécile Sorel and myself. She was a most marvellous person, magnificently dressed, with a most interesting face. I had seen her act and was very much impressed with her. She was very nice to me. She seized a large ham and said to me.

" Hold the bone while I carve it." I was at the other side of the table and grabbed the ham bone and pulled, as she had the fork in the ham. The bone was only an imitation one and came out in my hand and I fell over backwards. It was one of those very grand hams that had been filleted. She then grabbed me by the shoulder of my dress and said, " Take this off and dance." This amused me as I thought of Wassilieff's studio and my performances there, but I said nothing and did not dance. Lady Michelham was charming and asked me to come and see her at her home at Passy. I knew that she had the most wonderful pictures and was delighted. The party ended about four a.m. and I went home to Montparnasse. Some days later I went to see her. She had an enormous apartment and the footman showed me into a small room leading into a big drawing-room. I sat and waited. There were cases containing the most wonderful pottery and on the wall the sketch for Gainsborough's " Hay Cart," which is in the National Gallery. The sketch I thought very much more beautiful than the finished picture. The finished picture had, unfortunately, been so much cleaned that half the paint had been removed also. Lady Michelham came in and sent for some cocktails. We had a long talk about life and gossiped about our friends. She then asked me if I would like to see the rest of her apartment. We went into a huge ball-room with a very fine Lawrence portrait of a lady and many other splendid specimens of the English School. In a flat, glass case, in the middle of the room were the most wonderful jewels. There was one about an inch and a half long. It represented a semi-nude man. His torso was composed of a natural pearl. The head had been modelled in gold but the pearl was so shaped that it represented perfectly the body of a man. I don't think he had legs but a fish's tail that was made of gold. There were other jewels in the rest of the design. The case was filled with equally beautiful pieces of jewellery. I said, with a gasp, "Whatever are these?" As a matter of fact I had already guessed. Lady Michelham, whose memory was very bad, said, "I can't remember the man's name." I said, "Benvenuto Cellini," and she said, "Yes, that is his name." I said that I must be going, and she said, "Before you go my maid will give you a little box." I guessed that it would probably contain some clothes, as all my women friends were most thoughtful and kind and realized the importance of clothes, consequently I always looked well dressed. If one is smartly dressed, even if one lives in a garret, one can always ask more for one's pictures. The maid handed me a cardboard box about a foot and a half in length and a foot wide and three inches deep, which was so heavy that I could, only with difficulty, lift it. I placed it on the pavement outside and waited till a taxi appeared. When I got it home I opened it and found four most splendid evening dresses. They were covered in beads and that was why the box was so heavy. I tried them on and they fitted me perfectly. They were long and straight and all being French models would, to-day, have been most fashionable.

I had left the studio and was living in a small hotel in Montparnasse. I had behaved rather badly to the Pole and had neglected him. I found it much better to live by myself and to have no one to wait for one's arrival home. I found one day, at the Countess A's, Harry Melvill. She gave a cocktail party. Teddie Gerrard was there. I had met her during the War when she was in *Bubbly* with Constance Stuart Richardson and Arthur Weigall, the Egyptologist, who had designed the Egyptian settings. Sessue Hayakawa was also there. He was sitting on the floor on a small stool by the fire-place and I sat on a mat beside him. He was very fond of painting and we talked about art. He was most charming and very intelligent. It is such a pity that one never sees him now as he was such a good actor. Harry Melvill I had met in London just after the War. One day I was going to Chelsea on the top of a 'bus and in front of me was a very smartly-dressed, elderly man, with a fat, rather elderly, lady. She looked rather like Marie Lloyd. They talked and laughed a great deal and I wondered what they were doing on a 'bus, they looked much more like people who would own a Rolls-Royce. A few days later Mr. " Bogey " Harris, whom I had met at the Omega Workshops with Mr. Fry, asked me to lunch at Treviglio's. Treviglio's was at that time frequented by smart and amusing people; Lady Cunard went there a lot. I got there rather early and sat alone at a table and waited. Presently, to my astonishment, the elderly man I had seen on the 'bus came in alone. He sat down and seemed to be

219

waiting for someone. Mr. Harris arrived and the elderly man and myself both rose to our feet. I was introduced to Harry Melvill and we all sat down together and had lunch. Harry was most entertaining and never stopped talking. Certainly no one wanted him to. I did not tell him until years afterwards about the 'bus incident as I thought that, perhaps, he did not want to be seen on that occasion. He laughed very much when I did. During the War he had been the head of the passport office in Paris, as he was too old to join the Army, in fact he was much older than he looked. He died, unfortunately, for all of us, last year. He was the kindest person imaginable. At the cocktail party he talked French incessantly to the French, lots of French. He spoke French very fluently and correctly but in the same way that he spoke English. Consequently, unless one was close to him one thought that he was speaking English. I met Mrs. Reginald Fellowes and she asked me to dinner at her home. Some days later I went. I wore one of my grand evening dresses and some large pearl earrings and looked, I thought, very fine. Mrs. Fellowes had an enormous apartment in the Rue de Galilée. Lady Michelham, the Princess Murat and Lord Wimborne were there and several other people. There were some fine Fragonards on the walls and the dining-room was decorated with large still-lives, representing pheasants and fruit and flowers. They were by some eighteenth-century Master and were very beautiful. I was rather terrified as there were three butlers and so many knives and forks that I felt myself turning pale with fright. However, after a glass or two of wine I regained my courage and did not eat my meat with a fish fork. Hugo Rumbold was there and he played some of his songs, including the Madame Tussaud song about the Chamber of Horrors. I sang some of my silly songs. I wandered through the rooms of the apartment and found a large life-size painting of Nijinsky; this was by Jacques Emile Blanche. I thought it very fine indeed and the best thing of his that I have ever seen. I arrived home about two-thirty, feeling very much pleased with life and with myself.

My friend, Marie Beerbohm, spoke to me often about two friends of hers, F. and R. F. was half French, his Mother being English, and R. was an American from Boston. One day at the Boeuf she introduced me to them. F. was one of the first people, with Fauconnet, the French painter who died, and who was a very fine artist, to discover the Douanier Rousseau. They had seen his pictures at the Salon des Indépendants and had written him a letter beginning " *Cher Maître* " and had bought a picture. F. was a great friend of Cocteau, Radiguet, Max Jacob and, in fact, had known everyone of interest in France for the past twenty years. They were both most amusing and intelligent and we had a wonderful evening. Marie Beerbohm was as witty as all the rest of her family and we all laughed so much that we went home quite exhausted. Marie lived in a service flat near the Avenue Wagram. She had a room and a bath. This part of Paris and the Bois de

Boulogne is very tough indeed, and it is round here that nearly all the criminals are found. The neighbourhood from the point of view of living there is very respectable, but there are side streets with very bad cafés frequented by criminals. One evening I was going out to dine with Marie, and we stood on the doorstep—we were both in evening dress—to wait for a taxi. Suddenly she ran across the street and stopped a taxi and then called for me. I ran across and found that she was being spoken to by a most dreadful looking tough with a real criminal face. He wanted to take us off somewhere in the taxi. We ran quickly back to her house and shut the door. We then asked the *concièrge* to fetch us a taxi.

I met at the Parnasse an American who had the brightest, reddest hair, I had ever seen. He had small blue eyes, the colour of a turquoise, and a freckled face. He was very tall and looked as if his arms and legs might come unhooked at any moment. He spoke very slowly. I had not been in love since the incident of the Pole and immediately on seeing this vision with such red hair, I began to "sit up and take notice." I have always liked red-headed people of both sexes. They seem to me to be very much alive and very intelligent. I met him a few days later. We arranged to dine on the night of the **Bal des Quatz' Arts**. I never went, for reasons that I have explained before. It was too rough. I still saw my Pole and worked at the studio, in fact stayed there sometimes. During the afternoon of the day of the ball, Arthur Rubenstein appeared.

He knew all the Poles in Montparnasse, who adored him. He arrived at the Parnasse about three in the afternoon. He ordered drinks all round and the saucers began to pile up. He explained to my Pole, whom I was sitting with, that he wanted to go to the ball and wanted to pay rather less than five hundred francs for his ticket. It is almost impossible for a man to get in who is not a student without having to pay an enormous sum of money. Even if hundreds of francs are paid, very often people are thrown out, the few clothes that they have arrived in being torn off them. It is also necessary to know the name of one's supposed Professor and the " massier " of the class. This has to be learnt from memory from one of the real students. Any woman can get in free as they are considered the property of the students to do anything they like with. My Pole was able to obtain a ticket for fifty francs and then the great question of costumes had to be discussed. The period, as I have said, was Greek. No other kind of dress is permitted after the students have decided on a certain period. My Pole was not unlike Charlie Chaplin, and Rubenstein, although of a distinguished and imposing appearance, did not look very like a Greek. They decided to go to the Bon Marché and buy suitable material and that I would make them clothes at the studio. I went home and waited for them, collecting needles, cotton, and scissors. They came back with yards of tussore silk, with red and blue swastika patterns on it, bunches of imitation grapes for head-dresses, and sandals and ribbons to put round their waists. I cut the silk in half and sewed each side up, leaving only a hole for the head, and holes each side for the arms. The ribbon was tied round the middle under the armpits. I made two wreaths of the grapes and the vine leaves, and helped them to paint their faces. They looked very fine indeed and were extremely proud of themselves. I dined with the red-haired American and we went to watch the people enter the ball at Luna Park. We did not see the Pole, or Rubenstein, but many wonderful costumes. An American got in without a ticket, as he saw the students unloading a wagon of champagne and helped them, and so got in without being noticed. I saw two English Guards' officers who had come dressed in togas made out of sheets. They could not have looked more like the Grenadier Guards in their uniforms than they did in the sheets. They got in safely. The American and I went to the Bois de Boulogne after and sat on a seat as it was a very hot evening. He lived in a Hotel which is on the Quays at the corner of the Pont Neuf, and near the statue of Henry IV. We went to Les Halles and bought two bottles of white wine which we took back to the hotel. His conversation I thought completely "gaga," but the red hair made up for it and we drank the wine. I stayed at the hotel and at eight-thirty in the morning we decided to take one of the river boats and go down the river. It was a beautiful day and very hot. I had on a pair of sandals which I had had in London and were wonderfully made. I had very nice feet with long toes and was very proud of them. I had a check dress, very tight fitting, with a long full skirt, and on the chest, round yellow buttons like marbles. He wore a bright green shirt and no hat. We had to change at Auteuil, as we had decided to go to St. Cloud. When we got there we lay on the bank of the river and waved a bottle of beer at the passing bargees, who seemed to be much amused at us. We then took the boat back and I returned to Montparnasse to hear what happened at the ball.

The cafés were filled—this was about twelve a.m.— with very dirty and very tired people most of whom were still drunk. Nothing much was to be got out of them. I knocked on the Pole's door but he was still asleep and so I went to the Academy and did some drawings. Later on I found the Pole at the Dôme and he told me what had happened. Rubenstein and he had collected Heifetz the violinist, and they had all gone together. They had a wonderful time and afterwards had gone to Montmartre to a night club. It was a place mostly frequented by French people and had a band consisting of a rather bad pianist and a rather worse violinist. Rubenstein said to the pianist, " Give me the piano," and the pianist, who did not know who they were, said, " Oh no, Monsieur, you might break it! " However Rubenstein sat down. Heifetz said to the violinist, " Lend me the violin? " and the violinist said, " Oh no, Monsieur, you might break its chords! " but Heifetz took it and they both began to play. They played Hungarian dances, and most marvellously well. The whole café was entranced. A distinguished looking diplomat wept, the pianist wept in one corner and the violinist in the other, and the ladies of the house were so filled with emotion that they paid for the champagne. The next day at the Dôme I met Eric Satie and told him the story. I spoke to him in French and finally explained, "*Et à la fin les 'grues' ont payé pour le champagne.*" He drew himself up and said, "*Mademoiselle nous n'avons pas de 'grues' en France,*" and I said, "How funny, we have lots in England." However, I managed to pacify him and we had a drink together. That evening I saw Russell Green at the Dôme. I said, "Hullo, how did you get to the Dôme?" He said, "Is this the Dôme? I thought it was the Rotonde." I said that I was glad that he had made a mistake as otherwise I should not have found him. He had never been to Paris before and said that he strongly suspected that the whole place was a fraud and that there was nothing really interesting to be seen. I said, "Have you any money?" He had a little and I said that I would show him the town as I knew it. He had taken a first in French at Oxford and spoke the most beautiful French. We started for the Bol de Cidre, off the Place St. Michel. Here Russell's French was not very well understood and so I did the talking in my bad French. We then went to some Bal Musettes and then to some low haunts in Montmartre. He was delighted. We started out again the next day, where I met him at the Dôme, and after ten days he went back to London a changed man.

One day I met P. G. Konody at the Dingo, a small café in the Rue Delambre. He speaks every kind of language perfectly, and is a charming and most entertaining person. He was in Paris for a few days on business and was at a loose end in the evenings. I said, "Would you like to meet Eric Satie, I have just left him at the Dôme?" Konody was delighted at the idea, as, of course, he had heard of *Les Six* and all the modern painters and poets and writers, but had met very few of them. We went to the Dôme and I introduced them. I then had an inspiration. I said, "Come back with me and see my French friend, F., who knows everybody in Paris, and afterwards, perhaps, we can go and see *Romeo and Juliet* at the theatre in Montmartre. It is a French interpretation of Shakespeare's play by Jean Cocteau." I rang F. up, and we took a taxi to R.'s flat in the Rue de Condé, where F. was staying. We had some cocktails in the garden. It was a beautiful place on the ground-floor, part of a very good eighteenth-century house, and had a courtyard covered in grass with a fountain in the middle. The fountain was very pretty and represented a Cupid pouring water. We said that we thought of going to *Romeo and Juliet* and F. said, "Ring up Cocteau and he will give you some seats if there are any going." I rang him up and told him with whom I was and he told us to come and that he would keep us two seats. We had a very good dinner and went to L'Atelier, the theatre where the play was on. The stage *décor* was done by Jean Victor Hugo. He is a descendant of Victor Hugo and has a most remarkable talent for stage decoration and costumes. The back cloth was of black velvet, and the floor also. The actors were dressed in black. The men wore black tights, and painted on the tights were legs drawn in the style of the Sumerian artists. I met afterwards Jean Hugo and told him how much I admired the stage setting, especially the legs. He explained to me that the actors' legs were so ugly he was forced to design new patterns for them. The effect was startling and it was almost impossible with the black tights against the black background to see what shape they really were. Yvonne George took the part of the nurse. I had met her once or twice at F.'s house. I will write a lot about her later on as she became afterwards one of my best friends. She was a marvellous actress and had one of the most expressive faces that I have ever seen. The show was great fun. I don't know what Shakespeare would have thought of it. We went to the bar afterwards and I introduced Konody to Cocteau and Yvonne. As we were already in Montmartre I suggested that we might do a tour of the night clubs. F. and R. came with us to Zelli's in the Rue Fontaine. Jo Zelli is an Italian and certainly has the night-club spirit. There is a bar with high perches on which, nightly and all night long, sit rows of drunks, mostly journalists. Very few French people are to be found there. There is a very large dancing hall with a negro band. I had been there once before with the Princess Murat and Lady Michelham. When I came with them Jo Zelli rushed up to them and screamed at the waiter, " Royal Box for the Princess "; I did not think much about that and we sat down at a table. On this occasion when I was with Konody, Zelli recognized me and said, "Royal Box for the Princess." I said, "Oh, Mr. Zelli, I think you have made a mistake, I am not a Princess," and then I realized that he always said that to any female who looked expensive or who was with expensive-looking men. We drank champagne and danced until very late.

One day F. asked Marie and myself to have some cocktails at the flat. We found Yvonne George there, Cocteau, Radiguet, Stravinsky and Diaghilev. They asked me to bring my guitar which I did, and sang the "Drunken Sailor," the "Servant Girl in Drury Lane," and the song about Nautical William. They were delighted with the tunes. Yvonne dressed herself up in cushion covers and a pair of white kid gloves, which she arranged on her head as a hat. She sang some of her songs and she, Cocteau, and Radiguet did an imitation scene from an imaginary play. They were very funny and we had a magnificent time. Marie and I stayed to dinner and we went to the Boeuf sur le Toit afterwards. A few days later I dined at the Boeuf with F. and R. and later on Satie came in. I wore my golden dress covered with spangles. Cocteau and Radiguet were there and also Diaghilev and Boris Kochno. Satie was very affectionate and planted his bearded chin on my shoulder, it tickled a good deal, but I did not mind. He asked me to dance for him and the pianist played a suitable tune and I did various snake-like movements and felt rather like Salome dancing before Herod. It was

229

great fun at the Boeuf when the dull people and the Americans went away and we were left to ourselves. Everyone did turns, either sang their songs, danced, or did acrobatics.

I was introduced one day to a very nice American called Frank. Curiously enough, two years before, I had seen him in a small restaurant and always liked the look of him. He used to roll his eyes about and get up and do ridiculous dances by himself when he had drunk a good deal of wine. He was tall, with large blue eyes, and wore old-fashioned knickerbockers, the kind that we christened " Minus twos " after the appearance of " Plus fours." I have recently discovered that his line of conversation and his method of dancing were strongly influenced by Mr. Groucho Marx. He was extremely funny and amused me. I was very broke and very bored with life in Montparnasse and, although I had a fine time with my French friends, and at the Boeuf sur le Toit, I felt that I was not making any kind of progress, either from the point of view of painting or finance. One day Frank said, " I am bored here, let's go to Brittany." I said, " All right, I have no money at all." He said, " That doesn't matter, I have a few thousand francs and can live on that for a month, come along with me." I bought some paints and a long roll of canvas which was wrapped round a wooden pole, and one afternoon we took the train to Brittany. We took some bottles of wine with us, as no one in France ever dreams of entering a train without some refreshment. We had to change at Rennes and also wait there for nearly an hour for another train. We went to the bar and drank some Calvados. We had decided to go to Douarnenez, which is a very long way from Paris and, it seemed to us, from anywhere else. We got to Quimper about seven-thirty a.m., feeling very tired, and changed for Douarnenez. Frank had had some friends who had stayed there and knew of a hotel. We had to walk over a huge suspension bridge to get to the hotel. The board and lodging was very cheap, about five or six shillings a day, and we took a very nice room at the back of the hotel. Douarnenez is at the mouth of a river and we were about half a mile from the port on a high cliff. There were no English or Americans in the hotel, for which we were very thankful. Frank spoke very good French as, when he had arrived in Paris with some friends, they had the sense to live in the workmen's quarters and learn French. He spoke in very much the same way as I did. He wanted to become a writer. He brought with him a copy of *Ulysses*, which he read every day while I worked. I think he was one of the nicest young men I have ever met, he never worried one or got on one's nerves. After we arrived we went to bed and slept for hours. The food was extremely good. Magnificent lobsters and course after course for luncheon and dinner. We drank cider for lunch, which made us feel very amiable towards the rest of the world, and sometimes sleepy, and wine for dinner. After dinner we wandered round the town and found the port. We discovered a little café kept by a charming lady and her daughter and filled with sailors. We

231

decided to come here every evening. It was right
on the quays and we drank Vermouth Cassis and
sometimes Calvados. I found many subjects to
paint and started by doing a water-colour. I then
found, in a little street leading up to the town from
the quays, a pale blue and cream-coloured ice-
cream barrow with white and grey stone houses
behind. I painted this every morning, starting quite
early. Frank sat outside the café, drank Vermouth Cassis, and read *Ulysses* until I joined him
when I had finished painting. I found life extremely
agreeable and remember my stay in Douarnenez
with the greatest pleasure. One day there was a
Breton fête and all the peasants came out in the
dresses of their ancestors. They looked wonderful,
and played the Cornemuses, which are little bag-
pipes, and very much like the bag-pipes that are
played by the peasants in Auvergne. The fête was
held in a large field some miles from the town and
we walked there and sat on long wooden benches
to watch the dances. A few days after we arrived
we found another little café near our hotel. It had
a penny-in-the-slot piano which played a strange
selection of war-time popular tunes, including an
English one; its respectable title I don't know, as I
can only remember the unprintable version of it.
The café was kept by two buxom peasant women
who wore, as in fact all the women did, little white
caps and black dresses. On the counter were
barrels of cider and in the café there were only
sailors and no women at all except myself and the
proprietresses. Barrels were used as tables and we

sat round them on small stools. The sailors always drank beer out of half-pint bottles. We ordered a round one evening. No glasses were provided so the *patronne* produced fifteen bottles for fifteen sailors, and they and we drank out of the bottles. The sailors danced together and I danced with Frank. We got on very well with them, especially when I explained that I was " Galloise." This was not strictly true, but I was certainly born in Wales and could say, " Good health " in Welsh, which pleased them, as it is the same as in the Breton language. This reminded me of a story that Cedric Morris told me. He is, of course, Welsh and when he was quite young his family sent him to France to learn French. Unfortunately, they chose Brittany as a suitable spot for his studies. When he got there he found that it was quite unnecessary to learn French as everybody understood Welsh and he returned to England knowing as little French as when he started out!

In Douarnenez there was no sand or beach from where we could bathe, but two miles along the coast there was a wonderful beach with two or three miles of hard sand. The sea was generally rough with huge breakers. I could not swim and was rather nervous. We were the only people on the sea-shore and took our clothes off. Frank could swim very well. The waves were much higher than ourselves. They were about ten or twelve feet high. Frank grabbed me round my middle and pushed me head first through the waves as they approached us and just before they broke. I never expected to come out alive. This, however, did not teach me how to swim.

Our hotel had a little café attached to it, and before dinner we would have *apéritifs* there, and I did drawings of the peasants. There was an enormously fat woman of whom I did many drawings.

We had been in Douarnenez for nearly three weeks, and Frank had to sail for America in about ten days' time. We stayed a few more days, and decided to see some more places, before leaving for Paris. We went to Concarneau, which is a most beautiful place. On the quays were about fifty old ladies and gentlemen with easels, all painting boats. This was a depressing sight and so we entered a small sailors' café and had some Calvados. The place was delightful, but the English and Americans awful. We spent the night there, and started the next day for Pont Aven, which I had read so much about in Horace Annesley Vachell's book, *The Face of Clay*. It was also the place where Gauguin and a large colony of artists had lived. It was a dreadful place. We went to a hotel which was full of really terrible English Colonels with their wives and daughters. The proprietor of the hotel recommended us to an old lady near by as the hotel was full, who let us a charming room, with lace curtains, family photographs, Virgin Marys, and Crucifixes. It was pouring with rain when we arrived; I think it poured for two days. I sat in our room and painted a portrait of Frank in oils with an oleograph of the Virgin Mary behind him. We crossed the road to the hotel for our meals.

PEASANTS IN A CAFE
DOUARNENEZ, 1923

Next to us was a really frightful family, an elderly, hard-faced Englishwoman and her daughter. They wore blouses with whale-bone to hold up the collars, which came up to their ears. The anatomy of their chests was quite hidden by whale-bones and stuffing. They gazed at us with horror as Frank and I held each other's hands and whispered into each other's ears during lunch and dinner. The next day was a fête and the Bretons danced reels and quadrilles in the street. We joined in, which again shocked the English. It seems unkind and rude to always be objecting to one's fellow country-people, but those one so often finds abroad are frequently a blot on the race and should stay at home in some dismal village from which they probably came. We had to go to Quimperlé to catch the train for Paris. Quimperlé is a pretty place on a river and we had several hours to wait. We found a church and sat inside, in fact I think we knelt down and said a prayer, I forget what for. We then sat gloomily in a café till the train came in. It was full and we had to stand or sit on the floor of the corridor all night, it was very uncomfortable and very much worse than my voyage to Collioure. We got to Montparnasse about nine a.m. Frank had to leave that same afternoon and we were both very sad. I shook him by the hand outside his hotel and then ran up the Boulevard Montparnasse to the Dôme. It is too dreadful seeing people into trains.

I found my friends and a woman I had not seen for some time who bought some of my Brittany drawings and gave me a thousand francs, which consoled me a little for Frank's departure. I visited the Pole, who, I think, had missed me a good deal. I started work at once and was able to afford a model. A Polish girl came and I painted her portrait in a fawn coloured " cloche " hat. I met, one day, a rich American woman. She was very amusing and had an enormous apartment near the Champ de Mars. She drank a great deal of champagne and asked me to paint her portrait. She was fat, very smart, and heavily painted. I was to be given four thousand francs. I got a large canvas and began. She sat very badly, and very soon got angry with me, as she said that I had insulted her. All her enemies were delighted with it. I went occasionally to her flat, but life there was much too rough for me. When she got angry she would become violent. One day she got annoyed with some man and seized some geraniums that were in a pot. She rooted them out and threw them at him, and the pot afterwards. Fortunately, the man had just slammed the door and the pot crashed against it as the door closed. She paid me about fifteen hundred francs, but I never got any more, and I believe that it was eventually hung up in the butler's bedroom. She afterwards lost all her money, got some kind of job, and behaved in a very courageous manner.

I met at the Dôme two very charming men. One was Meriel Cooper and the other was Ernest B. Schoedsack. They had just come back from the unexplored parts of Persia and had done their first big film called " Grass." Cooper was a small fair man with a large forehead, and Schoedsack was one of the best-looking men I have ever seen. He was six feet-five in height, and had the most beautiful eyes. I made great friends with Cooper. Schoedsack was known as " Shorty "; he adored very small women. Afterwards they both made the film " Chang," and the last one, and I think the finest, is " Rango," which " Shorty " made himself. He is a man with a most delightful sense of humour, as one can see in " Rango." He went afterwards on the expedition to the Sargasso Sea with Dr. Gann and, I think, is now married. I have never seen either of them since, but hope to do so some day.

I met Sinclair Lewis at the Dôme. He was with Stacy Aumonier, who is now dead. We had an amusing evening, and told stories of all kinds. Sinclair Lewis tells stories very well and has the most remarkable ones about life in the Middle West. He would come from time to time to the quarter and bring Mr. Howe of Ellis Island fame. One evening I came into the Dôme and found Sinclair Lewis and Mr. Howe. I was sitting with them when in came two young American " College boys." They were so impressed with meeting the great man that they sat silently and listened to him. This was quite right as he is well worth listening to. I had to go out and dine with someone, and came back about nine-thirty. I found, sitting at the back of the Dôme, the two " College boys," alone and looking very frightened. I said, " What has happened to you? " They unfolded the following extraordinary story. They had a good many drinks, and foolishly opened their mouths. One of them said, " Say, Mr.

Lewis, I guess that as far as style goes Flaubert has got you all beat, but as far as characterization goes you've got Flaubert all beat." Whereupon apparently an appalling battle started and Sinclair Lewis left the Dôme having practically won on a " knock out."

I met a young American, called John; he was a curious creature, not good-looking but tall, and with a very nice voice. He was a writer and wrote for Ford's paper, the *Transatlantic Review*. I liked him very much. He seemed to have almost every kind of complex possible; I thought him interesting. He lived near Paris in an old château, which was owned by a Greek lady and her husband, whose fortune was not so large as it had been before the War. They took in paying guests. They had several children who were very nice and well behaved. I went out to see him about once a week. All the *pensionnaires* had to speak French. There was a large garden, and after lunch we all played croquet, a game that I am very fond of. There was no grass on the croquet court, only hilly earth, and to get the balls through the hoops was purely a matter of luck. The château was of a very fine design and I should think late seventeenth century, with large windows opening on to the lawn. There were some very fine pictures, two small Gauguins, a Sisley, and a Manet. After the croquet game was finished we walked round the countryside, occasionally stopping to consume some Vermouth Cassis. In the spring the landscape was really beautiful, there were orchards everywhere, and one could see nothing for miles around but white blossoms. I never dared to try and paint them. Much later on, when I attacked a pear-tree in bloom in the South of France, to my astonishment I did, I think, the best landscape I have ever painted. Anyway, I sold it for twenty pounds and it was only a small one. I took the train back to Paris about eight o'clock with my arms full of roses which the Greek lady gave me. Sometimes John came back to Paris with me and we dined there and he went back later on. I enjoyed his company and we had a very pleasant and romantic friendship. I brought the roses to the Pole, who painted still lives of them when they were fresh, and through every stage of decay until they were quite dried up, painting about three different still lives out of each bunch of roses.

From time to time the artists hired the Bal Bullier and organized dances. One time the Poles would have a ball, another the Russians and various other nationalities. It was not necessary to wear the national costume, but everyone wore some kind of fancy dress. One day the Poles gave a ball. They hired a *salle* near the Porte d'Orléans, as it was not to be such a big affair as the Bal Bullier. I found, during the afternoon, Jemmett the " Chelsea giant." He was six feet-ten and used at one time to be seen each morning in Piccadilly wearing a top-hat and tail coat. He was a really magnificent-looking creature, as he was perfectly proportioned and very good-looking. I asked him if he would like to come with me and he said that he would. I had

239

not got a fancy dress and had not time to think of one, so I wore a very fine oyster-coloured evening dress. Jemmett appeared in very old tattered trousers, a check shirt, a cap, and a red handkerchief round his neck. Later on in the evening his braces burst and I had to stand on a seat and attach the braces with a safety-pin to his shirt. We found, at the Dôme, Claude McKay, the coloured author; we took him with us. It was surprising how good Jemmett was at folding himself up in a taxi. We took another woman with us as well and we all got in quite comfortably. When we got to the ball we found a Pole who was six feet five strutting about being admired by everybody. When I walked in with Jemmett the Pole became pale with rage and nobody took any notice of him at all for the rest of the evening. I danced with Jemmett. He danced beautifully, but my head only came up to his chest, so one could not see anything or anybody while one was dancing. I found I had lost my hotel key afterwards, and decided to go to the studio and stay there. I walked up the long flight of stairs which was quite dark. I lit a match and saw, to my surprise, standing motionless outside the studio door, a man in the uniform of a Samurai Warrior, complete with two swords sticking out, one each side of him. He explained that he had dressed in the studio and had left his trousers inside and was waiting for my Pole to come back. We both waited and finally he arrived. I put on the uniform the next day and looked very odd in it and the Pole did some drawings of me.

240

I met James Joyce one day; Ford introduced me to him. He was a most charming man and had a most beautifully proportioned head. I asked him if I could do a painting of him. He said that I could, but I sent telegrams to him and he sent telegrams to me, and all of them arrived too late or too early and so I never painted him at all. He dined every evening at the Trianon and one evening I did a drawing of him when I was sitting at another table and he did not know that I was doing it. It was a very good likeness and I believe was reproduced in an American paper. The drawing is unfortunately lost and I never got paid for it. I met him and his wife whenever I went to the Trianon which, alas, was not often as it was rather expensive. Joyce is the most respectable and old-fashioned man that I have ever met. He also has the most beautiful manners, which is a pleasant change from most of the modern young men. He has a most charming voice and occasionally will sing. I think he is a little older than I am, but we were discussing old-fashioned songs one evening, " Daisy, Daisy, give me your answer, do," and others of the same kind and I said, " Did you see many years ago a show that was a kind of Magic Lantern show with a ship going down? The ship was attached to the screen and heaved up and down and voices sang a song called, ' I'll stick to the ship, boys, you save your lives '? " It was a tragic story of a ship that sank and the Captain stuck to his ship because he was a bachelor and the crew had wives and families. Joyce remembered it and knew the whole song. I remembered only the chorus and we sang that together. I went to the show (it was called somebody's " Diorama ") with my Grandmother, who wept, as she always did, at the sight of a ship. Joyce, I have heard since, paid me a very nice compliment and said I was one of the few vital women that he had ever met. I don't know if that is true, but I have very big lungs and can make a great deal of noise if encouraged. Joyce spoke with the most charming accent. His wife was fair and extremely nice; he had two children, a son and a daughter, who did not speak very much.

Yvonne George had got an engagement in London to sing at the Alhambra, and I had decided to go to London anyway to try and collect some money. Yvonne was a great friend of the Countess A.'s and she said, " I will pay your train fare to London if you will look after Yvonne." We all met at the Gare du Nord. The Countess brought our lunch with her, and two bottles of champagne. When we got into the train, we discovered an old friend of ours who said, " Are you having lunch on the train? " We said, " No, we have got our lunch with us." He said, " Would you like some champagne? " And we said, " Yes." We had our lunch and he joined us afterwards, bringing some wine with him. The Countess had engaged a cabin on the boat for herself and Yvonne and they went below. I wandered up to the bar. There I found Sachy and Osbert Sitwell and Sir Gerald du Maurier and Sir James Dunn. We had a drink and I sat on the deck with the Sitwells. It was a beautiful day and the voyage was very agreeable. Yvonne had arranged to stay at the Hotel Metropole in Northumberland Avenue. The Countess had to stay with a friend of hers. Yvonne and I went to the hotel. I had a room on the fourth floor and she had a room lower down. We were very tired and so we both went to bed.

The next morning about nine-thirty I went downstairs and tapped on her door. The maid had drawn the blinds and outside it was completely dark. There was not actually a fog but an overhead one and it was just as dark as night. Yvonne gave a scream of horror and said, " This is dreadful, I shall return to France at once! " I said, " Give me some money and you will not want to return so quickly." I went to Soho and bought a bottle of pre-war absinthe, a copy of the *Matin*, and some Maryland *jaunes*. When I arrived back we pushed the bell and sent for the waiter and told him to bring some ice. We drank a few absinthes and felt very much better. The fog then lifted and we went to the Alhambra, where she had to rehearse. I sat on the stage and translated to the conductor. That evening she appeared and had an enormous success. After the first house, which I did not go to, but waited for the second one, Yvonne returned to the hotel, and, finding me alone, said, " Now take me to somewhere amusing, not the Ritz or places like that but somewhere that is amusing and unique." I had already been thinking of places to take her to that would amuse and possibly astonish her. I said that for the moment I had only three-and-sixpence.

She had just got some money from the theatre and produced a ten-pound note. At this time ten- or even five-pound notes were not, I think, legal tender. I looked in horror at it and said, "You must get some change for that," but she said that it did not matter. I had a horrible presentiment of the trouble that we might land in. We took a taxi to Dirty Dick's in the City, near Liverpool Street. I paid for the taxi which came to nearly three-and-sixpence. Yvonne was delighted with the City and could hardly believe that Dirty Dick's, with the mummified cats and rats, existed. She had not troubled to remove her stage make-up, which really was very sensational: bright blue eye-lids and enormous eyelashes. All the local custo-mers, sailors, bank-clerks, and old ladies in shawls stared in astonishment. We went in to the farthest bar, where there are festoons of dead cats and rats, old policemen's hats and huge keys, all covered with dust. Dirty Dick was the son of a rich City merchant and lived in the eighteenth century. He was engaged to a young woman who had died on the day of the wedding, and as he had sworn never to wash again, he became known as " Dirty Dick." All the cats from the neighbourhood crowded in through the windows and died there, and he kept a tavern. The port is very good there and we had several glasses and some sandwiches. Yvonne was blissfully happy. I was nervously watching the clock and wondering what would happen when the ten-pound note was produced. She saw the time and she said, " *Mon Dieu, je dois être à l'Alhambra en vingt minutes!* " She asked for the bill. The waiter looked at us as if we were crooks and sent for the manager who looked worse, and I said, " Stay here and give me the ten-pound note! " I rushed up the staircase and into the arms of a policeman. I said, " I am in Dirty Dick's with the Star Turn of the Alhambra and we only have

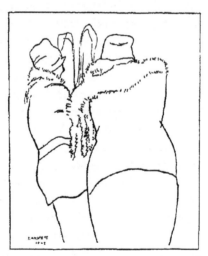

a ten-pound note and the manager thinks we are crooks and he won't change it." The policeman smiled and said, " Well, Miss, I know it's a bit 'ard on two ladies like yourselves. Take it to the Great Eastern Hotel," pointing out to me the way to get there. I ran round the corner and asked for the cashier. I was breathless by the time that I arrived and gasped, " Dirty Dick's, Star Turn, Alhambra, ten-pound note! " and I wrote all this information on the back of the note and he gave

245

me ten one-pound notes and we just got back in time.

Gwen Farrar was acting on the same bill as Yvonne. I went round to the theatre one day and arrived during the first house. Yvonne had dressed herself up as Gwen and was engaged upon imitating her in her dressing-room. She was a marvellous mimic. I left the Hotel Metropole, sold some drawings, and returned to Paris, leaving Yvonne and the Countess in London.

·*   *   *   *   *

One evening I was sitting in the Dôme with some Americans, Harold E. Stearns was there, and they were speaking of Hendrik van Loon, the writer. I had not read any of his works, but as it had been suggested to me on one occasion to do a book of drawings of famous people, I listened for all the information that I could get. I gathered that he was expected to come that evening to the Dôme and asked them if I might sit with them and meet him. It was rather like waiting for the arrival of the Almighty. About eight-thirty he arrived with his wife. I was introduced to them. I said, " Mr. Van Loon, may I do a drawing of you? " and he said, " Yes, certainly, will you have lunch with me at Foyot's to-morrow? " I was delighted. He was a very tall man and most awfully nice and amusing. Foyot's had probably the best food in Paris and is a nice, warm and comfortable restaurant near the Luxembourg Gardens. It is much patronized by the French Senators as it is directly opposite the

Senate. Some of the wicked English who used to dine there, on one occasion were discovered popping an indecent book through the Senators' letter-box. It was a French one too, which they had bought, and, owing to its incredible indecency, they were rather embarrassed with its presence in their hotel. I met Van Loon at one-thirty. He handed me a packet of a hundred blank visiting cards and said, " I dined last night at Larue with two friends of mine and we did a hundred and fifty drawings; I thought that you might find these useful for making drawings in public places." I thanked him and, I think, we did one or two drawings then to christen them. He also bought me a history book of his called *Ancient Man* which he had illustrated. He did very amusing little drawings. I wished that, when I had been a child, I had been given such an interesting history book, I might have taken some interest in the subject. We had ordered sole and on the first page he did a drawing of a sole and underneath wrote, " To N. H., in memory of a common sole." I was delighted and we had great fun. Van Loon drank Vichy water and I had some wine. Suddenly he said, " My God, this is Thanksgiving Day! I had quite forgotten it, I must give you a present, what would you like? " I could not think of anything for a minute, but after thinking a little I said, " I would like a guitar." He said, " That is splendid, I play the violin myself, and we will go and inspect the music shops." We went round the back streets in the neighbourhood of the Boulevard St. Germain which was quite near. I

247

tried all the guitars and Van Loon played all the violins. We could not find anything that we liked so moved on to the Boulevard Montparnasse. There were several shops that I knew of there, and we tried more guitars and more violins. Alas! we could not find a single guitar that we liked and I had to content myself with a large bunch of red roses. He came and sat for me a few days later and I did a drawing of him which was a bad drawing but a good likeness. I went often to his hotel near the Rue de Rivoli, and met his wife "Jimmy," who was charming and we all went to a Russian restaurant in the Rue du Bac and dined. I saw them quite often. One day they asked me to go to a large hotel in the Champs Elysées to dance and have tea or cocktails. Van Loon fetched me in the Daimler, which he always had in Paris. As we were walking down the corridor of the hotel leading to the ballroom I saw, walking ahead of me, a man with a wonderful figure and wide shoulders. I walked quickly on and caught him up and saw as I passed him that he was Carpentier. I saw him dancing afterwards. "Jimmy" and Van Loon's Dutch sister were waiting for us. I danced with Van Loon, who, like nearly all big men, danced very well. His wife and sister did not care about dancing. We all left together and stepped into the Daimler. As we drove away the sister said, "Hendrik, what kind of men are they that frequent this hotel; distinguished people, attachés at Embassies, I suppose?" Van Loon said, "No, my dear; bastard sons of bitches!" And Jimmy said, "Oh, Hendrik!"

248

Nancy Cunard was at this time in Paris and asked me if I would like to meet George Moore. I was very much thrilled and felt as if I was going to be introduced to one of the Old Masters. He stayed at Foyot's when he was in Paris. He was charming and asked me to lunch with him in the Place de l'Odéon. I showed him some reproductions of my paintings, they were nearly all portraits, including the one of Sickert, He said, " I see you are a clever woman, but why do you paint people larger than life? " We went after lunch to the Galeries Durand-Ruel, and Georges Petit. This was most interesting, as, of course, George Moore was known there in the days when he wrote his book on the Impressionists and the manager said, " Ah, Mr. Moore, do you re-member what Edouard Manet said to you that day in his studio in 1875? " Impressionist pictures were brought up from the cellars. Sisleys, Pisarros, Jondkinds and Manets, which I had never seen before. He told me how he had studied Art but had never found himself until he took to writing. He said to me, " My dear, you may do a lot with your talent and your life but not until you have got a point of view; some day you may develop one; *I* have got a point of view."

CHAPTER XII   SOUTHERN FRANCE AGAIN

THE Countess A. asked me if I would like to motor with her from Vichy, where she was about to take a cure, to Juan-les-Pins, where her brother-in-law had a house. She was going alone to Vichy for two weeks and I was to join her for the last week and we could motor South together. I had often wanted to see the Riviera, and was delighted. I arrived at Vichy one evening after a long dreary journey and she met me at the station. She thought that I was lost as the train was about an hour and a half late. She was not allowed to eat in the evenings, so I had to dine alone. After dinner we sat and talked till late in her sitting-room. The next morning she had to go off early to the cure, and I wandered about the town. It is a most dismal place, with many Arab chiefs; and in the gardens are kiosks, one side of which sit the chiefs and the other side their Arab servants. Everyone looked bad tempered and liverish; afterwards I was told that they were all suffering from that complaint. Before dinner we went to the Célestin Spring. The first day I hired a little mug and it was hung up on a hook with the other mugs. I, of course, was not a patient, but could drink the waters. I found it so agreeable as it poured out of the rock and had so much more kick in it than when it was bottled that I swallowed it in one gulp, to the horror of the attendant and the other patients. Afterwards I had to sip it.

I had arrived on a Tuesday and spent most of the

day alone. On the following Saturday the Countess said, " The motor will come round to-morrow morning and we will have lunch at Moulins. There is a fine cathedral and a museum and the food and wine are very cheap and good in the town." As we left Vichy I noticed that the whole population seemed to be leaving also. The Countess then explained that as the clinics were shut on Saturdays and the patients were free to do as they liked, feeling very hungry and well, they took any kind of conveyance to the country, where they ate and drank to their heart's content. We visited, first the cathedral, which has a very fine picture in it, and then the museum and afterwards a little hotel, where we had a magnificent dinner and very good wine. I think the whole bill came only to fifty francs. We stayed at Vichy for a week and then started for the South.

It was a most interesting voyage for me, as the Countess had studied architecture at the Sorbonne and knew a great deal about French history and painting. We spent the night at St. Nectaire in Auvergne; there is a most beautiful twelfth-century church, where, inside, the pillars are painted and in a state of almost perfect preservation; also a twelfth-century statue of Saint Baudîme. He is a most beautiful and rather terrifying figure and had had an adventurous career, having been stolen several times from his safe by robbers. We had lunch at le Puy, which is a most strange place. There are volcanic rocks, which are very high and steep, sticking out of the town; on these rocks are

251

statues and churches. I suppose one has to climb up them. They are very high and almost perpendicular. On the top of one is a statue which looked to me exactly like the Statue of Liberty, and apparently quite as large. It all looks as if it had been created by Gustave Doré. We found a museum with many Roman remains and visited the Cathedral. We walked round inside, the Countess explaining the architecture to me, and suddenly we were attacked by the rudest and ugliest priest I have ever seen. He flew at us and told us that we were disturbing the people at prayer. We could only see one person present, and he was asleep. The priest stormed and the Countess told him what she thought of him and waved a hippopotamus stick, which she always carried. She told me that she only wished that she had had the courage to beat him with it. She succeeded in frightening him into believing that he was going to be beaten and he finally slunk away. We were both trembling with rage and on leaving the church we found outside a stall, with hand-made lace and embroidery for sale. A small girl was standing by the stall. She said that her mother had gone home for a minute. We asked her what the priest's name was and told her what a rude, horrible man he was, knowing that this would be repeated to her mother, who would, in detail, explain the whole incident to the entire town. We gathered from the little girl that Monsieur B. was a far from popular figure and we left the town triumphantly.

We spent the next night at Alais and from there we went to Nîmes. We took rooms at the Hôtel de

Luxembourg and came out to a neighbouring café to have a drink on the terrasse and to buy some cigarettes. The Countess said, " Wait for me, I will go into the ' tabac ' and get a paper and some cigarettes." I waited and she stayed there rather a long time and came out laughing and said, " I have found two of your friends inside." I could not imagine who they could be. She would not tell me, but said that they were both men and that they had arranged for us all to dine together at a restaurant opposite the Roman Arena and then go to a travelling circus that they had found just outside the town. At seven o'clock we hired a horse-drawn vehicle that the Americans in Paris call a " seagoing hack " and drove to the restaurant. We went upstairs and there were F. and R. We were delighted to meet each other, and as we had a great deal to talk about, it was a most entertaining dinnerparty. F. and R. had just come from a place near Bordeaux, where Cocteau, Radiguet, and Max Jacob had stayed. The Countess had hired the carriage for the evening and after dinner we all got in and drove to a circus. Afterwards we went back to our hotel as F. and R. were staying there too. They had brought several bottles of wine, called *Vin de Carthagène*. They had bought it because they liked its name and also the shape of the bottles, which had spouts. The wine was very sweet and sickly. They also had a bottle of *l'Eau de l'Arquebuse*, which they had bought for the same reason. This was really terrible, and, as all the occupants of the hotel had gone to bed, we had to go to bed ourselves without a drink of any kind. The next day we had lunch at the hotel as both my friend and F. and R. knew the proprietor. He gave us a magnificent lunch and insisted upon us tasting all kinds of wine from his cellar. After lunch F. wanted to show me the Roman pond and fountain in the public gardens. Afterwards F. and R. had to go and we continued our pilgrimage.

We stopped at Tarascon where the Countess sent a postcard to Léon Daudet and went and looked at the fortress. We arrived at Avignon and took two rooms at a hotel where we found Tommy Earp and his wife. The next day we all motored to Villneuf and saw the frescoes in the monastery. We also went to see the Palais des Papes in Avignon itself. I have a horror of looking down from high places. F. has it too, and it makes him really ill if he is any higher up in a hotel than the first floor. The tower of the Palace is very high and has more than four hundred steps. I, feeling brave, walked up it alone as no one else had the energy. When I got out on to the roof I could see the country for miles around. There is a very fine early Corot of this tower in the National Gallery. There is no railing round the edge and I thought that I would like to see if I could really look down. I did for a second but ran very rapidly away from the edge and down the four hundred steps. The frescoes in the palace are most beautiful and perfectly preserved, having only been discovered under some whitewash, fairly recently. We went on to St. Rémy-en-Provence. The Countess and I photographed each other sitting on the Arc de Triomphe. We also saw the asylum that Van Gogh was in. Near St. Rémy is Les Baux, a lonely ruined town on a rock. Only about eighty people live there, it is most grim and sinister; and after drinking a bottle of very good white wine we were glad to get away from its gloomy atmosphere. We passed through Arles, which is a very bright and gay and paintable place, which can clearly be seen from Van Gogh's pictures. I was sorry that we could not stop.

We got to Aix-en-Provence at nine-thirty p.m. and took rooms at the Hotel des Thermes Sextius. Darius Milhaud was living at Aix with his family and we found him the next day. He said that he would take us and show us over Cézanne's house and then take us some miles further out to see Mont St. Victoire, the famous pink mountain. Milhaud came to our hotel and we started in the motor for Cézanne's house. It was then owned by some very *bourgeois* people. I believe they did quite a trade in Cézanne's hats. It was curious to see the garden, as everywhere one saw Cézanne's pictures—and how realistic they are! At the top of the house is a very small studio where he worked. On one wall was a large painting of a cow, most certainly not by Cézanne. We drove on, and saw, on turning a corner, Mont St. Victoire. It was a high and most beautiful mountain, much more beautiful and quite distinguishable from those surrounding it. We stopped at a little café from which we had a fine view of it. Cézanne used this café when he was alive. We drank some *Vin de Tavel*, which is a local wine, and found some old-fashioned postcards of the early 'nineties, representing the smart visitors to house-parties in the neighbourhood. There was a particularly fine specimen of a General's house-party, the ladies wearing leg-of-mutton sleeves and sailor hats. We then had tea at Milhaud's parents' house. Milhaud told us many amusing stories, one of Georges Auric, who was very absent-minded and who was asked to a party. By some mischance he was not introduced to the great man of the after-noon, the Academician, Edmond Jaloux. Jaloux came up to Georges and said, " *Je suis Jaloux* " and Georges turned round and said, " *De qui?* " Aix-en-Provence is a town of fountains. There are several in the main street, very pretty ones, covered in moss, with the water dripping from the moss.

We then started on the last lap of our journey. We had lunch at Brignoles, where all the English stop on their way South. There is a restaurant there famous for its *écrevisses*. We got to St. Raphael, where we sat in a café by the sea and had a drink. The weather was beautiful and we felt very pleased with life. Juan les Pins is not very far away and we got there about seven-thirty. Our chauffeur could not find the villa and asked an old man the way. He directed us and added, " *C'est la maison construite comme une ruine.* " This did not sound to us very promising. What he really meant was that it had a tower with battlements and although quite modern it was built like an old castle. It was on the sea with a little garden leading to the sea-shore. The Prince M. and his wife and daughter and a

256

crowd of others came out to meet us. The villa was filled up and so we had to stay at the house next door. This house was let out in rooms by an Austrian Countess. It had been sequestrated during the War. The Countess was a very beautiful woman with white hair. My friend had a room at the back. I thought the whole place most sinister. The room had a padded door with a tiny window in it that had bars for someone to peep through at the occupant of the room. All the windows and cupboards had wires over them; in fact it was a complete padded cell. My room opened out of it and faced the sea. Outside was a small conservatory and then a garden leading down to the sea-shore. At this time the Casino at Juan les Pins was only partially constructed. The beach was nearly empty most of the time. We had our meals with the Prince M. and his party. There was a Russian Baroness staying there who had gone through the War in the Russian Army as a Cossack orderly to a general. She had won the St. George's Cross. I saw a photograph of her in her uniform. She came from the Caucasus and was short but very strong. She gave me a Cossack's coat and some cigarettes. All the servants were Russians and in the evenings we would sit round a charcoal fire in the garden with our legs crossed and cook " Shlaslik," which is mutton and bacon put on a long skewer and held over the burning charcoal. We looked like a gipsy encampment. The Russian servants had mostly been officers during the War and had either to be servants or to keep restaurants. When the whole party went into Nice the servants would spread themselves round the drawing-room, drink the drinks, read the newspapers, and smoke cigarettes. Our rooms always gave me a strange, creepy feeling. One evening I decided to go to bed early and went to my room about nine-thirty. Some hours later I woke up and found myself staring at the window, which was a part of the conservatory. I was so terrified that the whole bed shook and it was some minutes before I could turn on the light. I opened the door of my friend's room and saw that she was sound asleep. I thought that there were probably burglars, as she had some valuable jewellery. I did not think any more about this until the day we left, and on our way to catch the train at Antibes for Paris, a Russian lady, who had been a member of the house-party, said, " Oh, you know your house was haunted and the last people had to leave? " I had cold shivers down my back. I suppose that at some time something awful must have taken place in the house. I hear that now it has been turned into a restaurant, as no one would live in it.

F. and R. were staying at Nice and came over to see us often. Sir Hugo de Bathe was at Antibes and came over too. At an enormous house in Juan itself lived the Hudnuts. Mr. Hudnut's daughter had married Rudolph Valentino. Sir Hugo knew them and one day they asked him if he would bring his friends to tea, meaning all of us. Half the party were thrilled but the other half were too lazy and comfortable at home to move. As most of our party were poor and the Hudnuts were rich we decided that, at least, we must make a good impression. Three of us actually went: Sir Hugo, who took us, a Russian Count, and myself. We brought two motor-cars with us. The house was enormous with a huge marble hall with life-sized bronze statues in Watteauesque costumes. Mr. and Mrs. Hudnut were there, Valentino and his wife, and two English people from Nice. Everyone was rather nervous. In the middle of the room was a grand piano Sir Hugo was looking very imposing in an enormous check overcoat that looked rather like a horse blanket, and of which he was very proud. He explained to the company that I sang sea shanties and other songs. I was horrified that I should be made to perform. Valentino sat me down at the piano and sat on the piano stool with me. He poured me out some whisky to encourage me. His wife, Natasha Rambova, sat on the other side of me. I have no voice but the songs were funny and I can sing in tune, so I got away with it. I found Valentino charming. He was tall and fine looking, but, of course, his face was *photogenic* and looked much finer on the screen than it did in real life. At this time I had never seen him on the cinema as I hardly ever went at all. I think he was rather pleasantly surprised that I didn't go into raptures over his performances on the screen. I talked to him a good deal about myself, which seemed to amuse him and we got on very well together. After tea and some cocktails we drove away to a café to find our friends, who were anxiously waiting to hear how we had got on. I was taken to

Nice. This was very interesting to me, as, when I had been in Russia I had read the life of Marie Bashkirtseff and was very interested in her. A great part of her life was spent in Nice. My Countess's mother-in-law, who was staying at the villa, was a Russian lady of nearly eighty and had known the whole Bashkirtseff family and told me a great deal about them. There is a fountain in Nice in memory of Marie. I was taken to see this and to the Museum, where there are some of her pictures and a large marble figure of her in a smart dress with a bustle. I am now severely reprimanded, if I ever mention this lady's name, for being old-fashioned: but I still have a great deal of admiration for her character. If she had only had the sense to realize that during her life-time the great man was Edouard Manet and not Bastion Lepage! She fell in love with Lepage and was completely influenced by him. In any case both their paintings seems to lack sensibility so completely and to be so *sec*. Whatever critics had to say about her, she did influence the fashions of her time and attained the most amazing amount of knowledge during her short life.

I was taken to Monte Carlo also, which I thought was a charming place, and filled with comic policemen and the strangest old Englishwomen who earn their livings at the Casino. We saw them parading about the town. I saw one with black stockings and white shoes, a white coat and skirt, a large hat with purple flowers in it, and a purple spotted veil. The whole head-dress looked like a meat safe covered in muslin. The Lower Corniche was the most terrifying road that I have ever been driven on and the Prince drove faster than anyone I had ever driven with. He tore round the hair-pin bends just missing the other cars. It was rather a nerve-racking experience. We had been away from Paris for five weeks and had to go back. We took the train from Antibes as the motor had been sent back a few days before. We had a *wagon-lit,* which I found a pleasant change from my journey to Brittany and Collioure, as one went to sleep in a comfortable bed and woke up in Paris.

In the late autumn Paris was very pleasant as all
the tourists had left and only the serious people remained behind for the winter. There was a Russian
Ball at the Bal Bullier, arranged by Larionof. The
balls at the Bal Bullier were the best of all if one got
in intact. Outside one had to wait in a queue,
sometimes for nearly an hour. One very cold winter
night we had to wait for a long time and the people
behind started rushing the doors. If I hadn't been
protected by two men and a policeman I think I
should have been killed; as it was, a great many
people were badly huit with the broken glass. B.,
my old friend, the man who had played soldiers
with Tuohy and the champagne bottles outside the
Dôme, were at the Ball. When he got excited, after
Mandarin Curaçao, he had a passion for climbing.
He would climb anything, trees, church-steeples,
pillars, anything he could find. He found a row of
pillars holding up the balcony and swarmed up one.
After becoming rather tired he descended slowly on
to the head of an infuriated Swedish diplomat. It
required a great deal of tact and some champagne
to calm the Swede. The little dwarf who played in
Romeo and Juliet was there. He was about three feet
ten high and had a large head. He came dressed as
a baby and wore imitation hands and arms and a
baby's mask over his face. Many people really
thought that he was about four and said, " *Va te
coucher! Où est ta Maman? C'est un scandale.*" The

dwarf was certainly not younger than thirty-five.
He is an excellent actor and I have seen him in
several French films. I knew him quite well and
one day he came to the Dôme in a pair of check
plus-fours with a little gun. He said that he had
been shooting sparrows on his estate; he looked
very funny.

My friend Marie was staying at Foyot's and introduced me to a rich man who bought pictures and
had a magnificent collection of old Masters and
sculptures. He was a great friend of Augustus
John's. He asked us to dine with him and we took
him afterwards to see some friends of Marie's,
George Adam and his wife, Pearl, at their flat.
Marie's rich friend came to my studio and bought
some drawings. He knew a great deal about food
and drink and whenever one dined with him it was
a wonderful experience. I took him to see the
Countess A. They got on very well, but I think she
found him a little out of date. One day I dined with
him and we decided to go to the Swedish Ballet. It
was not supposed to be very good but some of the
décor was interesting and also the music. During the
interval we went to the bar where everyone met. I
found the Countess A., Lady Michelham, and, in a
corner, James Joyce. I introduced them. Joyce
was rather frightened of them at first, but not so
astonished as when, a few minutes later, Valentino
came in and I introduced them both. They were
the last people in the world who I should think
would have met in the ordinary way, and they were
almost speechless.

It sometimes occurred to me that I should go back to England and live there and that I was not really getting anywhere either in life or in painting. Of course, life in Paris for foreign artists is extremely difficult if they have not enough money coming in regularly to pay for food and lodging. I could just scrape along. When I exhibited at the Salon d'Automne or the Salon des Indépendants I had good notices and encouragement from people like Friesz and Brancusi, and now and then did a drawing or a portrait which I sold. I had heard that things were brightening up in London. The Countess A. asked me to spend a few days at her country house near Versailles. It was a large converted farmhouse, the sitting-room had been a barn and it had been built with paving stones outside and looked very much an English country house. It was in the middle of a large orchard, one part of which was just a field of rose-bushes. There were several white goats, including a huge billy-goat, who was tied up with a chain; he smelt horribly and would make a dive at anyone who approached him.

I had often spoken of Ronald Firbank, and the Countess was most anxious to meet him. He had taken a house at Versailles from a French Colonel, and we decided to call upon him. I wrote him a note to say that we were coming. We went to Versailles the following day. When the motor stopped we saw a tall figure peering through the curtains. We were shown in. Ronald was in a particularly nervous mood that day and shook us by the hands and rushed to his writing desk, seized a stuffed bird of paradise, and pressed it into the hands of my astonished friend. He hardly spoke at all, but we asked him to lunch the next day, which was Sunday. One or two people had been invited to lunch from Paris to meet him and we waited and waited. After nearly an hour late Ronald appeared in an ancient barouche which he had hired. He refused to eat or to drink and hardly said a word. The minute coffee was finished he presented the Countess and myself with a copy of his latest book and made a dash for the barouche, which he had kept waiting, and returned to Versailles. I was severely reprimanded for producing an obvious lunatic, but Ronald was a person who was so temperamental that he could really not be relied on to do anything at any stated time.

In the afternoon Cécile Sorel came to tea with "Coco" Chanel, the *Couturière*, and Monsieur and Madame Van Dongen and several other people. Everyone spoke French and after tea we drank cocktails and danced. Van Dongen danced with Sorel, they both danced marvellously. Van Dongen is very tall and very thin, with a long beard. Sorel was not very tall but with a most elegant and serpent-like figure. Everyone stopped to watch them and no one else had the courage to dance. The Countess motored me back to Paris the following day.

A negro night-club had been opened by Bricktop, a coloured singer. Her name was explained by the fact that as she was not entirely coloured her hair was slightly reddish. One night after dinner

I went with the Countess. It was a gay and lively
place and many English people who objected to
spending the night in bed went there as it kept
open as long as anyone was there. I saw across
the dance floor, sitting at a table with two South
Americans, a very beautiful girl. She saw me and
we stared at each other. I waved to her and she
waved back to me. This was a most remarkable
girl who had been at Brangwyns at the same time
as I had. She was Irish and came from a very
good family. She was about fifteen and a half
or sixteen when I had known her first. She astonished and rather frightened the whole Art School.
I had not seen her for years. Even when she was at
the Art School she was pursued everywhere by
men; she was even stopped in the street. She was
supposed to be engaged to a *bourgeois* little man whom
I think she had met at a dance. He was at the time
engaged to some very dull girl. I think it was out of
pure devilry and perhaps the feeling of irritation
that such a silly, stupid woman should have got hold
of any man that she encouraged him. She was so
good-looking and attractive that it needed very
little encouragement, if any. The wretched man
asked her to marry him and she accepted. Of
course, she did not care at all for him, and I believe
that, in despair, at the other girl having refused to
have him back, he jumped off a Transatlantic liner.
I used to gaze in admiration at her and wish that
I was so beautiful. Now that I am so much older I
wonder if it is such an advantage and think perhaps
I. am better off as I am. We rushed across the

"NOW THAT I AM SO MUCH OLDER I THINK PERHAPS I AM BETTER
OFF AS I AM"
(1932)

dance floor, nearly upsetting the dancers, and embraced each other. She did not look more than twenty-two and was marvellously dressed; she had two large, real pearl necklaces on, and diamond rings. She had been for some years in South America and had had so many adventures that she said it would take weeks for me to hear them all. I had always called her Prudence; we christened her by that name at Brangwyns because her conduct was so rash. She had been a dancer in South America and had danced with Pavlova's troupe. She had now become an acrobatic dancer and was looking for a job in Paris. She had arrived at an hotel with two monkeys and a snake, and a very old and wicked-looking Spanish woman, who was her maid. The old lady looked exactly like the keeper of one of the more sinister " Joints " in Montmartre. The hotel did not consider very highly the idea of lodging the snake and the monkeys, but they said that they could stay for the night. The next morning Prudence went out, taking with her the maid, who had never been to Europe before. When they returned they found the whole hotel in an uproar and a miniature Niagara Falls pouring down the main staircase. The monkeys had got into the bathroom and turned on the taps and hidden themselves. The snake's behaviour was beyond reproach and it lay curled up in an armchair. I introduced her to my friends, who were delighted with her. Her descriptions of her adventures were most amusing and she did not mind telling them with the fullest detail.

I must say that I think that the fullest details can be told to a select company of sympathetic people, but not written down for everyone to read.

She had just taken an apartment in the Bois de Boulogne on the ground floor. It was horribly dark and the lights had to be turned on almost the whole time. I went to see it the next day. The monkeys had a whole room to themselves and lived in a large wooden cage that had been made specially for them. The snake had disappeared, apparently up a pipe in the bathroom. We put mice at the bottom of the pipe to try and entice it out, but nothing happened except a horrible smell and we think it must have stuck inside and died there. She had an instructor who taught her acrobatic dancing; he had worked in a circus. A mattress was placed in the hall, which was large, and she, in a bathing dress, would do remarkable feats with her anatomy. We christened the instructor Adalbert, because his name was Albert. He would roar instructions at her. Acrobats are fiends and nearly always want everyone else to become one. Prudence and Adalbert did their best to induce me to break up my extremely well-preserved anatomy, but I firmly refused. I introduced her to many people and they all liked her and found her most entertaining. We also went about a good deal together and I had a wonderful time.

I saw Pascin from time to time. His studio was always filled with the most extraordinary mixture of people. He had the genuine descendant of the Baron Munchausen, who was a shy young man, many Germans, generally some negresses, and several artists' models. One day when I arrived a terrible battle was in progress between a young lady from the south and another one from the north. Hair was being pulled out and they had to be forcibly separated. There was a very amusing young model who came from the north, who was known as " *La fille du curé*." At any party she would always undress. She was quite small in height, had long golden hair below her waist, rosy cheeks, and a fine and not too much developed figure. She was a most charming and unspoilt creature. She had been at the Folies Bergères and danced very well. On this occasion there were three very *bourgeois* negresses sitting in a row. Pascin had collected them from some place in Montmartre, certainly not a night-club, for they were the height of respectability and looked rather startled at the chaste but nude dance of the *Fille du curé*. Pascin said that there was a party that we must all go to, the other side of Paris, near the Rue de Vaugirard, and that we should take our food with us. We collected string bags and baskets and the *Fille du curé* and the negresses and went shopping. We bought sausages, wine, olives and ham, and took several taxis, as there were about twelve of us. The party was held in a large studio. The three negresses sat in a row and said nothing. *La fille du curé* stoked up the fire and removed her clothes. No one took much notice of her as we had seen her performances so often. The host told us to collect some more people, so several of us went to the Dôme and the Rotonde. I found there a well-dressed young Englishman who had just left Oxford. He came along. He looked so respectable that we made him dance a tango with *La fille*. I think he felt that he really was starting out on a career of adventure. Pascin suggested that we should remove the negresses' clothes. We approached one and induced her to remove her dress. She wore purple cotton underclothes and looked so dreadful that we urged her to replace it. Parties in Paris are always supposed to be so wicked and immoral, but I can't say that I have ever, during the whole of my career, seen or taken part in anything worse than I have so far described. It is true that I have been asked to places where I suspected that things would get rather rough and so have refused.

Pascin asked me to sit for him. He did a portrait of me which he did not like and, I think, destroyed it. One day I was dining in Montmartre with him and some of his German friends. After dinner we were sitting in a café drinking coffee and he was talking about Les Belles Poules, and how he had done many drawings there. I said, " What kind of place is that? " He said, " *C'est un bordel: est-ce que vous n'avez jamais été là?* " I had to confess that I had not. He said, " Then we will go now. We will go back to my studio and get some paper and pencils and spend the evening drawing the girls." The Belles Poules is near the Boulevard Sébastopol and we went down a long passage. The *patronne* was a most evil-looking old lady, exactly like a drawing by Toulouse-Lautrec. The walls were covered with tiles, representing the Palais de Versailles. Floating on the lakes were swans and seated on their backs were nude ladies, clothed only in black stockings. This made a strange and rather beautiful background for the inhabitants of the café. A very loud mechanical piano was playing. We sat down at a table and the girls stood in a row in front of us. Everyone who comes in has to choose a girl to drink with and dance with. There were about eighteen of them, very heavily painted and with very little on. They all wore socks and high-heeled shoes. Their hair was most elaborately curled and some wore coloured bows of ribbon; it would have made a marvellous painting. They lined up and said, "*Choisissez, Monsieur, 'Dame.*" I chose a large, fat one, with red hair and Pascin chose a small and I thought, rather disagreeable young woman. They said they would like some wine. We asked them if we might do drawings of them. They were delighted and sat motionless for about ten minutes. All the other girls crowded round and left their men and insisted on sitting for us too. They took each of our drawings, folded them up and put them down their socks. They kept their money there and, as we explained that we found their conversation and company quite sufficient, we had to produce ten francs from time to time. At 12 o'clock we were quite exhausted, I had done eighteen drawings. I took a taxi and went home. Pascin stayed behind and made friends with the red-headed one, who told him the story of her life. Poor Pascin is now dead. He became very depressed and suffered a lot from his liver and, I think, felt that he had worked himself out. He hanged himself and cut his throat.

CHAPTER XIV   HYÈRES AND NICE

F. and R. had gone to live in the South of France. They had taken a small villa some miles from Hyères, on the coast, and had frequently asked me to stay with them. I was generally in debt in Paris and could not go, but one day an Englishman came over and bought a painting and I wrote to say that I would come down. I took a train for Toulon; it was, of course, late and I had to take a taxi eventually from Hyères. Harry Melvill was staying there too. The Villa was owned by an eccentric Professor of Harmony from the Sorbonne, Monsieur Koechlin, who appeared generally with a sack. There was a fat and most wonderful cook and two Russian men servants. The only shop was the Post Office, kept by Madame Octoban. She was the postmistress and had a café, also a shop. Round the countryside were dotted villas. In order to get to the Post Office we had either to walk along the sea-shore or along the railway line. A very small train crawled along an absurdly small line at the bottom of our garden. That was at the back of the house, the front looked on the sea. We could bathe from the rocks below. F. refused to, as he said that no one would admire his figure, but R. and I did, and lay about on the rocks in the sun.

Georges Auric, I knew, was coming to stay after Harry Melvill had left, and about a week after my arrival he turned up, I had met him often at the Boeuf, but I did not know him at all well and regarded him as a rather terrifying person. The day after he arrived, F. and R. had to go to Cannes. They had seen a most beautiful old Château with ninety acres of land, on the top of a hill. It had not been inhabited for a long time and was for sale. They said that they would be gone for a day or so and told Georges and I to take care of the house and entertain each other. They left early in the morning and I gave one despairing look at the fat Georges, and went into the garden and sat under the trees amongst the freezias, which were in bloom and smelt very nice. I was wondering whether or not to just walk away into the landscape and not come back at all, when I heard, " *Je cherche après Titine* " played, not once, but thirty-five times on the gramophone. I thought that Georges must either be a very interesting person or to have become suddenly demented. I returned to the house and the Russian butler brought us some cocktails. Neither Georges nor I knew how to open the shaker. We finally discovered and made some more and by the time that lunch appeared we were on very good terms. He explained at lunch that he had just come from Monte Carlo, where he had been with Diaghilev, Stravinsky, and the ballet, and had written two acts of a new ballet called " *Les Matelots.*" It was all about sailors and sounded most interesting. He said that he had come to stay with F. to write the last act. He said he had so far got no ideas about it and was getting rather worried. I said, " When we have finished lunch I will teach you all my English sea songs, you will soon learn the

274

accompaniments and that will give you an inspiration." I whistled him the tunes and in a hour or
two he could play the accompaniments marvellously
well. I did a drawing of him playing the piano,
which eventually appeared in the *Burlington Magazine*. That night there was an appalling thunder-
storm. Georges was terrified and pulled the blinds,
and hid in a dark corner with his head covered up.

The next day F. and R. returned and were
delighted to find how well we had got on. We
spent the rest of the day singing the songs to them.
Georges worked hard at his ballet. He managed
to weave into it nearly all my songs so cleverly
that it was almost impossible to detect which
was which. The *finale* was most impressive, and
one could easily recognize " Nautical William."
Georges said, " If you see Diaghilev don't say anything about the third act!" Later, when I went
back to Paris I went to the first night, and after the
ballet, in the promenade, Diaghilev came up to
me and said, " And how is the fair young lady? "
which is a quotation out of the song. The ballet
was a great success and, I think, one of the best of
the post-war ones. Georges refused either to walk
or to bathe and spent all day at the piano composing.

Drieu la Rochelle lived a few miles away and
came over to see us. He was a most brilliant writer
and spoke English very well. F., R., and I walked
daily up and down the railway line. We walked
one day in the opposite direction to Hyères. F.
said there was a place called Le Datier. The
railway was very near to the sea and all the places

that it stopped at consisted of just a house or two. I asked why Le Datier was particularly interesting. He said that there was a very large date palm and a very old negro with white hair. We got to the station and saw the date palm. Beside the palm was a farmhouse and in the farm-yard, sitting on the doorstep and feeding the chickens, was the old negro. There were a few tables in the yard and we sat down to celebrate our arrival. The old negro had been in France for years and was married to a Frenchwoman. We did not like to ask him if he had brought the palm with him from his native country as it looked too old. Afterwards we took the train back. It rattled horribly and was very uncomfortable. When we took our walks along the railway line we walked in single file. I went first, then F., and lastly R. F., who was a great expert on women and clothes, gave me instruction on how to walk. He said that I carried myself well, and knew how to wear my clothes, but my principal fault was that I swung my arms like a windmill. This I endeavoured to correct.

Our villa had a little stone terrace outside with a few steps leading to the garden, which contained two orange trees with about half a dozen oranges on each of them. We gazed through the window in admiration at our beautiful oranges, and as they got riper I longed to eat one, but this was strictly forbidden. In any case, F. pointed out, they would be very sour. One day our landlord appeared with his sack. We went for a walk and when we came back we found no landlord and no oranges.

The cook said that the " *Vieux Monsieur* " had taken them away in his sack. F. and R. had to go to Nice to see their tailor and buy various things, and as I had to go back to Paris in a few days they said that we would all stay at the Hotel Westminster. I had a room on the front with a bathroom and they had a room next to mine.

The Hotel Westminster is filled with nice English families, so we did not spend much time there. The meeting place for all our friends was Chez Vogade, in the Place Masséna. Here we saw daily Cocteau, Milhaud, Poulenc, Stravinsky and his family. They all came to the tailor for their clothes. Stravinsky had a wonderful tweed coat of all colours. F. ordered a pair of burnt sienna plus-fours, which very nearly fitted him. At any rate they were all delighted with themselves. I found Frank Harris and his wife at Vogade's and had tea with them. The next day was the Carnival. It was a glorious spectacle with enormous figures of the most beautiful colours; I should imagine very much like a Roman festival, the sculpture of the figures was magnificent. We wore wire masks with faces painted on them. On one day of the carnival little balls of plaster confetti are thrown by the population at each other and anyone else who is there. The moment the confetti hits you it becomes powder and it is extremely dangerous. People have had their eyes injured for weeks afterwards. We dined at Caressa's, near the Place Masséna, and walked round the town. We found somewhere in the back streets a café with the noise of a mechanical piano and went

277

in to find French sailors, the " Marine Militaire " dancing. We joined them and bought them drinks. R. and I then went to the bar of the Hotel Negresco and sat amongst the Americans and English. Unfortunately, I had to leave the next day and my friends saw me off at the station. I started on the dismal return journey to Paris. I had stayed nine weeks with my friends who seemed to have liked my company and asked me to come back as soon as I could.

CHAPTER XV

PARIS AND BRITTANY

THERE were two very nice American boys called Ralph Sabatini and Julian Levy. They were friends of Frank's and also spoke very good French. We spent a lot of our time together; they were both talented and very enthusiastic about everything. Ralph wanted to do a copy of the Uccello in the Louvre. This is the other half of the one in the National Gallery, but it is in very bad condition, whereas the one in London looks as if it had been painted only recently. Ralph bought a canvas half the size of the original; this was about eleven feet long, and we set it up on an easel in the Louvre. The attendant of the room he was working in came up to him. On seeing what he was about to do he explained to him that during his career in the Louvre he had seen many people start copying this picture; so far, he had never seen anyone finish it. I don't know how many times Ralph went to the Louvre, but I remember that, one day, Julian and I arrived at his studio near the Sorbonne and there it was, half finished. We condoled with him and he said that he had bought a large number of photographs and had already put indications of the colours on the canvas and proposed finishing it at home. Julian and I were delighted; we said that we would come and help him. Julian went out and bought some bottles of wine and we all three started. We worked away for hours, it was great fun, and it really developed into a most extraordinary picture. I would

279

do a helmet, Ralph would paint the body, and Julian would do the legs. It was an imposing picture, distinctly reminiscent of Uccello, but somehow different. Ralph took it back to America with him and, I believe, sold it to a museum. Ralph and Julian both went back to America, unfortunately, and the detachments of Americans sent over got steadily worse and worse.

One day I found Tuohy in Montparnasse. He said that he and a friend of his, Kinko, an Irish girl, and two other friends were taking a cottage in Brittany on an island called Bréhat. They asked me to join them, but I could not for some reason or other. One day the Dingo, where I went often, became inundated with most of the crew of the American flagship " Pittsburg." They talked to everyone, they fought and drank, they ate beef-steaks with bottles of tomato sauce, and bought everyone drinks. All the ladies from miles around arrived, and the Quarter brightened up. I made friends with a fat electrician, who was charming, and made more noise after, as he described them, " a flock of ginfizzes," than anyone I had ever met. I painted his portrait, which he sent to his Mother; he also paid me for it. The sailors who did not get fighting drunk I found very amusing, and quite different from any other kind of person that I had met. My fat friend, if he was not on leave at a certain time, would send his friends to me to look after. He sent two ridiculous little creatures one day, who were about eighteen. I looked after them and told them where to go. Even in London

280

when I got back in 1926, I found two American
sailors in their bell-bottomed trousers and white
hats waiting for me in the Fitzroy Tavern, much
to the amusement of everybody. I found it rather
embarrassing as I did not know what to do with
them.

My friend Prudence was still in Paris and was
engaged to perform at the Four Hundred Club.
She worked daily with a pianist in a large room
which was let out for dancers to rehearse in. I
went, in the afternoons, to watch her. I went with
my French friends to see her the first night. She
looked perfectly beautiful, although I do not really
like acrobatic dancing; I think it is ugly and un-
gainly. We then went to the Jardin de ma Soeur and
to Montmartre.

One day Tuohy and Kinko came from the island
in Brittany in their two seater Citröen. They said,
" Come back with us." I took my water-colours
and a rucksack with a few clothes and got in. One
of us had to sit on the back of the seat on the folded
hood. They both drove in turns and one or other
of them would change places with me. I was delighted with the idea of seeing Brittany again.
They said that there was no need to hurry and that
we could take our time and see some of the towns
on the way. We spent the night at Dreux. Tuohy
told me that they had invented the " Anti-omelette
club," as none of them liked omelettes. The first
thing to do on arriving at an inn or restaurant was
to say, before stepping inside, " *Pas d'omelette s'il
vous plaît.*" He said that, frequently, when motoring

281

up the drive, approaching the hotel, you could hear them beating up the eggs. At Dreux we had no omelettes. We spent the next night at Mayenne, which amused me as this was where Edgar had been stationed after he left England and I had received from him many picture postcards of the place. We went further and further north and finally came to Paimpol, which was not far away from the island. We stopped for a drink and then drove to l'Arcouest. The motor was put into the garage there and we took the " Vedette," a small motor-boat, to the island.

Bréhat, at this time, was quite unspoilt, and a few French people came there year after year. There was a hotel and café by the port and a comfortable hotel with bath-rooms somewhere else. We walked down a path as there were no roads and only one horse and cart on the island. We came to the square where the Town Hall was, a rather battered-looking thatched house which was labelled " MAIRIE " in stone letters. Just outside the square was a rather new café. In the square was a covered-in terrasse on one side of the path leading to an inn, and on the others, chairs and tables under the trees. We rested ourselves and I was introduced to Madame Balet and her husband, who had been a chef. We then walked across the island through flat fields. The house was the other side and faced many little islets, mostly uninhabited and consisting of yellow-ish rocks which became as bright and yellow as gold when the sun shone. It was a most beautiful place. The sea was so blue; I thought a much finer blue than the Mediterranean. The whole atmosphere of Brittany reminded me of Wales and I felt quite at home there.

The house was in a row with three or four other houses. I slept in a large room underneath the roof with beams; it had windows on each of the four walls. Our house was surrounded by a small garden and not attached to the houses each side. I found many subjects to paint and started some watercolours. There were some charming French people who lived on the island and we had *apéritifs* with them at Madame Balet's before dinner. There was Monsieur Negroponte, who was really a British subject, having been born in Egypt. He had hàd a son in an English regiment during the War, but he could only speak a very little English himself. He had been a very good-looking man when he was young and still was most amusing and attractive. He wore a sailor's peaked cap and a check coat. There were some French painters there and a French marquis who lived in a château near Guingamp, not very far away on the mainland. They gave dinner-parties at the hotel with enormous fish, cooked specially by Monsieur Balet, and to which I was sometimes invited. The native women, mostly the older ones, wore the national costume. Black clothes and enormous black poke bonnets with strings under their chins. I did some drawings of them. Tuohy wrote most of the day and I drew and painted. Sometimes we took the boat to the mainland and motored round the countryside. Kinko knew Brittany very well and had, in fact, written articles on it for papers. The Bretons liked us very much and I always said that I was Galloise and they said that they were Irlandais. The Bretons and Tuohy understood each other perfectly.

At l'Arcouest, where the " Vedette " crossed to, was a hotel, and we used to have drinks, not with the tourists, but in a little side bar where the sailors went. The patron had a *chien de chasse*, a setter, of which he was very proud. His wife had a short, fat, white dog who wheezed. One day the patron went off to *faire la chasse*, taking both the dogs with him. To his horror his famous setter had no scent at all and the short fat dog was the success of the party. His wife laughed loudly when they came home. One day Kinko was expecting some money from her Father and, as Tuohy was working, we went together to the Post Office, which was near the square. She found it waiting for her and spoke of three hundred francs. We went to the dull new café and started to celebrate the event. We had also promised to buy the lunch. We arrived home rather later than we intended and, after eating, retired to rest. During the afternoon Kinko said, " I have mislaid my money, perhaps I have dropped it or hidden it somewhere." We searched the house and could not find it. We consoled ourselves by playing Mah Jong. None of us really attained great proficiency in this game but we liked handling the pieces. The next morning I was in the kitchen. The fire was not lit and it had not been cleared out since the day before. It was an old-fashioned stone stove, built into the room with a hole underneath with a grating for the ashes to drop through. I saw, sticking out, a piece of a five-franc note. I put my hand in and there was all the money including a five-pound note and several hundred-franc notes, some tens, and the five-franc one that had only had its edge burnt. This find, of course, called for another celebration. Hiding money reminded me of the Modigliani hundred-franc note and that " It's an ill wind, etc.," but we were pleased that it was us who found it rather than the rather bad-tempered and incredibly inefficient charwoman.

I found an old friend of mine whom I had known in London during the war; I had known him with Constance Stuart Richardson and Mario Colonna. He had been to Spain and had taken the most beautiful photographs of Spanish architecture. He already knew Tuohy and Kinko but they didn't know that I had known him before. He knew everyone as he came to the island every year. He said that he would come and cook us a Hungarian goulash one evening, and told us what we must buy and that he would bring the other ingredients with him. We spent the day getting food and drink in and arranged the whole dinner with different kinds of wine. The goulash took a long time to make and the smell from the kitchen was terrific. Finally it appeared and we all stuffed ourselves. During the night we suffered from the effects of the Paprika and in the morning felt very ill. It took us three days to recover. It was, unfortunately, too hot and too rich for us.

One day a most curious thing happened. We

were celebrating someone's birthday at Madame Balet's and came home rather late. I carried the lantern, with which we crossed the island at night, because it was completely dark if there was no moon and impossible to find the path. I carried a ship's lantern; we used it as light in the sitting-room as there was no gas or electric light. We crossed the fields, and on the other side was a narrow path, on one side was the hedge of a garden belonging to a house. Suddenly, in the middle of the path, we saw two creatures. They were about eight inches long, like lizards, with high front legs like chameleons. They had broad black-and-yellow stripes all over them, long tails, huge eyes that they rolled at us and long tongues which shot in and out. This really was a startling spectacle in the middle of the night, and we all turned rather pale and walked on in silence. I went to the café the next morning by myself, as I had to go to the Post Office, and I asked Madame Balet what the curious creatures were that we had seen the night before. She said that they were Salamanders and that it was very rare to see them as the Bretons kill them. They are in the arms of Francis I, who was the first king to put down the Bretons.

We bathed from the rocks in front of the house, but we had to wait till the tide came up and it was about twenty feet deep, so I could only cling on to a rock as I could not swim. We bathed also from a little beach at the back of the island. This had sand and I could go in up to my neck. Tuohy swam very well and would swim far away to a rock. One

286

day he swam out of his bathing suit. Kinko and I
stood on the sea-shore and laughed at him as he
swam after it.

One morning we decided to do a tour of Brittany
in the motor. We started off early. We stayed
the first night at Morlaix, a town which I wanted
to see, as it was there that Tristan Corbière lived,
and I knew his book of poetry, *Les Amours Jaunes,*
quite well. Sophia Brzeska read them all the time
to me when I was with her at Wooton-under-
Edge. It is rather a beautiful old town with some
very fine old carved houses. The hotel was very
expensive and filled with very dull French *commer-
çants.* We went to Roscoff, which has been completely ruined by the English. After Roscoff we
motored through wild moors and hills. This landscape might easily have been Ireland or Wales.
At Huelgoat is an extraordinary valley with huge
rocks. They said that they were of volcanic origin.
There is one particularly large stone which is called
" *Le Rocher tremblant.*" This, if pushed in the right
place, rocks to and fro. The guide could do it but
we could not. We saw many churches with painted
wooden sculptures and effigies of the Breton Saints.
We found a church at Pleyben with a statue of
Saint Herbot. He is the patron of cows, and on a
stone table under his effigy were a collection of
cows' tails, offerings to him for his kindly services in
saving their lives from various diseases. Many of
these statues are of the fifteenth century. In the
Chapelle de Notre Dâme du Huat are the statues of
six saints in painted wood. They stand in a row:

Saint Lubin, who deals with every kind of affliction; Saint Mamert, who takes upon himself all troubles of the stomach, and is seen holding his entrails in both hands; Saint Meen, who looks a little " gaga," and represents La Folie; Saint Hubert, who gives his protection to those who are bitten by dogs; Saint Livertin, for the maladies of the head, is represented holding his head with a pained expression on his face; lastly, Saint Houarniaule, who protects people suffering from fright. We visited Douarnenez and I took Tuohy and Kinko to see the old ladies in the café on the Quays. (I wished that Frank had been with us.) They remembered us both and were most pleased to see us. We went to Pont Croix, where all the houses are white with grey stones down each side. There is a marvellous church porch here. We got to the Point de Raz, which is the most western point of France. In the distance is the island of Ouessant, in English, Ushant. This gave me an unpleasant feeling as I remembered the name in connection with history at school. This island has two or three hundred inhabitants, who are very poor indeed, and, until two hundred years ago, were pagans. The sea is so rough between the island and the Point du Raz that, sometimes, it is impossible for them to come ashore for months. Even the men in the lighthouse quite close to the Point are cut off for weeks at a time. We had some wine at the hotel near by and then became very courageous and said that we would like to walk round the Point. One has to take a guide. I was extremely surprised on returning to find myself alive. It is a most terrifying experience. We had to walk along a very narrow path. On one side of the Point was a whirlpool which churned and seethed and the water dashed nearly up to our feet. The path was on the edge of a precipice with no protection whatever. I ran along it quickly, as I really felt as if my last minute had come. We asked the guide if people ever fell over or got giddy. He said that six had the previous year and when once they went overboard they were gone for ever, as they were dashed to pieces immediately on the rocks below. We were led on and round the end of the Point; we had to cling on to rocks and grass. This continued until we were nearly completely round the Point. We immediately returned to the hotel and had some more wine to calm our shattered nerves.

We came to a strange place with savage dark people and strange old ladies, wearing antique costumes of, I should imagine, the eighteenth century. With difficulty we found someone who spoke French. The place was called Ploneour. Outside the church was the funniest War Memorial that I have ever seen. It must have been sculptured by the local stone-cutter. It represented two soldiers standing each side of a tablet, on which were written a list of the names of the dead. The two soldiers were identical and were exactly like the wooden soldiers in the song. I wish I could have taken a photograph of it or that I had had time to do a drawing. We came to another strange place called Ile Tudy. Here the origin of the people

appears to be unknown. They are very dark and
unlike the Bretons. It becomes an island at high
tide. We went to Bénodet and had to cross a river.
To do this one had to take a large ferry boat. We
drove the car into it and as we were waiting for it to
start I did a drawing of the opposite bank, with
large trees, a white hotel, and a red gipsy caravan.
I painted it when we got home and was quite
pleased with it. We passed through La Forêt,
which is a very pretty place with the slowest hotel
in the world. It is true that in France if you do not
arrive between stated hours you have to go hungry.
We only asked for bread and cheese and cider and
we had to wait about an hour, which was very bad
indeed for our tempers. Our tempers were marvellous and even when we had punctures and break-
downs and lost our way we never got cross with one
another.

We spent the night at Concarneau. The line of
old ladies and gentlemen were still there and gave
me the appearance of never having moved since the
last time I saw them. I noticed that their painting
had made no visible progress. I expect they are still
painting. We stayed the night in a hotel overlooking the fortress, which looked beautiful with the
grey reflections of its walls on the blue waters. We
had one look at Pont Aven and Kinko and Tuohy
thought that it was as dull as Frank and I had found
it. We found ourselves at Hennebont. It had a
fine fortress and was free from foreigners. We
visited a café and found there all the maids of
the opposite hotel. They seemed never to have seen

anything like us before or, in fact, to have encoun-
tered any English. We entertained them and ourselves to Vermouth Cassis, which seemed to mount
to their heads with great rapidity. They got very
talkative and most confidential, and we became
rather nervous in case the angry patron, or worse
still, *patronne*, of the hotel came and objected to us
leading the staff astray. We rapidly entered our
motor and drove away before trouble took place.
We were punished for this disgraceful behaviour
and, on the road to Auray, had three punctures and
arrived all in the vilest of tempers. We found a
horrible hotel all got up in oak and plates on the
walls like something that is labelled in England,
" Ye olde," etc. With difficulty we got some food
and hurried rapidly away to Vannes where we
spent the night in a very good and inexpensive
hotel. We had been on the road four days and had
not lost much time, but the money was getting very
short and we had to hurry. We left early the next
morning and as we were nearing home we had a
puncture. There was enough money to pay a man
to mend it and we arrived home with exactly four
francs. I don't think the whole tour had cost more
than four hundred francs for the three of us. I had
done quite a lot of work, nothing very large or
important, but some drawings of sailors and some
very nice water-colours of the island. For about
thirty or forty years bad painters from all nations
had found the island a paradise of " pretty " subjects. I thought the subjects were pretty too, but
oddly enough, seemed to find different ones from

the old gentlemen and old ladies who, I expect, would have been horrified. I had been on the island for five weeks and had to return to Paris. Tuohy and Kinko motored me to Vannes, where we spent the night at the hotel and I took the train from there to Paris. On my way to Paris I saw one of the most beautiful sights that I have ever seen. As the train approached Chartres there was a large plain, with corn that was just ready for cutting. It was about seven-thirty and a most perfect evening. The sun had nearly set and all the corn was a bright golden colour. The sky was purple and suddenly, on the horizon, I saw, first one and then the other spire of the cathedral of Chartres rising slowly out of the field of yellow corn. The spires of Chartres are both different and one is taller than the other.

I felt very bored with Paris. I met a very nice man called Dreydell, he is now also dead, as so many people in this book are. He bought some drawings of mine and took me to the Boeuf and to Montmartre. I saw the Dowager Lady Michelham at the Boeuf. She was with Ethel Levy and she introduced me. I talked a great deal of rubbish but they didn't seem to mind and gave me some champagne. I met with Lady Michelham several very nice Americans, including Jeff Crane and his cousins, the Pattersons, who came from Dayton, Ohio. He had a friend called Jeff Dodge, who had a beautiful apartment in the Boulevard St. Germain. It had a garden, and instead of flowers in the flower beds there was planted thick ivy. In the middle was a fountain with a Cupid. We sat in the

garden when I visited him and drank cocktails.
He had the most beautiful furniture and pots filled
with flowers and leaves carved in Chinese jade,
some of which had come from temples in China.
These Americans were very kind to me and bought
drawings and Jeff Dodge asked me to paint his
portrait. I started it quite well but I forget why I
never finished it. Perhaps it will be like the portrait
of the Old Master who painted a gentleman when
young and then, thirty years later, added grey hair
and some wrinkles, and I will finish it when I am
sixty!

A grand birthday party was given in an Ameri-
can's flat and I was asked for some unknown reason.
I arrived in my workman's trousers, dressed as an
apache. The butler looked rather alarmed, but the
guests liked it. I had three hundred francs in my
pocket. We had a magnificent dinner with champagne and brandy and danced, and about two a.m.
I left. I went to a cochers' restaurant near the
Gare Montparnasse, which the inhabitants of the
Dôme visited after two a.m., to eat soup *à l'oignon*.
I thought that I might find someone that I knew.
The patron knew me and the inhabitants were
delighted. The *clientèle*: chauffeurs, workpeople,
apaches and the ladies from the neighbouring
houses. The ladies wore bedroom slippers, no hats,
and shawls. I sat down with them and drank white
wine and ate snails. By this time the wine had gone
to my head and, as two policemen had come in and
were drinking at the bar, the patron asked them if
they would be kind enough to see me home, as I only

lived a few doors away. The policemen were much amused and both offered me their arms. I gave them a few francs and they left me at my hotel. If anyone is behaving in an eccentric fashion and obviously enjoying themselves, I have always found the French willing to join in the fun. Of course, now and then foreigners' perfectly innocent intentions have been mistaken, and everyone has ended " *au violon.*"

Jeff and I used to go out for terrific evenings in Montmartre. We would put on our best clothes and dine at some grand place and then " do " the mountain. One night, very late, almost five-thirty in the morning, we went to a negro cabaret and restaurant. It was kept by a very pale negress and her husband, who was very black. We had some champagne and Jeff said to Palmer, the husband, " Well, Palmer, it's a curious thing, every day Florence gets whiter and whiter and every day you get blacker and blacker." And Palmer said respectfully, " Yea, Mr. Crane."

I had met at Pascin's a little clown called " Charley," he was at the Cirque de Paris. He had a partner and they were funny at times. I was discussing him with Iris Tree one day and said, " It's a curious thing that Charley has not made a greater success." And Iris said that, " If you were going to be a clown at all you had either to be very funny and original indeed or not a clown at all." At any rate he was a most amusing companion. He had crossed America several times with circuses on the road. He spoke five or six languages and, I believe,

was actually a Belgian Jew. He was often with
Pascin and his friends. He collected pictures, which
he succeeded in wangling out of painters. He has
one of mine which he acquired in a very artful
manner. I was with an American judge one evening
and we went to the circus. Charley was really funny
on that occasion and extremely vulgar. We went
round to his dressing-room, which was a wonderful
place. It had all his properties hanging upon the
wall. An enormous cardboard razor and a pair of
imitation breasts made of papier mâché, which hung
up on a string and a miniature fire engine, a
miniature hearse, which was used for the funeral of
a flea (I forget how this tragedy took place), and an
imitation Turkish bath, in which a body was taken
out boiled to death. Sometimes, if Charley was in
a good temper, he would give one some relic with
which one could play awful jokes on one's friends.
We asked Charley to come to Montmartre with us
after the show. He came with us during the interval
in his costume to have a drink at the bar of the circus. Descamps, Carpentier's trainer, was nearly
always there and all kinds of sporting people. We
sat up at the bar and bought Charley and the other
clowns drinks. I found the circus people most charming and unpretentious. They are a most cosmopoli-
tan race and they all speak so many languages that it
is difficult to know which race they belong to. After
the performance we collected Charley and took a
taxi to Montmartre. When we got into the taxi
Charley found on the floor a garment of some kind,
and when we passed a bright light, Charley held it

up and we saw that it was a black female coat with a
cape attached, very fashionable at the moment.
Charley said, " You can have it if you give me a
picture in return," and I said, " All right! " I
rather regretted it afterwards, as Charley came to
my place and chose a very nice oil-painting. He
had paintings by half the well-known artists in Paris,
which he had wangled one way and another. There
was a story of a very famous painter who was a terrible drunkard. His pictures are now worth thousands
of francs. He will give them away if he is not
prevented from doing so. He lives in Montmartre
with his Mother and his stepfather. He is one of
those unfortunate people who, like my Australian
soldier, simply cannot drink a drop, without having
to continue. A friend of mine was at his house one
evening and Charley came in. She noticed that his
pockets rather bulged. He went out of the room
and then came back. Presently loud shrieks were
heard. These were from the unfortunate painter
who, although a man of nearly fifty, was being
unmercifully beaten by his stepfather for having
exchanged a picture for a bottle of drink. This
poor painter had a miserable life. One night he
was found by Rubézack, wandering in the Rue de
Vaugirard, in the pouring rain terribly drunk with
carpet slippers on and no hat or coat. Rubézack,
who was quite penniless, led him to the Rotonde in
the hopes that he would find a picture-dealer or
some kind person to pay the taxi to Montmartre.
Several dealers refused, although they had made
fortunes out of his pictures. Finally a collection was

made amongst the artists and Rubézack, my Pole, and someone else took him back to his Mother's house. His Mother was very grateful to them and offered each of them one of his water-colours in return for their kindness, but they said they were old friends of his and refused to accept anything. I am afraid that I should have taken one as they are very beautiful and I have always wanted to buy one.

Van Dongen I saw sometimes at the Countess A's. He and his wife gave receptions every Monday evening. He had an enormous house and two studios. He and his wife sent me a permanent invitation to come every Monday. I was delighted as it gave me the opportunity of showing off all my grand evening-dresses. I had nine at this time. I knew that the person whom Van Dongen must meet was Prudence and that he would love to paint her. I went by myself the first week and when I got there Van Dongen said, "Look what I have got for your benefit," and I looked up to the gallery and there were the musicians from a Bal Musette. One man with an accordion with bells on his ankles and a man with a violin. These bands are wonderful to dance to as their sense of time is perfect, and the French workpeople dance so well. At one time Ford hired a Bal Musette once a week and invited his friends, but it ended in a disturbance between the intellectuals who wanted to talk and the dancers who wanted to dance and to drink. Van Dongen's parties were the best that I have ever been to. There was plenty of champagne, the only drink to have at a party.

Unfortunately there are those that it makes ill, but I think that they are in the minority. There were the most beautiful and elegant collection of women I have ever seen. One South American had a Lanvin dress of white silk with an enormous white bow, edged with black, that covered nearly the whole of her skirt and looked like a huge butterfly. Van Dongen introduced me to a few people, including a most charming Frenchman who wrote a great deal about the discoveries of Glozel and the tremendous controversy there was about them. He sat with me and pointed out all the celebrities and introduced me to anyone I wanted to meet. There was an electric gramophone and a Breton singer, a woman who sang Breton songs and was very celebrated on the music halls. André Warnod was there with his wife. I told Van Dongen about Prudence and the monkeys and how beautiful she was, and he asked me to bring her and ask her to dance. She came with her dancing clothes and her accompanist. Most of the audience sat on the floor. She was an enormous success. If she had done nothing except stand still and smile she would have brought any house down. The women were most enthusiastic. I have found that Frenchwomen suffer much less from jealousy of other women than most other races. If I happened to look rather better than usual or had a dress that suited me they would crowd round me and be so sweet and kind. I think it is really because they are so sure of themselves and the idea that they should have a rival in any shape or form never enters their very elegant heads. Any-

298

way I have always been devoted to them and wish there were more of them over here. One evening I brought Peter Johnstone, who is now Lord Derwent, with me. He had a most terrific success, especially as he spoke such excellent French. I also brought an American opera-singer who sang. I think in the end, as so often happens, Van Dongen's hospitality was abused by " gate crashers," and the parties came to an end. Madame Van Dongen is one of the most charming and most elegant women I have ever met, and I had the pleasure of seeing her quite often when she was in London a few years ago and showing her a few of the sights. Van Dongen painted a portrait of Prudence. It was an enormous canvas, I should think over life-size, in a green satin dancing dress and a green satin top-hat. I sat behind him and drew his back. He looks very funny when he paints. He wears a hat and a long black coat like a house-painter. He begins a portrait by drawing it in charcoal; in one hand he holds a large feather duster with which, now and then, he dusts the charcoal off and corrects the drawing. The extra-ordinary sureness with which he applied the colour astounded me and I began to think that if I sat behind him and watched long enough I should also become a society portrait painter. The portrait was exhibited at the Salon.

One day I went to F. and R.'s flat and found Radiguet, Yvonne George, Cocteau, Marie Beer-bohm and several other people, and we had some cocktails. I sat and talked to Radiguet. He asked me when I was going to draw him. I had arranged for him to sit some time before, but he had not come. I said that I would some day soon. Ten days afterwards I heard that he was dead. He had been taken ill at Foyot's, where he had been staying; a doctor had not been sent for until he had already got pneumonia and a few days later he was taken to a nursing-home. The following day his Father had arrived and the door was opened by a hospital nurse, who said, " *Est-ce que vous voulez voir votre fils, il est dans le mortuaire?* " Radiguet was the eldest of the children and adored by his Father and his brothers and sisters, and it was a terrible shock. Marie Beerbohm told me of his death and asked me if I would go with her to his funeral. We did not look forward to it as we knew that it would be a very sad affair. This was in the month of November, and one morning at nine I fetched Marie and we went to the church, which was near the Etoile. It was foggy and raining. The church was filled with white flowers and near the altar was the raised platform, waiting for the coffin. The church was crowded with people. In the pew in front of us was the negro band from the Boeuf sur le Toit. Picasso was there, Brancusi, and so many celebrated people that I cannot remember their names. Radiguet's death was a terrible shock to everyone. " Coco " Chanel, the celebrated dress-maker, arranged the funeral. It was most wonderfully done. Cocteau was too ill to come. We waited some minutes for the arrival of the body, in its white coffin, covered with white flowers; it was carried up the aisle and placed on the platform. After a short service we walked round the coffin and shook the Holy Water over the coffin, the men walking one side and the women the other. We could hardly see, as Marie and I and everyone else's eyes in the church were filled with tears. We had to walk round the church and shake hands with the relatives. It was the most tragic sight that I have ever seen. Radiguet's Father and Mother were there, and then his four little brothers and sisters, the youngest being about six, stood in a row, their faces contorted with weeping. Marie and I burst into tears and went out into the street to see the procession start off. The hearse was covered in white and was drawn by two large white horses, like those in the war picture by Uccello in the National Gallery. They stood patiently and waited. The coffin was carried out with its white pall, and on it was one bunch of red roses. Many wreaths were carried out, and by the time the procession started the white hearse and a carriage following were covered with white flowers. We walked down the boulevard, following the procession, and waited and watched the hearse and the long train of mourners disappear into the distance on their way to Père Lachaise. It was not yet ten o'clock and still pouring with rain. Fortunately, in Paris, the cafés are open all the time, so we went to the Café Francis, which is near the theatre Champs Elysées, drank some brandy, and sat silently gazing at the rain. Cocteau was terribly upset and could not see anyone for weeks afterwards. I wrote to him in February and asked him if I could come and see him. He wrote me a charming letter:

"25 *février* 1924,

CHÈRE NINA,

Je suis toujours très malade et sans courage.
Téléphonez un matin.

De cœur,
JEAN COCTEAU."

I went to see him and he had grown thin and worn.

One day I received a cheque for a painting. It was in American dollars and I asked Harold Stearns where I could cash it. Harold said, " Come with me." We went to the other side of the river to a bank and cashed it. I think it was for about eight hundred francs. We visited the New York Bar and Henri's Bar and drank champagne cocktails, which certainly went to my head. Harold was not affected, as he had one of those heads which are only to be found attached to the bodies of Americans whose families have been in America for not less than two hundred and fifty years and want some " hitting." We came back to the Dôme in a taxi and a friend of his met me inside and said, " I am with Leonard Merrick and a friend of his, and they have come to find you." I didn't know him but, of course, had read his books. Apparently my friend did not know him either and he had heard that I was a desperate character and was to be found at the Dôme. I introduced myself and he introduced me to his friend, who was Edith Evans, who has since become a famous actress. I said, " I am awfully sorry but I am afraid that I have had too many champagne cocktails and may fall asleep

or scream, will you meet me here to-morrow? "
They were charming and said that they would and
I was conveyed home to bed. I saw him several
times, and the day he left Paris I had luncheon with
him and he gave me a hundred francs and asked me
if I would buy myself some flowers. I did, but a
very small bunch, and lived in comfort for the rest
of the week. I have never seen him since but hope,
perhaps, that he will see this book and know that I
have not completely vanished.

I don't much like writing about funerals, but I
shall have to because Erik Satie died and I thought
that I ought to go to his. He lived at Arcueuil with
his umbrellas and was to be buried there in the
village church. I took a train on the morning of
the funeral at the Gare d'Orléans by myself. On
the platform waiting for the train was the painter
Ortiz de Zarate. I found that he was going to the
funeral too and so we got into the same carriage;
I was glad to have someone to go with. When
we got to Arcueuil we asked the way to the church,
which was about ten minutes' walk. The ceremony
had already begun. The church was filled, there
were politicians and all the *Bœuf*, Brancusi, Cocteau,
Moïse, Valentine and Jean Hugo, Yvonne George,
Wassilieff, all *Les Six*, and the Ecole d'Arcueuil,
Erik Satie's own school of musicians, of which
Sauguet is the only one whose name I can remember. This was the second funeral I had
gone to, and, although it was very sad, as I missed
my afternoon séances with Satie at the Dôme,
he was an old man and had lived his life and

had had a lot of fun, it was not so tragic as that of Radiguet, who was so young. After the service we started for the cemetery, which was about a mile away. The men followed on foot first, walking four abreast. There must have been at least fifteen hundred people present. Afterwards walked the women. Yvonne George, Valentine Hugo, Wassilieff and myself headed the procession. There were many very respectable French *bourgeoises*, all dressed in deep mourning. These I found out afterwards were the wives of all the keepers of cafés in Arcueuil where Satie had had *apéritifs*. At the cemetery we stood by the graveside and saw the coffin laid in the grave and shook the relatives by the hand and went back to Paris. I had a most beautiful letter from Satie that he wrote me on one occasion when I asked him to come to a ball that I was arranging with some Americans. I said that I would " dance like the devil " for his benefit. Alas! he could not come as it was a very late affair. He answered my letter and said that he was sure that it was impossible for me to " Dance like the devil " as I was " *beaucoup trop gentille.*" Unfortunately, I have lost it.

I was at this time very broke and very gloomy. F. and R. asked me to stay with them in their castle and I very much wanted to go. I was in pawn at my hotel and could not move, so had to wait patiently until something turned up. A very nice Englishman, Dreydell, turned up whom I had met before. He suggested that I should have an exhibition in London that he would arrange for me to

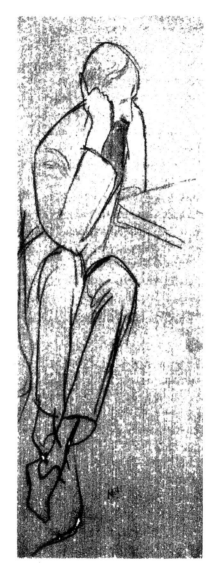

LYTTON STRACHEY

Drawing in the possession of Philip Gosse

have at the Claridge Gallery, in Brook Street. I had a good many oil-paintings that I had never exhibited before, and quite enough for a good exhibition. He bought a still life of mine and paid me twelve hundred francs. I was delighted and wired immediately to F. that I was arriving at any moment. I paid the hotel bill and felt very light-hearted and free again. The next day I caught a violent cold and that evening had to go to bed with a high temperature. I was living alone at that time in the Rue Campagne Première. In the same hotel lived three people who were charming, but generally spent every night dancing and drinking in Montmartre, arriving home at seven or eight in the morning. They generally bounced into my room to inform me of the scandals of the night, which they managed to hiccough out. At seven a.m. they arrived in evening-dress. I said I was very ill. They were very upset and brought me a bottle of brandy and tottered off to their beds. I looked at it and decided that I should, on the whole, prefer a lingering death rather than a sudden one and went to sleep. I managed to sleep all day and at six-thirty a doctor friend of mine happened to call and see me. He gave me one look and said, "Have you any money?" I gave him fifty francs and he went out and bought various pills, potions, and appliances, and within ten minutes my temperature was considerably less. By this time my neighbours had come to, and were appalled to think that they had not fetched a doctor in the morning. I suggested that they should have some brandy and console themselves as it wasn't really very serious. The same evening the doctor came to see how I was, and he and a friend of mine finished the brandy and staggered home arm-in-arm.

CHAPTER XVI   SOUTH AGAIN

I BEGAN to pack my things and think about the South of France. The Pole saw me off at the station. I armed myself with a bottle of red wine. The train was full and the only seat I could find (I travelled, of course, third class), was in a carriage filled with French sailors. In the corner was a very small ginger-haired French soldier. I sat down in a corner. The sailors opened their bottles and offered me some wine. We then all drank together. They were all Bretons and we talked about Brittany. Next to me was a very good-looking, golden-haired sailor, who got very drunk, and, after making an unsuccessful attempt to kiss me, fell asleep with his head on my lap. I felt slightly embarrassed but thought it better to remain still, hoping that eventually he would become conscious and that I could change my position. The other sailors and the little soldier were already asleep and I lay my head against the window and slept too. About five in the morning I woke up and from the opposite corner of the carriage the soldier spoke to me in the most perfect " Oxford English." I thought, " Good God! He probably knows all kinds of people that I do and here am I with a sailor asleep with his head on my lap." I asked him why he spoke English and he told me that he had been brought up in England and that his Father was a Frenchman, and he, being a French subject, had to do his *Service Militaire*. He had been in Egypt before in some kind of political job

and had to leave it to join the Army. He said that
the food was very bad but his family gave him
money so that he could feed himself. He was perfectly charming and at Toulon the sailors got off,
feeling rather ill and bad-tempered, and the soldier
and myself continued, standing in the corridor, talking and looking at the landscape. When I arrived
at Cannes, my friends were waiting for me on
the platform. The soldier got out and I introduced him to them. We asked him to have a drink
with us but he had to wait for another train to
take him to Nice and had not got time. F. was
not at all surprised to see me with a French soldier,
as he is one of those sensible people who are not
at all surprised at anything.

I was very dirty indeed and I had some food at
the Café de Paris, which is, or was—I think it no
longer exists—opposite the Casino. We then
motored to the house, which was on the road to
Grasse, but about two miles from the main road.
It was a most beautiful old house, built about 1802,
on a hill surrounded by mimosa trees, which were in
full bloom. The yellow flowers in the sunlight were
so bright and dazzling that one had to blink one's
eyes for a few seconds before one could see. In the
front of the house was a hilly lawn with some big
trees. The whole lawn was covered in the biggest
and sweetest smelling violets that I have ever seen.
There were several farmhouses on the estate, quite
near the house, surrounded by olive trees and
a small, strangely shaped, and very fat donkey with
an enormous head. I did not get on very well with

it as, whenever I sat outside and attempted to draw, it would lay its head on my lap or try and swallow the Indian ink. There was also a tame sheep which was very fond of walking into the drawing-room and tucking itself up comfortably on the sofa. This had to be discouraged in wet weather as it did not wipe its feet. I had the most beautiful bedroom with a large and very comfortable bed. I also had a bathroom to myself and a kind lady came and asked me if I wanted any mending done. I felt that at last I had arrived in Paradise. The house had a wide winding staircase. The rest of the house had been painted with coloured patterns which, unfortunately, had disappeared, principally owing to the damp. At the back of the house was a lake filled with fish and a small and very beautiful island with mimosa trees on it. On the far side was a bed of irises. We were on the top of a steep hill and the ground sloped down. The other side of the pond, behind the irises, which could be seen from the house, we could see in the distance the sea, and at night the Esterelle. At one side of the house was a valley and, in the distance, more and bigger mountains. These had snow on the top of them, and in the early morning were the most wonderful colour. Near the house was a pear-tree in bloom. I think I have already mentioned that near Paris, there were orchards filled with pear blossoms which I never had the courage to paint; but every day I looked at this tree and determined to try. For the background there were trees on the hill as it sloped towards the valley, and over their tops were the distant snow-

309

capped mountains and the blue sky. To my surprise I found that blossom was very much easier to paint than many other subjects and it turned out to be, I think, one of my best pictures. Even F. liked it. It is now in the collection of Roy Randall. We had breakfast in our pyjamas and dressing-gowns and then walked about the estate accompanied by a very fat white mongrel, which waddled and wheezed, and was called Zézette. Poor Zézette very much shocked the smart French people who visited us, as they expected that F., with such a fine château, would have, if not Borzois in attendance, at least Alsatians or something rather grand.

I worked in the morning and afterwards we sat in the sun and drank cocktails till lunch. The cook was a fat Frenchwoman and I have never eaten so much or such good food. I felt myself growing fatter every day, which indeed I was. I am afraid that I slept generally during the afternoon. Every evening I insisted on putting on one of my nine evening-dresses, and had great pleasure in sweeping up and down the wide staircase and imagining that I was rich. F. would put his head out of his sitting-room now and then and hand out instructions on the subject of deportment. F. and R. never worried about changing and generally had dinner in their ordinary clothes and espadrilles. After dinner we sat in a little room which has now, I believe, a mosaic floor designed by Picasso. F. would discourse on life and the beastliness of the human race and R. and I would listen. Once I inadvertently mentioned my admiration for Marie Bashkirtseff as a person, and was so shaken by the torrent of abuse that I received from F., that I had recourse to the brandy-bottle for a few minutes to recover. I think, and still do, that F. is the most intelligent person that I have ever met. He seemed to have read everything that had ever existed. I had the sense to make notes of many of his views and of all the books that he mentioned, all of which I shall certainly not live long enough to read. We read Fantomas, that series of French " bloods " in forty-two volumes, all of which Max Jacob and Cocteau have read. F. drew most beautifully and did two paintings of me which he never actually finished because he decided that he could not attain to the perfection of his original conception. He might have been a great artist if he had not been so intelligent and so critical. R. was a portrait painter of considerable talent and had had a good deal of success in Paris and, in fact, had made quite a lot of money, but being so far from anywhere and managing the estate, he did not paint very much.

We motored into Cannes one morning to do some shopping and have some cocktails at a large hotel on the Promenade. It was filled with English and Americans; one could easily pick out the English as they all sat with small bottles of champagne in front of them instead of cocktails, a habit of which I thoroughly approved. F. heard from Francis Poulenc to say that he was coming to Cannes to stay with his Tante Léna, who was eighty, and F. wrote and asked him to stay with us for a few weeks.

I knew him quite well and was delighted, as he was most amusing and intelligent, as all *Les Six* were. We went to Cannes to fetch him from his Aunt's house. He had a room next to mine. It was a small room papered with the most wonderful eighteenth-century wall-paper, with a landscape continuing all round the walls. It looked like a Henri Rousseau and had large snakes and huge trees and alligators coming out of the water. F. was very proud of this room as it had a wicker bed. I believe that it was actually very uncomfortable, but F. showed it to everyone with great pride.

Poulenc composed all the morning; I painted the pear-tree and F. came and gave first Poulenc, and then myself, advice on our respective arts. It was delightful to paint in the sun and hear pleasant music at the same time, and I was perfectly happy. I taught Poulenc some of my songs, which he invented accompaniments to, and I sang them sometimes to the French people who visited us. Poulenc was terrified of birds and one morning, at about five o'clock, I heard a knock on my door, and there was Poulenc, who said, " *Venez ici, j'ai peur,*" and under the water-pipes of his room was a fluttering sparrow, which he could not bear to pick up. I put my hand underneath and took it out and threw it out of the window. By this time the cook, who slept underneath, had heard voices and poked her head out of the window. She looked up in astonishment and saw our frightened faces and the fluttering sparrow.

We went to Grasse one day and found Nicole

Groult, the dressmaker, and Madame Jasmy van Dongen. They arranged a luncheon-party at the hotel, which we went to. There were only French people present and we had a wonderful time. Poulenc and I found some gambling machines in the bar of the hotel and proceeded to lose francs until we were dragged away by F. and R. Grasse is a dreadful place and smells of bad scent. I asked Poulenc to sit for me, which he did, for an hour every day. I thought that he should wear a button-hole, and we all walked round the estate to choose a flower of a suitable colour. The ground was covered with wild anemones of all colours and I chose a pinkish purple one, which looked well on a grey-green suit. The portrait was a very good like-ness but a drawing I did I liked better. The drawing was reproduced in the *Burlington Magazine* some years ago, with one of Auric also.

Madame Porel, the daughter-in-law of Réjane, came to lunch one day. She was very chic and very nice. Harry Melvill was staying in Cannes at the time and came over frequently to see us. One day he came to lunch and said that he had just been to see Monsieur Patou, the dressmaker, and that Mon-sieur Patou had been talking about the Queen. We asked what he had said, and Harry said, " He said that the Queen was forty-seven, and I said, ' But Monsieur Patou, the Queen must be more than forty-seven,' and Monsieur Patou said, ' I am not talking about her age, I am talking about her bust.' " When Harry talked about the happenings of the evening before, or the present time, he was

313

very funny, but he had a large stock of old stories that got a little wearying after a time.

My birthday is on the same day as F.'s, but he is older than I am. It is Valentine's day, the fourteenth of February, and he arranged a birthday party. We asked Harry Melvill, a French Countess and her husband, and a tall and distinguished Englishwoman who was staying at Cannes, and we hired a waiter from the hotel at Grasse. The waiter proved to be quite mad and very inefficient. Speeches were made and we drank a magnum of champagne and walked and talked in the garden afterwards. One day we went to Nice to see Monsieur Gentilhomme, the tailor. We went to Vogade's, where we found Honegger and Stravinsky. Stravinsky had to be fitted at the tailor's and we all went round there, where he was to meet his wife and children. He had with him two little pictures that he had just had framed. They were sewn in needlework and designed by his two small daughters. They were very beautifully drawn and he was very proud of them. His eldest son came to meet him with his Mother. F., R., and I went back to Vogade's and talked to Honegger. We asked Stravinsky and his wife to lunch with us at Faletto's, a restaurant on the road from Nice to Monte Carlo, in a week's time. A few days later a motor-car arrived at our house and Stravinsky and his son appeared. This was before dinner. We always had a tin of caviare pressé which I had to spread thinly on toast. Stravinsky seized a spoon and dug spoonfuls out of the tin and then played on

314

our harmonium the fair tune out of Petrouchka.
They stayed to dinner, Stravinsky sat beside me and
presented me with a glass cigarette holder.

Picabia, the Dadaist, lived not far away from us
and we went with Harry Melvill to his house. The
house was so full of things, ornaments, pictures,
furniture, that it was almost impossible to move
without upsetting something. He came to lunch
with us and brought with him Marthe Chenal, the
famous opera-singer. She sang the "Marseillaise" on
the steps of the Madeleine during the War, and had
a wonderful voice. She was the most magnificent-
looking creature, very tall, with a wonderful figure
and a beautiful and very animated face, with curious
purplish-red Medusa-like curls all over her head.
Poulenc tried to induce her to sing, but she would
not, but asked us all to a box at the Casino at
Cannes, where she was playing "Carmen." Poulenc
sang his latest songs which were composed for the
words of some old and rather naughty French
poems of the sixteenth and seventeenth century,
which delighted Chenal, and I was finally induced
to sing my sailor songs which Poulenc played for me.
Poulenc's Tante Léna was invited to the Opera also
and asked us if we would like to come and dress
at her flat at Cannes. She was the sweetest old lady
I have ever met, very active and talkative, and was
so kind and nice to me, treating me as if I was a young
thing of twenty. She came and brushed my hair
and helped me to dress and we all went to the
Café de Paris and dined. I really did feel like a
jeune fille being chaperoned and out for the first

time. I wore a magnificent white dress with white beads on it, very long. My hair was cut quite short with two side whiskers, known by the apaches as *Rouflaquettes*. I had enormous pearl earrings, a large pearl ring, and a very good imitation gold chain bracelet, all of which had been given to me by R., F., and Poulenc one day, when they left me alone at the Café de Paris, and went out and showered false jewellery upon me, with which I was delighted; and they really looked magnificent with my fine dress. Chenal was a splendid actress, but looked really almost too big for the stage. Afterwards we went to the Casino and had supper with Chenal and Picabia and his wife and several other people. I induced Picabia to dance. He assured me that he had never done so before, but he got round somehow. He was much shorter than I was, and rather fat.

Chenal hired a motor-boat sometimes and took her friends to the smaller of the two islands opposite Cannes, called St. Marguerite. She invited us all to lunch with her one day. F. was not feeling well and so Poulenc and I went off in the car together. We had to meet at a small café and had to explain that F. could not come. One motor went back and Poulenc and I got into Chenal's Hispano-Suiza, which was very large and grand. There were Picabia and Gaby and two other people. It was a beautiful day and very hot. On the island is a little restaurant by the sea and under some trees we had the *spécialité de la maison*, which was lobsters done in a special way. Everyone was French except

myself. From St. Marguerite we could see in the
distance, in the Golfe Juan, some warships. We were
told that they were English. After lunch we visited
a monastery and then took our motor-boat. Chenal
suggested that as we had plenty of time we should
return by the Golf Juan and visit the warships. The
first one had not a visitors' day, but the second one
was the " Royal Oak," and we climbed up the side.
A petty officer said to a sailor who had helped us up,
" Do they speak English? " And I said, " I am
English," whereupon they were delighted. So were
my friends, and we saw all over the gun-room and
climbed up and down ladders. When we got to
Cannes we went to the Casino. One can play boule
without a special ticket, but for the roulette and
more serious gambling rooms one has to have one.
Chenal was charming and bought me a season ticket
for a month, not that I ever gambled, but it was
most thrilling to watch the faces of the Greeks and
serious old ladies at the most serious table of all,
where the chips on the table staggered me. We
saw the ex-King of Portugal. We had to wait
a little before the really serious table started. On
each place is a card with a name on it, and I saw
the names of several very well-known people.
Eventually the table filled up. There was a very
smart old lady with a large hat covered in flowers.
She had the most sinister face I have ever seen, and
completely expressionless. There were two elderly
Englishwomen, who looked like governesses, and had
piles of chips in front of them. Poulenc played
boule, I did not play anything, but continued to

watch the roulette. Our motor came to fetch us, and Poulenc and I drove back to the Château.

The next day we had arranged to meet Stravinsky, who was to have lunch with us at Faletto's. He lived at Montboron, which was near by. The restaurant was called the Pavillon Henri IV. There was a tiny bar and outside a small paved terrasse with a few tables. We could see the whole of the Cap Ferrat from our table. Stravinsky arrived very flustered. He told us his troubles, which were many and varied. He had quarrelled with his cook, which he did once or twice a day, as he was always late for meals. His whole household worked all day. The girls drew and embroidered their drawings. One son painted and the other composed and his wife dealt with the whole family. He was hiding from Diaghilev. He had just returned to Nice and had had an appointment to lunch with him at the Reserve. We had nearly, at the last moment, decided to go to the Reserve, and we breathed a sigh of relief, as Russians have a habit of getting very excited indeed when awkward situations arise. Stravinsky explained that if he met Diaghilev, Diaghilev would disturb him and upset him doing his packing. He said, " *J'adore faire ma valise, c'est la seule chose qui vraiment m'amuse.*" He told us that he had invented a most beautiful suitcase, all the fittings were made of silver and all the bottles and little boxes inside were square. He said that it was called *Le modèle Stravinsky* and was sold by a firm in the Champs Elysées. He explained that he did not possess one as the firm was so mean that they had expected him to buy one at some enormous cost.

Cocteau came over from Monte Carlo and joined us after lunch. I met a Frenchman I had known slightly in Paris, who had a villa and one of the most beautiful gardens in the South of France. He lived on a hill above Cap Martin. He asked me to lunch. I mentioned, at luncheon one day, the name of the man, and a French woman present said, " How odd! I and my husband are lunching with him the same day; will you come along with us in our motor? " We started the next day, and as we were driving through Monte Carlo we saw Cocteau. We waved to him and he came and spoke to us. As he smiled we noticed that his gums were bright red. As we drove on the Frenchwoman said, " *Tiens! il a ses gencives peintes* " (his gums are painted). I said, " I wonder what he has done to them? " Cocteau was always finding new stunts and jokes to astound the *bourgeois*. He was going to lunch at a large hotel and we wondered what the effect would be on the guests. I told F., who was very interested, but we did not mention it to anyone else, knowing that repeating things leads to trouble of every kind. Unfortunately, the Frenchwoman repeated this incident to Harry Melvill, who did not get on at all well with Jean. They both liked talking all the time and consequently it was very awkward when they were both at a rather small party together. Harry was delighted and told everyone. We went to Villefranche one day to see Cocteau and Georges Auric, who were staying there. There we found

319

Harry at a corner table. Jean came and joined us and, after lunch, he took me aside and said, " Come upstairs, I have something to show you." We went upstairs and on the washstand were tubes and pots of bright red paste. This was the secret of the *gencives peintes*. He had found, at Nice, some tooth-paste which, if rubbed hard enough and long enough, made the gums bright red. F. and I immediately on our return journey stopped at Nice and bought some. We went home and scrubbed and scrubbed. The effect lasted about half an hour and as we did not propose to spend the day cleaning our teeth we abandoned it.

One morning I was standing in the middle of my room with no clothes on, assuming a variety of poses and looking at myself in two mirrors, so that I could see the effect all round. The window was open and suddenly the round red face of a workman appeared. He had come up a ladder and was engaged in painting the house. I stood still with shock, and so did the astonished workman. I then walked up to the windows and closed the shutters. I told F. and Poulenc, who were delighted. I suppose the workman told his mates who were working on the estate, because, afterwards, they always laughed when they saw me. I had a letter from the English-man who said that he had arranged for me to have an exhibition at the Claridge Gallery in April. I painted two pictures during my visit, as well as the pear-tree. They were of the farm-houses with olive trees and I sold them all in London.

I packed up my possessions and returned to Paris

PORTRAIT

321

to collect my work for the exhibition. The Pole saw me off at the Gare St. Lazare. I entered a third-class carriage and in it I found a young man, Hans Egli, whom I had known for some time and who had married one of my friends. He was coming from Switzerland with his youngest child, who was about a year old. He had with him also one of my guitars. I had some wine with me. Some other people entered the carriage and I felt rather embarrassed as I was sure that they thought I was the mother of the infant. A business man with a grey moustache was sitting beside me. My friend handed me the baby, who roared. I wished I could have jumped out of the window. The business man smiled and I handed him the baby. Hans and I, much relieved, took down the guitar, and I opened the wine. The baby was entertained by the business man and we drank wine and sang songs till we reached Dieppe. We got to London at 7.30 a.m. It was cold and dreary and raining slightly. I took a room in a hotel and went directly to bed, wondering what my exhibition and the future would bring forth.

INDEX

Lightning Source UK Ltd.
Milton Keynes UK
UKHW022032240621
386089UK00004BA/725